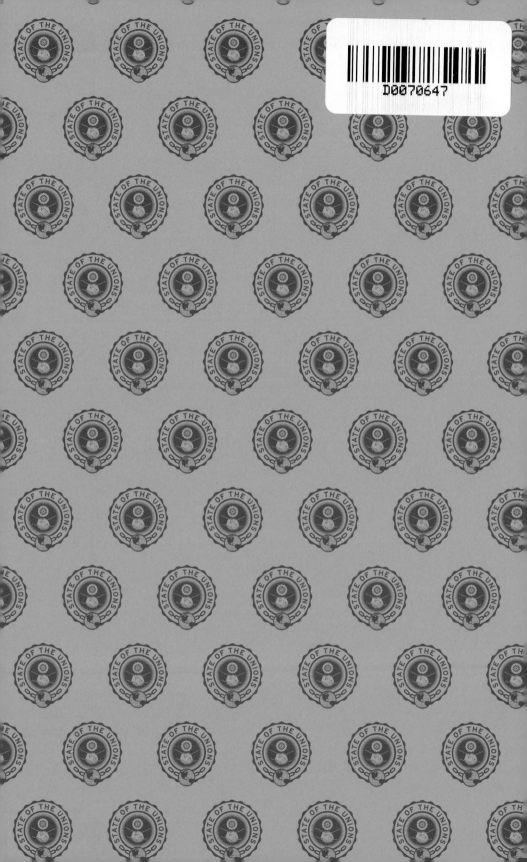

"In *State of the Unions*, Phil Dine offers a compelling tale of the modern American labor movement. With shrewd political insight, he argues that while unions have and continue to face challenges, they aren't waning in power. Rather, they continue today as an effective, strong voice for American workers and an important constituency in the Democratic Party. Dine's account shows that the unions are still very much a key player in politics at all levels."

SENATOR EVAN BAYH (D-IN)

"*State of the Unions* reinvigorates the argument for the need to rebuild the labor movement in the twenty-first century. Through a compelling mix of stories, Phil Dine gives an intriguing new perspective on labor's declining numbers and the ill effects for our country if we let this trend continue."

DONNA BRAZILE, POLITICAL COMMENTATOR, CNN AND ABC NEWS

"*State of the Unions* is not just the clearest evaluation of the U.S. labor movement at the turn of this century, it is also a roadmap. If labor can find a way to energize and, in doing so, rebuild America's working class, *State of the Unions* should be recognized for its contribution. Workers, management, politicos and all the other Americans searching for something lost but not forgotten need to read this book. Delta catfish and firehouse chili might just be the cuisine of a New America."

HON. JACK BUECHNER, MEMBER OF CONGRESS, RETIRED, MO-2ND

"*State of the Unions* highlights many of labor's greatest achievements, yet also painstakingly describes the current struggle that labor now finds itself mired in. During our history, the strength of organized labor has led to a growing American middle class that has been crucial to the vitality of our democracy. However, worker's rights in this country have been under assault and many worker protections that unions fought so hard to secure have disappeared. Philip Dine delves deep into labor's struggle to remain relevant in the face of lax enforcement of labor laws, trade deals sending jobs overseas, and the widening income gap that threatens the future health of our democracy."

CONGRESSMAN BILL DELAHUNT, MA-10

"The author enters areas few media professionals have ever even visited. In this astonishing new book about labor values, union ownership, ethnic relations, community support, globalization, and open communications, Philip Dine shows how a strengthening of the labor movement can help preserve the American middle class. He also illuminates the American trade union movement's involvement in the spread of democracy during the Cold War even as he lays out a strategy for going forward."

"*State of the Unions* is a fascinating tale of America's unions and how and why they need to be heard in a time of growing gulfs between America's haves and have-nots. It's a lively read that should be of interest to people who either know a lot—or nothing—about the trade union movement."

"Why has organized labor suffered such a precipitous decline in recent years? Does it matter? And if it matters, what can be done to swing the pendulum back? Phil Dine provides answers to those questions and makes a compelling case—to borrow a sentiment expressed fifty years ago about General Motors—that 'What's good for organized labor is good for the country!'"

"Phil Dine has produced a *must read* for both union members and members of the press. *State of the Unions*—with its keen observations and thoughtful conclusions—could be a primer for labor leaders and labor reporters. Except that it's so well-written and entertaining, it beckons anyone who works for a living to bring it to the beach."

"*State of the Unions* is an insightful view of and commentary about what ails labor, where it is going, and where it might go in conjunction with sound policy. This is mandatory reading for all who want a hands-on practical assessment by a solid investigative reporter and observer of labor in our society."

"Phil Dine offers an insightful, riveting, reader-friendly examination of organized labor as it exists in today's political and economic climate."

"Philip Dine on the labor movement is a *must read* in Washington."

"In *State of the Unions*, Philip Dine challenges organized labor to respond to the business and political 'forces arrayed against them' that work to undermine unions and workers. His words should be heeded if unions are to survive and grow into the twenty-second century."

JOSEPH J. HUNT, GENERAL PRESIDENT, INTERNATIONAL ASSOCIATION OF
BRIDGE, STRUCTURAL, ORNAMENTAL AND REINFORCING IRON WORKERS

"In *State of the Unions*, Phil Dine offers critical yet sympathetic reflections on the contemporary U.S. labor movement. Based on his personal experiences as a labor reporter, he weaves together compelling tales of union success with biting commentary on labor's shortcomings. Most notably, Dine argues that unions should aggressively promote a message that champions the dignity of workers while exposing growing income inequality and corporate excesses. *State of the Unions* should be of great interest to labor leaders, scholars and students, as well as citizens concerned about the future of our democracy."

RICHARD HURD, PROFESSOR OF LABOR STUDIES, CORNELL UNIVERSITY

"When I read Phil Dine's account of the largest strike by black workers in Mississippi's history, I was swept back to the summer of 1990 standing in a cotton field in Indianola, Mississippi as hundreds of striking workers sang "We Shall Overcome." The memory of the hardworking black women brings me to tears to this day when I recall their courage and determination to create a better life for their families and children. Phil Dine tells their story as no one else can. He too stood with me in that cotton field and proved once again that the pen is mightier than the sword."

G. NEEL LATTIMORE, FORMER PRESS SECRETARY
TO FIRST LADY HILLARY RODHAM CLINTON

"Philip Dine has written a provocative and riveting book on the current state of the labor movement. His analysis and recommendations should be robustly debated inside and outside the world of labor. All progressives should welcome such a debate. Indeed, the future of the social justice movement in this country depends, in so many ways, on rapidly growing and increasingly influential labor unions. Especially pertinent are Dine's observations regarding the communications challenges that face even the most effective unions.

If the labor movement and the progressive community at large are to prevail, we must strategically "frame the terms of the debate," "define the issues from our perspective," and "put a human face" on those issues. If we do, we can win the hearts and minds of the American people. If we fail, our right wing adversaries will turn back the clock on social justice for decades."

RALPH G. NEAS, PRESIDENT AND CEO, PEOPLE FOR THE AMERICAN WAY

"Phil Dine combines personalized stories from his years covering labor issues with insightful analysis of the labor movement and its leaders, creating a lively and indispensable guide to the present and future of unions. Labor unions are misunderstood and hardly covered in today's news, but remain a key part of our politics and society. *State of the Unions* brings the people, the issues, and the problems to life."

NORMAN ORNSTEIN, RESIDENT SCHOLAR, AMERICAN ENTERPRISE INSTITUTE

"Anyone interested in the fate of the American middle class in today's cutthroat global economy needs this book. Phil Dine shows how the decline of job security, retirement and health security, and safety at work for average Americans parallels the decline of trade unions. He presents a compelling case for why unions are essential to America's future and explains how labor's failure to communicate has cost it influence with the public, politicians, and in the marketplace. *State of the Unions* is rich with insights into our present predicament."

HEDRICK SMITH, AUTHOR, *RETHINKING AMERICA*

"Few topics are more important in defining today's America than the links between the travails of the middle class and working people, the decline of the labor movement, and increasing economic inequality with all its political ramifications. *State of the Unions* does a masterful job of pointing out those links and showing how labor can revitalize itself so it is in a position to tackle the problems."

CONGRESSMAN CHRIS VAN HOLLEN (D-MD)

"Phil Dine has written a book worthy of attention and study by the labor movement, its friends, and all those who care about social and economic issues in America today. It is a lament about the decline of labor and all that this means for workers, their families, and America. It is also a passionate plea for labor to do what is necessary to become a strong and effective voice for working and middle class Americans once again. It offers prescriptive ideas and practical strategies of how labor can reinvent itself and be a greater presence in the national dialogue. It also provides real world examples in which labor has done this in politics and organizing. These are models for the future. *State of the Unions* is an important book.

JOHN CALHOUN WELLS, FORMER DIRECTOR OF THE FEDERAL MEDIATION AND CONCILIATION SERVICE, 1993-1998

STATE
OF THE
UNIONS

HOW LABOR CAN STRENGTHEN THE MIDDLE CLASS, IMPROVE OUR ECONOMY, AND REGAIN POLITICAL INFLUENCE

PHILIP M. DINE

New York   Chicago   San Francisco   Lisbon   London
Madrid   Mexico City   Milan   New Delhi   San Juan
Seoul   Singapore   Sydney   Toronto

This book is dedicated to my wife, Debbie, and to our children Alexandra, Jessica, and Joelle.

The **McGraw·Hill** Companies

1 2 3 4 5 6 7 8 9 0   DOC/DOC   0 9 8 7

ISBN-13: 978-0-07-14844-0
ISBN-10: 0-07-148844-8

McGraw-Hill books are available at special quantity discounts to use as premiums and sales promotions, or for use in corporate training programs. For more information, please write to the Director of Special Sales, Professional Publishing, McGraw-Hill, Two Penn Plaza, New York, NY 10121-2298. Or contact your local bookstore.

This book is printed on acid-free paper.

CONTENTS

FOREWORD   ix

ACKNOWLEDGMENTS   xiii

INTRODUCTION   xvii

CHAPTER 1
DEAD MAN WALKING   1

CHAPTER 2
DELTA PRIDE   57

CHAPTER 3
HEARTLAND VALUES   107

CHAPTER 4
FROM DIALOGUE TO DIVISION   145

CHAPTER 5
UP ON THE ROOF (OR SILENCING
THE WORKING CLASS)   175

CONTENTS

CHAPTER 6
JOE T! JOE T!   211

CHAPTER 7
WHAT IT MEANS FOR THE FUTURE   249

NOTES   259

BIBLIOGRAPHY   265

INDEX   269

FOREWORD

Growing up in St. Louis in the 1950s, my father was a milk truck driver and a Teamster and we thought we were in the middle class. My father would often say to my brother and me: "Never forget—we have food on the table and clothes on your back because I'm in a union that can get me fair pay for my hard work." I never forgot that, and after my dad's back was injured (hauling heavy loads in those pre-OSHA days), he lost his Teamster job and we never again enjoyed those "middle class" wages.

The year 2007 is a long way from the 1950s, but I believe labor unions remain just as crucial today in building and maintaining the middle class in America. Even though the percentage of private workers in unions has dropped from about 35 percent in the 1950s to less than 8 percent today—unions continue to play an essential role.

The role of organized labor has changed for two simple reasons. First, some employers have become more enlightened and treat workers better without a union. Second, a combination of labor laws that discourage workers from voting for unions and foreign competition that intimidates workers from voting for unions have reduced the number of unionized workers.

Nonetheless, an America with fewer unions and union members will result in a lower standard of living for all Americans. To stop and reverse this trend, American organized labor must adapt and reform itself to move the numbers of unionized workers—and therefore the American standard of living—back up. As Phil Dine so astutely points out in this book, unions and union leaders that better understand and define a positive, modern role for organized labor to meet these multiple challenges will succeed in reviving the number of unionized workers and in lifting standards of living in a highly competitive global economy.

Unions will always be essential: First, to give a voice to the voiceless when employers are hostile and unfair to workers, and second, to better motivate and organize workers to increase productivity with employers who "get it" and understand that their workers are essential stakeholders in a shared enterprise. The most enlightened employer I've ever met always says the biggest task of management is to get all of the workers to think like owners.

We are also seeing a new role for many unions to manage and be responsible for health benefits and pensions for workers, where these programs traditionally were the responsibility of employers. As global competition has put downward pressure on "fringe benefits" more and more employee benefits are being dropped by employers and creative unions are seizing this part of compensation into their suite of services.

Many Americans would believe that unions are an anachronism—entities passed by because of more enlightened employers or because of fierce global competition. That view fails to recognize that if union membership continues to decline, fewer employers (unions do as much for unorganized workers as they do for organized workers) will remain "enlightened" and if we fail to resist the downward pressure on standard of living caused by globalization, America and the world will fall to the lowest common denominator.

Understandably, capitalism will always tend toward pushing down worker compensation to increase profits. Rule of law and labor unions constitute the only available counterforce for a greater sharing of the wealth, thereby ensuring we have demand as well as supply.

Business leaders intellectually realize that robust middle class demand is essential for a highly successful economy, but without organized pressure from unionized workers business will always opt for micro-profits over macro-demand. Said another way, only society's legal authorization of economic power for organized workers saves business from overwhelming the most essential tool for sharing the wealth and creating healthy demand in the overall economy. Understandably, individual businesses must focus on their individual profits over the health of the overall economy.

Yet, capitalism without rules soon creates a concentration of wealth and power that chokes and destroys capitalism itself. Capitalism with rules remains the only proven and reliable path to prosperity and well-being for everyone blessed to enjoy such an economic system.

This book explores a subject that is grossly misunderstood and rarely studied. Mr. Dine has expertly cleared up many modern misconceptions about the role of unions in the past and has ably explained how some unions are successfully redefining a vital role for the future. Ideally, books will open our eyes to information most of us have never seen and inform us about important—but unnoticed—developments. This book fulfills that role very well.

I can still hear my father, Louis Gephardt, getting out of bed at 3 a.m. and tiptoeing out of the house to get to Pevely Dairy in St. Louis to drive his truck on that retail delivery route. Because he was in a union, his son got a great education and got to be a candidate for President of the United States. Phil Dine's book makes us understand that the American economy—built strong on the back of a stable middle class— still depends on having strong unions. Unions must and will change with new circumstances, but to misunderstand their crucial role in maintaining America's economic strength would be a serious mistake.

RICHARD A. GEPHARDT, MEMBER OF
CONGRESS (D-MO), 1977 TO 2005;
HOUSE DEMOCRATIC LEADER, 1989 TO 2003
AUGUST 2007

ACKNOWLEDGMENTS

This book could not have been written without the patience and understanding of my wife, Debbie, and our three children, Alexandra Jennie, Jessica Lilli, and Joelle Samantha, who saw far too little of me (or maybe that's just my perspective) as I worked on it.

I'm responsible alone for the opinions or conclusions expressed in this book, but credit for any felicitous phrasing, organization, or tone must be shared with my wonderful literary agent, Victoria Pryor, whose guidance, insight, and tact were invaluable, the highly skilled McGraw-Hill editor I was privileged to work with, Jeanne Glasser, and the entire McGraw-Hill team. Neil Levine's counsel also was most helpful.

While this is the first book I've written, journalism is a great preparatory course. I've had the chance to work with some top-notch journalists over the years, too numerous to mention. Among the best have been editors such as Laszlo Domjan and William B. Ketter and reporters like Bill Lambrecht and Fred Hanson; most memorable was the legendary Joseph Pulitzer, Jr., even if encounters with him were hardly an everyday event. The newspaper his grandfather founded let me define the labor beat broadly to include political, social, and racial components and report on it widely, from Mississippi to Budapest.

I don't dare attempt to mention all the union leaders, staffers, activists, intellectuals, or rank-and-file workers who've been generous with their time as I've worked the labor beat, but perhaps the most pivotal were the local ones who early on decided to trust me. Once the traditional labor-media frostiness was thawed, straightforward St. Louis union leaders like Bob Kelley, William Stodghill, Jerry Tucker, Bob Sansone, Richard Mantia, Andrew McKenzie, Tom Harvill, Lew Moye, Dennis Skelton, Joan Suarez, Len Terbrock, Ted Zlotopolski, Duke McVey, and Herb Johnson provided an entrée into the world of labor.

Among the unsung heroes of the nation's industrial relations system are the labor lawyers and mediators with agencies like the National Labor Relations Board and the Federal Mediation and Conciliation Service. Those who ran these institutions over the past 20 years, such as Jerry Hunter, Bernard DeLury, William B. Gould IV, and John Calhoun Wells, were generous with their time and knowledge. Less unsung but also helpful were labor secretaries such as Robert Reich and the estimable congressional leader Richard Gephardt, who as much as any public figure understands the ties between labor-management relations and a competitive U.S. economy. Officials at the U.S. Chamber of Commerce and the National Federation of Independent Business have always been willing to put things in perspective.

Journalists who cover labor are few and tend to be there because they care about the beat (it's certainly not the glamour or career path), and you can't help but learn from smart veterans like Frank Swoboda. I've also benefited at various times from the counsel of those in a variety of fields, including Suzanne Berger, Gerald Serotta, Stanley Lugerner, Tim Bross, and Warren Talbot.

Discussions about politics, labor, and economics with Kim Dine, the best public servant I know, the remarkable Kretzmer family, and the intellectually curious Joe Denaro have been instructive for me. And I've benefited immensely from the work on labor and industrial relations of academic experts such as Richard Hurd, Robert Bruno, Harley Shaiken, Kate Bronfenbrenner, and Ray Hilgert.

My appetite for the field was first whetted at the Massachusetts Institute of Technology, notably by graduate courses on comparative industrial relations taught by Ezio Tarantelli, whose contribution was unfortunately cut short by the terrorist Red Brigades in Italy.

Because of the hospitality of the labor federations—whether socialist, Social Democrat, or conservative—two years of academic research on labor unions and immigrant workers in France and Germany provided me with insight into how unions actually function.

Most of all, I must pay tribute to the memory of my parents, Joe and Laurie Dine. My father, who had a half-century career in print, radio, and television news, was the bravest and gentlest man I've known. He headed for years of combat in Europe just a couple of years after my mother fled the Continent barely ahead of the Holocaust. Their courage, wisdom, sense of justice, and extraordinary love have been an unending source of inspiration.

INTRODUCTION

Things were breaking up after a news conference at the National Press Club in downtown Washington, D.C., where the Teamsters had made their case yet again for getting out from under what they regarded as the onerous federal stewardship they'd been subjected to since 1989. Seated in the back row, I'm trying to shove the handouts and my notebook and other items into my shoulder bag when I hear this booming voice:

"Hey Phil, where've you been?"

I glance up and see none other than the Teamsters' president, James P. Hoffa, son of the legendary Jimmy Hoffa, shoulders about six feet wide, looking me right in the eye. The man's not making small talk; he's got a message to deliver, so he doesn't bother waiting for a reply.

"You used to write about me," Hoffa continues, still smiling but a trace of menace creeping into his tone. "Remember, Barbara's watching. She reads everything."

Barbara would be his sister, Barbara Hoffa Crancer, who had returned to school after having kids and is now a judge in

St. Louis. My paper's her hometown paper. Mrs. Crancer is a nice lady, to be sure, but there's something mildly unsettling about the notion of her reporting to her brother on whatever I write. Or miss.

His point made, Hoffa pivots and leaves the room, followed by his somewhat surprised entourage of union attorneys, advisers, and Teamsters officials.

I shook my head. Here's the bearer of one of the fabled names in labor history—make that in American history—presiding over the storied International Brotherhood of Teamsters, 1.4 million members strong, and he's not only aware of what some individual reporter writes or doesn't write, he's practically pleading for more coverage.

Now it's true that I hadn't published a word about him for several years, in part because post-9/11 reporting exigencies meant spending time with then–Defense Secretary Donald Rumsfeld. The thing is, I could have written about Rumsfeld every day for 20 years, asked questions at each of his frequent Pentagon press briefings, and he still wouldn't have had the vaguest idea who the hell I was—or cared enough to find out. But after I ignored Hoffa for all this time, he not only remembers, he's what, hurt?

This, of course, has nothing to do with personalities—Hoffa is no more sentimental than Rumsfeld—and everything to do with the institutions they represent. Rumsfeld was constantly harassed by droves of reporters, so his imperative was to ward them off. If Hoffa is plaintively looking for a reporter's glance to be aimed his way, it's because the attention of any assignment editor or producer worth his or her salt is focused elsewhere and not on a labor movement in pre-cipitous decline.

Indeed, the once-proud American labor movement has faded before our eyes, wounded on all fronts. It represents a shrink-ing share of the workforce.[1] It has an ever-tougher time hold-ing its own in collective bargaining with employers. It has proven utterly incapable of stemming the flight of good jobs overseas. It endures crushing political defeats, including the 2004 presidential election when despite a then-jobless recov-ery and an unpopular war, it couldn't push its candidate over the top. At the same time, labor itself is fragmenting. Its recent split into two competing federations deprives the union movement of the one attribute it retained—*unity*—making it all the more vulnerable as its adversaries gain in strength.

The unraveling of the labor movement is no small matter. Unions have had a lead role in establishing many of the most fundamental and valued features of today's society. The eight-hour workday, five-day workweek, paid vacations, retirement and health-care benefits, safety regulations, bans on sweatshops or child labor, protections against employment discrimination, and other workplace advances now taken for granted were the result of struggles—invariably protracted, often bloody, and sometimes even deadly—by workers and their unions.

Labor also has played an integral part in the expansion of the middle class, a phenomenon that helped define America and that has been key to assuring its political and social stability. The breakthrough contracts Hoffa's father negotiated in the 1950s reverberated well beyond labor's immediate ranks, exerting upward pressure on the incomes and benefits of tens of millions of working families. That was possible because of the leverage wielded at the time by labor, which represented 35 percent of all workers and an even higher portion in key industries.

In a profound sense, the labor movement has been an indispensable part of the history and fabric of the United States in ways extending far beyond the workplace. This is due in large measure to the peculiar nature of trade unionism in this country. The goal of unions in much of Europe and elsewhere has been to overthrow—or at least fundamentally alter—the social order and economic system, but America's unions have fought to improve and expand them, and to do so incrementally at that. Having bought into the system, they haven't tried to redefine or disparage the American dream, but rather they have allowed more people to realize it by raising the living standards of workers, integrating waves of immigrants from around the world, and narrowing racial and religious divides. Though often faced with strenuous opposition from entrenched and privileged interests, unions have helped create the social and economic mobility that has set the United States apart from more stratified European societies.[2]

It is no overstatement to say that labor has contributed mightily to what has made America work—and what has made it unique.

Yet despite this backdrop, labor's current plight is both broadly misunderstood and badly underrated. The prevailing wisdom is that organized labor's long and steady slide reflects a loss of relevance. After all, unions long ago fixed the abusive practices that gave rise to the labor movement in the first place: hazardous working conditions, unpaid overtime, and arbitrary discipline. At this point labor seems to be hanging on for reasons of power or personal gain or simple institutional habit when its reason for being has expired.

Lest anyone doubt that labor is no longer needed, it would seem that the proof is in the numbers: only one in eight workers these days bothers to join a union. You have to ask, if the very people labor is supposed to serve and protect no longer care, why should anyone else? And so there are those who believe that labor's demise is a ho-hum development that is both inconsequential and inevitable.

Granted, one might argue, labor once mattered and even waged some heroic battles, but that was back then. Doesn't the fading of labor's vital signs show that it has outlived its usefulness and that the country has moved on? This, after all, is twenty-first-century America, a place of shifting work patterns, of rapid economic change, of the exodus of traditional manufacturing jobs, and of startling technological progress— all occurring at a time of globalization and a new international division of labor. Isn't the vital role unions used to play in the past—when employers were cutthroat and government fronted for business interests, income gaps were enormous, and immigrants were exploited, class distinctions were sharp, and miners risked their lives to make a living—all part of a bygone era?

Not necessarily. The very gains that fundamentally changed the nature of our society and the conditions of employment for nearly all Americans—union or not—are now under unrelenting assault from employers and political foes. Living wages, enforcement of health and safety regulations, the retention of good jobs in this country, pensions earned during a lifetime of work—these and more are seriously threatened. It is no coincidence that gains in these areas were made as unions flourished and that those gains are now coming undone as unions decline.

Right here in the United States of America, worker casualties on the job edged upward recently, interrupting what was assumed to be an irreversible, decade-long trend toward an ever-safer workplace.[3] Since 2002 improvement in the fatality rate at work has stopped; in fact deaths rose for part of that time. This reversal of what seemed the natural course of events is directly related to the waning influence of unions. And the fact that you're shaking your head right now, in part because you wonder how more American workers could have died daily—16 a day, seven days a week, from job-related accidents alone—without your having heard a word about it in itself reflects labor's problems. As does the fact that on January 3, 2007, the AFL-CIO and the United Food and Commercial Workers (UFCW) took the extreme measure of going to court to force the Occupational Safety and Health Administration (OSHA) to honor its own regulations requiring employers to pay for workers' safety apparel.[4]

The risks associated with working are not merely some abstract statistical concoction. Though virtually no one made or at least expressed the connection, the deadly year coal miners experienced in 2006, starting with the Sago tragedy of January in which 12 miners died after a mine explosion, was closely intertwined with labor's sagging fortunes and diminished clout. If unions represent fewer miners and more mines are nonunion, it should not be surprising that this has consequences well beyond wages and benefits. Individual miners concerned about safety deep in the shafts have fewer opportunities to raise those concerns and less protection if they dare to do so. Even more important, on a federal level, there is less of a counterbalance against industry pressures for relaxed enforcement of the rules or for appointment of employer-friendly regulatory boards and dimmer prospects of enacting laws that would actually improve the status quo.

Labor's vulnerability played an equally pivotal, if similarly neglected, role in the fate of thousands of Gulf Coast workers in Hurricane Katrina's aftermath. Because of labor's perceived weakness, these individuals faced the loss of prevailing wage provisions—meaning that at their time of greatest need, their earnings risked decline. At the last minute, this was averted. And it's not only union members or even blue-collar types who find themselves affected by the growing absence of a foil to corporate power; as the economy evolves, white-collar workers are increasingly feeling the impact of the lack of an organized mechanism to push back. More women, across various income levels, went bankrupt in 2005 than graduated from college. Near record low shares of the economy are going to wages and salaries, while the highest portion in modern times contributes to profits.[5] Such trends led to the formation of a national organization—United Professionals—in the fall of 2006 that is aimed at helping white-collar workers collectively assert themselves; people who the founders said had "felt they were immune" to economic dislocation. While not a union, it was formed with seed money from the Service Employees International Union (SEIU).[6]

The point of all this is that, while it's indisputable that labor's strength is eroding, the need for a credible advocate for the American worker is growing steadily. Rather than becoming irrelevant, unions are increasingly needed by workers because they are taking it on the chin—with virtually no institutional means of fighting back. The very problems that beset workers and unions in the past are precisely the same ones that are driving the need for a renewed labor movement today.

Unions are needed not only to address the specific policies and practices that are hurting workers but also to address the processes that produce them. A major American strength, even if not uppermost in the popular consciousness, long has been how the nation's tripartite labor-management system works, with business, labor, and government each providing checks and balances. Input from each provides a self-correcting element to both workplace practices and national policies, helping make the U.S. economy the envy of the world while also averting the kind of class strife evident elsewhere. To the extent any one of those parties is not a full participant, it skews the outcome of work-related decisions. The competing parties may reap short-term gains as a result, but the ultimate effect is to throw a structure that has been a bulwark of the U.S. economic model completely off balance. And this very disequilibrium is at the heart of what many people correctly sense is going dramatically wrong in the United States.

Skyrocketing salary gaps between the rich and everyone else[7] and elections that focus on diversions such as gay marriage and flag burning to the exclusion of important mainstream issues such as how to improve access to good health care and save manufacturing jobs are among the distortions that occur when power is overly concentrated. Society's long-term interests aren't served when corporate economic power is unbridled or when political actions on job-related matters are one sided. The problem is not whether to agree with all—or indeed any—of labor's positions or whether to criticize management—which is merely doing what it is supposed to do: advance its own interests. The problem is that for all intents and purposes, management now has the playing field to itself. If any entity is to be criticized, it is labor for failing to fulfill its end of the bargain. In essence, this criticism recognizes the truism that an indispensable part of the genius of free market economies and democratic political systems is that the best policies emerge from vigorous debate and genuine competition.

Fine, you might say, but what of that 87.5 percent of employees who don't join unions? Assuming that in some theoretical sense unions continue to have a role to play, aren't workers in practice voting with their feet? Their behavior, it would seem, suggests that however persuasive the argument that unions are still necessary, their decline is inevitable—because their own potential clientele is turning its back. The shrinking numerical strength of unions reflects workers' perception of them as dinosaurs.

Case closed.

Except that this is not what's happening, popular myths notwithstanding. A closer look at what workers are saying about unions and, more broadly, at why the unionized portion of the workforce is slipping, paints quite a different picture. Polling in early 2007 by Peter D. Hart Research Associates shows that a record number of nonunion employees—some 53 percent—would favor, and join, a union at their workplace given a fair chance. Why then aren't they?

In this book, we'll get into the hidden side of labor's falling numbers. The decline in union membership is a function of the current state of hand-to-hand, union-management combat. It is far easier for workers to form a union in virtually any other democracy than in the United States where the legal path is cumbersome and laborious. Theodore St. Antoine, law professor and former dean of the University of Michigan Law School, says that the "intensity of opposition to unionization which is exhibited by American employers has no parallel in the western industrial world."[8] Aided by employer-friendly labor laws and helpful (pro-business) federal regulatory board members, companies increasingly succeed in thwarting organizing drives at their job sites, suffering at worst a slap on the wrist well down the road if these employers have improperly intimidated or coerced workers. Corporations and employers have grown more emboldened ever since the federal government took on the Professional Air Traffic Controllers Organization (PATCO) in 1981. And so the United States has a high, and rising, number of worker rights violations.[9] From a purely economic calculation, the infrequency of any significant penalty makes it a worthwhile cost of doing business (CDB) for employers to abridge the right of their workers to form a union.

Admittedly, this is easily done—in part because there's little resistance from the very workers whose rights are being restricted. And why is that? From the perspective of employees, it makes little sense to risk unionizing under these conditions since they are unlikely to be around if and when the disputes are eventually settled. This is particularly the case in service jobs, food, low-level health-care, and similar job classification areas in which there are high turnover rates. Ironically, these are precisely the growth sectors in today's economy because the jobs generally aren't exportable, so membership growth in these areas would have a major impact on general union membership. Yet under the best of conditions, service sector jobs are inherently difficult to organize because of the transient nature of that type of employment, the dispersal of work sites, and the typical low pay and high sense of vulnerability often tied to a large immigrant presence. In addition to those employment issues, aggressive employer behavior vis-à-vis unionization efforts and limited governmental enforcement of the laws combine to impede ongoing organizing efforts while deterring any new membership drives, and the consequences are enormous.

Meanwhile, in that part of the private sector where labor traditionally has been strong and worker rights tend to be better protected—the industrial trades—union losses aren't the result of workers leaving the unions but rather the result of manufacturing and production leaving the country or ceasing for other reasons. It is the exporting of jobs and the closing of plants, not individual decisions by steel or auto workers, that are driving down the sizable share this sector once contributed to labor's overall ranks. Labor Department figures show a net loss of more than 3 million manufacturing jobs—disproportionately union jobs—since manufacturing employment peaked in 1998, with perhaps half having gone overseas.[10] And while globalization and national wage disparities spur the loss of these jobs, public policy also plays a role in that employers are not dis-

couraged from—and in some cases are even rewarded for—
sending jobs overseas. Sometimes those jobs are reimported
back into this country in the form of foreign auto makers setting up plants, but this often takes place in southern, right-to-
work states, precisely because labor practices and laws work to
complicate any union efforts that represent those workers.

In both the service and industrial sectors, the combination of
employer behavior, public policies, labor laws, and economic
trends depresses membership in unions. Bottom line: plunging
union levels don't reflect workers' opting out of unions but
rather a stacked labor-management deck at a time of a shifting
balance between manufacturing and tertiary sector jobs. Ford is
shedding workers, Wal-Mart is taking over small-town America,
and unions haven't yet figured out how to organize workers
where employers have dug in their heels and face few reprisals
for doing so. Labor, it must be added, is far from blameless for
its plight; unions have often been poorly led in ways that compromise their ability to attract new members despite the difficulties workers face. Moreover, labor's weakness is hardly a draw
for potential members, particularly given the difficulties and
risks they may encounter if they try to form a union.

The question then shifts from whether unions are still relevant to a more practical line of inquiry: What must labor do
to regain the strength to carry out functions that appear to be
as urgent now as they have been in a long time? With workers' gains under assault even as unions find themselves on the
defensive, how can the labor movement revitalize itself so it
can secure its own institutional future—and therefore be in a
position to defend that of its members? Examining that question will be a key focus of this book. Unions are on the bub-

ble not because their mission is obsolete but because at present they are not a match for the forces arrayed against them—forces whose very actions demand a response on behalf of workers. Magnanimous corporations, after all, haven't suddenly decided to fill the vacuum left by a weakened labor movement and represent the interests of workers, nor has America overnight become a safe haven for employees. And if the need for what unions do remains as pressing as ever, it follows that labor's decline *can't* be inevitable.

And yet labor leaders are doing their best to make it seem that way. For years, they were in vigorous denial about problems afflicting their movement, worried they might embolden their foes. Recently, though, the situation has grown so threatening that they have not only finally acknowledged their plight but have embarked on an unprecedented effort to turn things around. However, their earnest and energetic, but thus far misguided, search for an answer has produced little more than a split into two competing federations—something labor can ill afford in its already-weakened state. This is another significant development that has been met with a shrug as the unavoidable throes of a fading movement. In fact, it reflects some poor decisions by labor. The internal debate proved counterproductive because the premise on which it rested reflected less a thoughtful analysis than false choices among squabbling labor leaders who wanted to focus on politics, or on organizing, or on collective bargaining to secure labor's future. There was also a good measure of personality conflict and power struggle at play here. As a result, absent any realistic and serious proposals to turn things around, labor's grand debate has devolved into a futile food fight.

Until labor properly assesses the dilemma it is in—including recognizing that all these traditional goals are currently beyond its limited capacities—and finds a mission that fits, any effort to right itself is doomed to fail. But once it does right itself, it has the potential to not only rejuvenate itself but to serve as an agent of broad change, as I will explore.

Even with a constructive mission in hand, however, labor will still have to learn how to accomplish a few basic daily tasks, such as how to craft and communicate a message that will give Americans some clue to what unions are all about. And labor will have to learn how to reach the electorate in ways that resonate with voters. As important as it is that labor become a player again, it won't happen until people know, for example, when job safety is eroding, and how to turn that situation around becomes part of the public dialogue.

Fortunately, amid its string of recent failures, labor has some striking successes from which to draw, cases it could use to inspire the public about the role it can play in today's society, while also examining those successes to derive lessons for its own future conduct. Unfortunately, it has consistently failed to do either. This book is, in part, an attempt to chronicle some of these successes and consider how labor might use the lessons they offer to again find its voice and its footing.

Over the past two decades, I've had the good fortune to occupy a front-row perch—too often surrounded by empty seats—from which to observe many of labor's struggles and vivid personalities, the devastating defeats delivered by its weaknesses, and, occasionally, its against-all-odds victories.

I followed as a small but determined firefighters' union scrambled the political calculus of the last presidential contest. The International Association of Fire Fighters (IAFF) devised a plan that allowed Iowa's firehouses to unleash a band of novices—softball players and military veterans, soft spoken and boisterous—who knocked the larger and more experienced ranks of two dozen other unions for a loop in the nation's critical first primary in 2004. The firefighters lived up to their professional credo of never giving up, of leaving no man behind, even when everyone else counted out their candidate. The union threw away labor's generic playbook and developed a strategy that maximized the unique strengths of its members while minimizing their gaping weaknesses—and meshed it all with the peculiarities of the state and the type of primary. Since stealth played a part in the plan, the media essentially missed the story. Now, as new elections approach, valuable lessons could be gleaned from what transpired in this remarkable case.

In the Mississippi Delta, an impoverished region seething with hostility to organized labor—what little exists, in any case—I watched as 900 women mustered the courage to take on their employer, a cooperative of wealthy white men who exercised control over all aspects of the women's work lives. Just years removed from the cotton fields and now working in the region's new cash crop—catfish processing—these women waged the biggest strike by black workers in Mississippi's torturous racial history. They had no choice, as they saw it, because this was a fight for their very dignity; if they didn't stand up now, one said, they'd always be treated as "field hands." They faced not only the 180 farmers who employed them but also an interlocking legal, economic, social, and political nexus of power in an area largely bypassed by the civil rights movement, rendering them all the more vulnerable.

It was a brave fight, but one that realistically they couldn't win—not with banks run by the cooperative's directors threatening foreclosure on their homes and not with the mayor doubling as the firm's attorney. And yet, many weeks after they had begun subsisting on donated bags of groceries, one chilly night in December the women joyously crowded into a church to approve and then celebrate their new contract. This was a triumph that would alter their relations with their employer, their place in town, and perhaps most significant, the way they regarded themselves and what they could accomplish together. It was also an outcome that could not have been achieved without the innovative and bold strategy devised by their food workers union.

Inside the International Brotherhood of Teamsters (IBT), I've observed from up close how the fear that once pervaded this muscular union—where dissent could mean broken legs—melted away as the rank and file asserted itself under the watchful eye of federal officials wary about organized crime's possible return. A vigorous brand of democracy has gradually caught on in what was the most authoritarian of unions, with the tyranny of Mob-approved leaders yielding to grassroots scrutiny of those who would run the IBT. Italian learned during a stint as a lifeguard in an area south of Naples, Italy, helped provide me with insight into the feelings of colorful, connected—and unsuspecting—old-line Teamster chiefs who spoke frankly about these unsettling developments. Imagine, their hold on the union loosened as ordinary truck drivers and delivery service drivers actually were given a say in its direction. Uneven progress in enacting internal reform and in achieving accountable governance are, it should be noted, matters that still cause unions problems and render them susceptible to conservative criticism—however unfair—that labor "bosses" make decisions for the workers.

Covering the Teamsters is an endeavor like few others in journalism. Writing about former Secretary of Defense Rumsfeld or his successor Robert Gates and the nation's military establishment involves a formal process that is facilitated by a Pentagon press pass—obtained with a mass of paperwork and official approval—to enable a reporter to attend the buttoned-down press conferences and hear the carefully phrased spin. Getting into Teamster events, on the other hand, requires something quite different: being personally vouched for as "a good guy" by someone whose word matters. That, and often only that, leads the doorway-sized guards to quietly slip from your path.

Farther away, I watched the American labor movement delicately help sow the seeds of democracy in Eastern Europe by providing quiet assistance to fledgling free-trade unions in Hungary and its neighbors. The risks were substantial because if this had become known, it would have imperiled the work being done—to say nothing of the Eastern European workers themselves, engaged in the most subversive actions imaginable under regimes whose legitimacy rested on their claim to be the sole representative of the working class. I saw firsthand both the hatching of this effort in the United States and the empowering impact it had on the workers who eventually challenged the hegemony of the Communist regimes and their unions. Since then, I've looked on as the American Federation of Teachers (AFT) and other unions have fought for worker rights and freedoms elsewhere around the world.

And yet, I've consistently been startled at labor's failure to tell these stories, most of which are surely as novel as the negative trend in workplace deaths. If episodes like these—of success and even heroism—were to become part of the public parlance, they would chip away at labor's image as a hidebound institution no longer needed or incapable of achieving anything worthwhile. The likelihood that the stories of the Mississippi catfish workers or the firefighters or even the East European role of the AFL-CIO are news to well-informed readers speaks volumes about labor's inability to get its story out and its resultant decline. Indeed, labor's poor relationship with the media reinforces the aura of silence that surrounds unions, except for incidents of corruption, strikes, picket-line violence, layoffs, or the like. Labor's complicity in the muzzling of the American working class amounts to self-inflicted damage that unions can ill afford, particularly in today's wired world.

This strange situation is, for those few who still cover labor, a double-edged sword. Trying to report labor's story, I've had phones slammed, expletives screamed at me, and doors shut on me; I've been pushed in front of oncoming buses and almost shoved off a hotel roof by unionists who apparently felt their frustration couldn't be adequately reflected in a mere letter to the editor. The flip side of this is that because there is so little competition among reporters trying to get a labor story, with persistence there can be unusual access. And once inside, there is nothing formulaic, nothing rehearsed. I had entrée, sometimes exclusively, as labor leaders and activists, together with academics and union members, sought a way out of their morass, engaging in brainstorming sessions in Washington and New York and elsewhere in 2004 and 2005. If the passionate and unvarnished discussions never produced a creative way to turn the labor movement around, they at least shed a great deal of light on labor's travails—and its thinking. Then I witnessed organized labor begin to fracture, and I was present as the Change to Win federation was formed in St. Louis in fall of 2005, exactly a half-century after the AFL-CIO's founding unified labor.

And there, late on the first day of the federation's maiden convention, Jim Hoffa comes bounding through the revolving doors in the downtown hotel that was hosting it, entourage around him. It's been several years since our previous encounter, the one at the National Press Club.

"Phil," he booms, before lowering his voice. "Barbara was here earlier. She's looking for you."

CHAPTER 1

DEAD MAN
WALKING

It was a frigid Monday evening in January, and the firefighters of Iowa were, as usual, poised for action. The person they aimed to rescue, however, wasn't a fire victim but rather a languishing political candidate. It was caucus night, the world was watching, and these firefighters hoped against great odds to turn months of intense preparation into concrete electoral results. Observers may have written off the man they supported, but if these firefighters were to give up on him as well, it would violate the most fundamental ethos of their profession. So on this night, it was full steam ahead. With little fanfare, they had been deployed throughout the state. Each firefighter knew his role, and now they would see whether it would all come together.

In the town of Ottumwa, a county seat of nearly 25,000 residents above the southeastern border with Missouri, a 245-pound behemoth named Ricky Kleinman had just slipped into the library at Evans Middle School lugging a cooler of iced tea and water. With the caucus still a couple of hours away, the place was empty, but the town's senior firefighter was determined to hunt for any possible edge. Taping up one last poster for his candidate in a strategic spot might lure an extra supporter or two, and who knew how critical that might be once residents started streaming into the library to vote for the next Democratic presidential nominee.

"Competitive" doesn't begin to describe Kleinman, a mountain of a man (despite a name that means "little man" in his ancestral Germany) who had dominated Iowa's softball diamonds for the past quarter century, willing his team to victory nearly every game. Initially his team was sponsored by Pepsi, then Coca-Cola, finally the local Coke and Frontrunners Bar—but through it all he kept piling up the W's. Now embarking on a new type of mission, he knew he couldn't allow himself to be out-hustled. Dousing flames or fanning batters was old hat; if this political rookie felt particularly driven on this evening, it was because his outsized personality had landed him the daunting role of local caucus captain for his side.

One hundred miles northwest in Des Moines, Kleinman's counterpart was an unassuming Navy veteran named John TeKippe, as softspoken as his colleague in Ottumwa was boisterous. Intimately familiar with aircraft carriers but himself a neophyte in the political arena despite being active in his local firefighters union, TeKippe was girding himself for the task ahead. These caucuses require a good bit of public interaction, and TeKippe speaks in tones so measured one must pay close attention to hear him. Diverse political strands coexist in Iowa's capital city, and he suspected—correctly, as it turned out—that he was heading toward a nail-biter of a contest.

While these two men were feeling the pressure, in the suburb of West Des Moines, a free spirit named Bill Post had no particular cares. And that made sense because Post expected to play a marginal role when the local caucus got underway. He might have been, after all, the newest Democrat in all of Iowa, having signed up only the day before at a political rally at the fairgrounds he attended with his wife. That appearance, out of character for him, sparked some ribbing at the firehouse, and Post—not one to shy away from the limelight—hoped to keep the notoriety going by showing up here this night. He also had a more serious motive: A gnawing concern that firefighters weren't getting what they needed to protect the homeland in these suddenly dangerous times. His union, the International Association of Fire Fighters (IAFF), had recently been sounding the alarm bells on that issue, and Post, newly promoted to lieutenant, felt obligated to do his bit to rectify the situation. He didn't know it yet, but his bit part was about to expand. Post would be unexpectedly thrust onto center stage in the auditorium of the Rex Mathis Elementary School to deliver the most important speech of his life—with almost no time to prepare.

Meanwhile, the IAFF president, Harold Schaitberger, who had helped forge the plan these men were carrying out, worried whether everything possible had been done to prepare the territory for the task at hand, and he wondered what the mood would be around the table the next morning when he had breakfast with Des Moines area firefighters.

What linked these men together was their participation in an ambitious, if unorthodox, political effort during the 2004 presidential election that was carried out—and that remains—largely under the radar screen. And yet, given the impact it had, their actions merit a closer look for possible clues as to whether, and under what conditions, labor retains its ability to influence electoral outcomes, and why it so rarely manages to do so. These are questions that go to the heart of labor's revival as a force in this country—and even to its very survival.

Iowa's votes had barely been counted when I began investigating the unusual dynamics behind the outcome. I was tipped off the next morning by labor backers of the candidates blitzed by the firefighters. "We never saw them coming," one said. And so I would spend the next days and months trailing Schaitberger, speaking with key players in the Iowa caucus, and watching firefighters operate behind the scenes. My goal was to piece together what they had accomplished in Iowa, how and why they had done so, what they were up to for the rest of the primary season, and what it all meant.

"Wait," you might say, signaling for a time-out. "Firefighters? Leading off a book about the labor movement and its future? Who even knew firefighters had a real union, or cared about politics? And Harold *who*?"

Precisely. Armed with precious little in the way of resources or experience and led by a union president nobody had heard of, once they decided to take the plunge, the firefighters had to rethink labor's traditional assumptions. They couldn't simply throw manpower and money at the campaign, couldn't rely on typical, labor-intensive (no pun intended) door-to-door canvassing, or telephone banks. Not only hadn't such approaches proved very successful for labor in quite some time, for the firefighters these were not even options. They had to apply their imagination to the chores ahead, figure out how to get the most out of what they brought to the fight, and create an impact far beyond their numbers. If this was to work, they had to use the qualities of a Ricky Kleinman, a John TeKippe, and a Bill Post to sway residents in ways that would compensate for the expensive advertising or mass rallies the union couldn't undertake.

And because so much was at stake, making it work was imperative. The firefighters' belated entrance into the national political arena, 86 years after their union was founded, was no whimsical choice. This was the first presidential election since the attacks of September 11, an event that had transformed their world overnight. They were America's first responders in a brand-new age of terrorism; with 343 of their brethren having perished at the World Trade Center, they felt that the politicians weren't providing the resources that would let them do the job with which they were now tasked. The levels of training and equipment, in their view, didn't match the political rhetoric or the demands being placed on them. The U.S.–led war on terrorism had cast elections and legislation in a more urgent light for the union and its members, so their voices needed to be heard and their concerns incorporated into the discussion and decision making at a national level.

But how? Where and when should they start, with what strategy and which tactics, and with what forces leading the charge? How could they make a difference as opposed to making fools of themselves? Indeed, with labor's political influence ebbing year after year—with *experienced* union activists failing to sway electoral outcomes—on what basis could this collection of newcomers, who constituted barely one-sixtieth of the union movement, realistically hope to have any effect whatsoever?

And those were only some of the obstacles they would eventually face once they actually entered the fray. The dismal early polling of their candidate, Massachusetts Senator John Kerry, signaled an uphill political struggle. Additionally, even within organized labor, the firefighters were taking on two dozen of the largest and most powerful unions that were backing rival candidates and apparent frontrunners Howard Dean and Richard Gephardt. These unions possessed far greater resources and boasted multitudes of veteran political operatives within their ranks.

As it turned out, the firefighters—a mere 2,400 strong in Iowa—packed a bigger wallop than anyone else. Than *everyone* else, in fact, combined. They managed to sustain and then rejuvenate Kerry's flagging campaign. They brought thousands of Iowa residents to his camp, and then on caucus night their peripatetic presence proved to be the X factor. The meticulously planned effort overwhelmed their stunned opponents in virtually every nook and cranny of the state.

They amazed everyone—even themselves—by fundamentally altering the national political calculus—something the entire labor movement hadn't been able to do in eons. Kerry, whose support only months earlier was in the single digits both in Iowa and nationally and whose appearance was so listless he was dubbed "dead man walking," would sweep to victory that night. This victory's dimensions and unexpected nature essentially catapulted him to his party's presidential nomination and ushered Gephardt and Dean out of the race, the former immediately, the latter soon afterward. When the votes were counted, the forces of Harold *Who?* routed Jim Hoffa and Andy Stern (president of the Service Employees International Union) and other labor luminaries who had appeared to have all the advantages in their corner.

The firefighters' unlikely and largely unheralded work didn't stop there. They continued to build on their momentum in equally effective if less dramatic fashion in the next primaries. Behind the scenes, the union's leaders prevailed on the entire labor movement to follow their example and endorse Kerry. Though treated by the media and other observers as a ho-hum fait accompli, the AFL-CIO's eventual decision to endorse Kerry early in the primary process marked only the *third* time in its history that the labor federation had taken such action. And the other two occasions involved sitting or former vice presidents—Al Gore and Walter Mondale—rendering what the firefighters achieved inside the labor movement as notable as what they did in the campaign itself. The IAFF succeeded not so much *despite* its small size, meager resources, and lack of a track record; rather, it turned those shortcomings into an advantage by proving to be strategically flexible and organizationally nimble enough to adapt to the various challenges at hand, thereby soundly whipping its more ponderous adversaries.

What the little band of firefighters accomplished in the snows of Iowa contains a treasure trove of material waiting to be mined at a time when organized labor has lost its electoral compass. But the episode has been left largely unexamined. That is understandable, given the IAFF's lack of prominence and its quasi-underground approach, combined with organized labor's recent split, the desire of union power brokers to forget what was largely an embarrassment, and the media's consistently poor coverage of virtually everything involving labor.

Yet with labor's ability to influence events increasingly questioned, and indeed its very survival in doubt, this episode should be examined.

This success story could not have started on caucus night, and in fact it did not. For months before the caucus, firefighters in Iowa had been quietly assembling their forces, planning their activities, seeking out likely supporters among neighbors, and generally laying the groundwork for the caucuses. One element in particular bears mention because of its simplicity yet effectiveness: The "Carloads for Kerry" program asked each participating firefighter to pledge to bring to his caucus site at least five residents exclusive of IAFF members. The tactic served as a *force multiplier* for the undersized union, and it caught other candidates off guard. This program would not have blossomed as it did without the unified structure, discipline, and cohesion that characterize their union—and the trade itself. Nor would the ride-along program have resonated among the state's voters if it hadn't tapped into the confidence neighbors and acquaintances have in their local firefighters to begin with. Helping Kerry reach required thresholds at sites throughout the state, and doing so early on election evening, allowed caucus leaders like Kleinman the luxury of focusing on prying supporters away from other candidates.

Regrettably little attention has been given to what the firefighters did in Iowa; exceptionally little, in fact, given the circumstances. These were colorful men engaged in a high-stakes political gambit, and the anonymity that surrounded their work was striking. To the extent they were noticed at all, it was inevitably the presence of a handful of them at a particular event, not their overall role or strategy in the campaign, that brought attention. And in those fleeting instances, they were often referred to by cable news anchors as "volunteer firefighters." Being ignored was one thing but this misleading, even dismissive, reference rankled. "I'd rather they call us cops," said one firefighter.

Sadly, it was completely predictable that their story would be overlooked, given the media's tendency to downplay or flat out miss what America's workers and their labor unions do. This is exacerbated by the failure of unions themselves to communicate what it is they stand for and what they're up to. For two decades, I've watched these twin trends reinforce each other, creating a downward cycle in terms of what the public learns about labor—and, thus, what it thinks of labor. It's by no means the only reason labor is in a tailspin it can't seem to get out of, but it sure contributes, and unlike the more systemic hurdles unions face, it's something that labor could readily change.

Though, on a personal level, who's complaining? One consequence of the neglect was that Harold Schaitberger, a figure out of central casting who'd have to be invented if he didn't exist, was available for generous stretches of time as the campaign unfolded. A sturdy, mustachioed old-school trade unionist, he had an emotional bond with his members, even if most didn't know his dramatic personal story.

Decades before, as a troubled teenager he had been given shelter by a kindly firefighter—a twist of fate that eventually would lead him to his present position and the union to its political metamorphosis. Whether at union headquarters in Washington, at a variety of firefighter functions and strategy sessions, or even at chance encounters such as a Bruce Springsteen concert for Kerry in Ohio on the eve of the November election, the access was invaluable.[1]

The upshot of neglecting the firefighters' role in the last presidential race is that it facilitated the portrayal of labor's activities in an unduly harsh light as simply one more predictable instance of labor's waning clout. That depiction stressed the unfortunate side of several major unions' performance in Iowa and afterward, including their internecine bickering, their awkward here-today, gone-tomorrow endorsements and, ultimately, their candidates' flops at the polls: a simplistically negative spin. While these things indeed occurred, they were by no means the most compelling—or important—part of labor's role in the political saga of 2004. They were simply the most obvious, and they conveniently fit the prevailing storyline of a labor movement in turmoil and perhaps in inevitable decline. So why dig deeper?

As a matter of fact, Iowa proves the need to dig deeper; and for those in labor and politics—perhaps even the media—to review the lessons learned. Concerning labor's impact, Iowa and indeed the last presidential contest were far more complex than this would suggest. Yes, some unions bombed. Yes, there was some discord within labor. But there were also some astonishing achievements. A closer look would raise a series of intriguing questions: What decisions contributed to a less-than-desirable outcome for most unions; what specific tactics and strategies succeeded for the IAFF; and what does this indicate about labor's future political approach?

It's important to note that Kerry's eventual loss in the general election in no way negates what Kleinman and Schaitberger and their brethren accomplished, nor does it diminish the value of what knowledge can be extracted from the effort. On the contrary, the fact that Kerry turned out to be a less-than-superb candidate waging a flawed campaign only adds to the significance of what the firefighters and their union accomplished.

Let's examine it further.

The caucus in Ottumwa had barely begun, and Kleinman had already scored his first triumph as the last of the residents he single-handedly recruited marched through the doors of the school's library. When the overall attendance was established, those 16 would suffice to lift Kerry over the minimum needed to qualify as a "viable" candidate in a given precinct. Any contender with less than 15 percent backing at a caucus site is ineligible to secure any delegates from that location, costing him or her whatever support he or she did have—and freeing his or her supporters to make a second choice among candidates who qualified. As it turned out, several candidates at Evans Middle

School missed the cut-off, meaning that Kleinman had by himself outperformed their entire organizations in terms of preparatory work during the weeks leading up to the vote.

With Kerry assured early on of getting past the first hurdle, Kleinman turned to attracting available residents, but his inexperience led to a small blunder. Misinterpreting the rules, he declined an offer from supporters of Dean, who'd unexpectedly failed to make the grade, to join Kerry's team under certain conditions. He ploughed ahead, and soon his energy and contacts were adding new recruits. The group's growth became a self-fulfilling prophesy, luring those who sought a winner, and eventually he had landed 49 residents. This was almost half of the 104 present under the union's gold-and-black signs. Pumped, Kleinman wanted to take a break and call his daughter who was working at another precinct in Ottumwa, but he knew this was no time to sit on a lead—not with something even he hadn't envisioned in his grasp. Kleinman approached the Dean supporters he'd turned down, who had since become the subject of overtures from other camps, and returned with 4. This was enough to give Kerry 53—an absolute majority of the caucus attendees.

Meanwhile, in the Waukee Public Library outside Des Moines, TeKippe was embroiled in a seesaw contest. It's not that he'd put any less effort into the advance work; he wrote and hand delivered a letter to everyone in his precinct—at their homes or outside church—who had attended a caucus in previous years, explaining why he supported Kerry. Even so, things were highly fluid. Eventually, it all came down to 1 last holdout among the 109 caucus goers, a middle-aged Gephardt backer who was quickly descended upon as if by salivating recruiters surrounding a high school basketball phenom. TeKippe let his competitors overwhelm the poor fellow and neutralize one another before he ambled over with a more conversational approach.

"You're a big person. I know you'll make your own decision, but if you have any questions about Kerry, I'll be over here," TeKippe quietly said. He turned to leave, but the man chuckled and responded: "That's what I was waiting for. I'm tired of getting leaned on." Bingo: That made it 51 for Kerry to 50 for Edwards, again giving Kerry not only a win but an outright majority of the delegates: 5 of the 9 at stake.

Just a few miles away, Post's jocularity had vanished. Kerry's caucus captain had contracted a bad case of nerves about addressing the West Des Moines gathering, and with no time to spare, the contingency was to replace him with Post, easily the most garrulous among them. As the only firefighter present, they thought he might have a rapport with the crowd, that people might take him as something more than just another Kerry advocate. The drawback was that he knew little about politics and less about Kerry. Post had only five minutes to soak up their words, even as he simultaneously skimmed the firefighter union's "cheat sheet" he had brought along. What they didn't know was that among the courses he'd been taking at the local community college for his two-year degree in fire science was Speech 101—and Lieutenant Bill Post would acquit himself just fine in the two-minute address he was about to deliver. He may have known few details, he perhaps had little political polish, but he was enthusiastic, he was their firefighter, and he definitely had the jury's ear. When the dust settled here, Kerry had tied for first place with Edwards.

None of this, of course, was supposed to happen. Nevertheless, not only *did* it happen but similar scenes were replicated all over Iowa. The details differed from place to place, but throughout Iowa's cities and suburbs, small towns and rural areas, firefighters spearheaded what turned into a Kerry romp that surpassed everyone's expectations. He took 38 percent of the vote, besting Gephardt and Dean combined by more than doubling Dean's total and tripling Gephardt's. Iowa Governor Tom Vilsack, who remained judiciously neutral during his state's caucus season even though his wife endorsed Kerry, attributed the senator's success in the first instance to the personal attributes and unanticipated level of organization of the firefighters. They "willed it," he says—which is a sentiment shared by key operatives for the 2004 campaigns of Dean and Gephardt, including union officials who backed the two candidates.[2]

There are five concrete ways in which the firefighters' efforts boosted their candidate:

1. They turned out residents. Of the state's 1,600 firefighters not working on caucus day and hence available to take part in the Carloads for Kerry program, 800 to 900 did so. That produced at least 4,800 votes for Kerry, a highly conservative count because many brought more than 5 (and, of course, themselves), including a firefighter in Des Moines who lugged 43 acquaintances in a veritable caravan of carloads. In addition, other firefighters who didn't formally take part in the carload program went to the caucuses with a friend or two, adding more votes. And well before caucus day, the firefighters' voter identification and lobbying efforts had focused on getting com-

mitments from residents favorably disposed toward Kerry to attend caucuses on their own.

2. Because firefighters, by dint of their profession, are present across Iowa, they were uniquely positioned to boost Kerry over the 15 percent threshold in one site after another. Other candidates had their geographical areas of strength—Dean near university towns, Gephardt in areas with factories—but elsewhere they often lacked sufficient support to qualify for delegates. Having 14 percent of the caucus goers at a given precinct was as worthless as having none. The omnipresence of the firefighters helped Kerry achieve the required percentage per location, thereby ensuring that he would get the votes of nearly all residents who intended to vote for him.

3. That, in turn, put them in position to pick off the newly available supporters of opponents who hadn't made the cut at a given caucus site as well as residents who had last-minute doubts. The aggressive activity of the firefighters situated throughout Iowa resulted in a windfall. Entrance and exit polling showed that 38 percent of union household caucus goers had planned to support Gephardt but the Missouri congressman ended up with only about half of those voters by night's end because he often missed the cut-off. Since union voters were a quarter of the total Iowa turnout of 130,000, that meant that Gephardt sacrificed more than 5,000 votes from labor households alone during the actual caucuses. Kerry, meanwhile, saw his share of union votes rise from 21 percent to 29 percent—a bonus of 2,500. That amounted to icing on the cake delivered by the firefighters.

4. Prior to the caucus, during the dark days of winter, at a time when staffers were losing hope and all could simply have fallen apart, the firefighters were pivotal in maintaining the pulse in Kerry's campaign. Not only was Kerry distant in the polls, he seemed moribund and utterly incapable of changing the dynamics. While it's true that Dean's collapse and Gephardt's failure to expand his base much beyond labor later paved the way for Kerry's victory, it was doubtful for much of the precaucus period that Kerry would survive long enough to profit should such an opportunity arise. Over those discouraging months, the firefighters quietly provided spirit, the prospect of better days, and some organizational backbone. Since they never gave up, how could Kerry and his inner circle?

5. Beyond their internal effect on Kerry's faltering bid, they provided his campaign with public credibility at a time when people otherwise might have concluded he was a nonstarter. And there is evidence that their backing helped boost the senator's personal image and resonance among Iowa residents. Polling data suggest that women who saw Kerry surrounded by firefighters formed a more positive view of the candidate. On top of that, the IAFF, whose ranks contain a heavy dose of military veterans and reservists, shopped Kerry around not only at fire stations but also at veterans groups' halls. Even before all this paid off at the caucus, Kerry's positive ratings were rising, and he became an acceptable fallback choice. That put him in position to benefit once the Dean-Gephardt negative ads began turning many residents off, and it was reflected as he

moved up in the polls days before the caucus. On caucus night, as the two former favorites bottomed out, with the firefighters' aid Kerry was able to siphon off many of their fleeing supporters, helping account for his upset win.

In Ames, firefighter Mike Bryant, two decades on the job, exemplified much of this. Hauling 11 neighbors, he more than doubled the carload goal. At his tiny precinct, which offered only four delegates, that contingent was enough for Kerry to win a tough three-way battle with Dean and Edwards—and capture twice as many delegates as each opponent. It was an unlikely outcome, given the proximity of Iowa State University, where Dean appealed to the large student body. Bryant's effort in the first place says much about the nature of the tightly knit union and the bonds, among firefighters and also with the public, at play here. While some firefighters came to Kerry's camp through their own research, for others, such as Bryant, the imprimatur of the IAFF's endorsement did the trick. In his job, he says, he routinely relies on judgments made by those above him. Meanwhile, none of the Ames residents Bryant brought had ever been to a caucus, and furthermore, each was undecided when approached by Bryant, who said that his mere status as a firefighter appeared more compelling to them than any political argument he advanced.

This entire episode marked a seismic break from the firefighters' past. Nothing in their history suggested they would try something like it, let alone succeed. Ever since firefighters began organizing into clubs and associations in the mid-nineteenth century and then into unions at the outset of the twentieth century, they had focused on professional issues. That didn't change appreciably even after a charter convention of 24 locals in Baltimore in 1918 created the IAFF. The "International" stressed matters pertinent solely to its members, generating few waves in the larger labor movement. The union's issues of choice—a two-platoon work schedule, civil service protection, medical research on the toll of fighting fires; and those were the nontechnical issues—were hardly likely to excite the public either. Given the restricted nature of the union's policy interests, its political outreach was largely limited to city councils, county boards, and occasionally to state legislatures, with Congress at best an afterthought and presidential politics not even that.

So what prompted the union's abrupt reinvention, the firefighters' pedal-to-the-metal undertaking in Iowa? What led Kleinman to end up at the Evans Middle School library on a cold night in January or TeKippe to test himself in the public library outside the state's capital?

Two seemingly separate trends intersected to bring all this about. One was the expanding role of the firefighter professionals as first responders and homeland protectors, which altered society's expectations of them as well as the way they approached their job. The second was the internal evolution of the union itself.

The meandering path that led to the IAFF's political awakening began 40 years earlier when a struggling youngster in Fairfax, Virginia, sought refuge from a difficult and impoverished situation at home. A local firefighter named Thomas A. Gaines, Jr., decided the 16-year-old could benefit from an extra cot at the local firehouse and also from some mentoring. And so Harold Schaitberger's haven during his last two years of high school turned out to be a clean bed amid the camaraderie of men with structured and purposeful lives—which helped set his own course.

Too young to sign on as a firefighter after graduating, Schaitberger bided his time with a stint as a grocery store clerk. But, impatient, he falsified his birth date so he could join the force a year before reaching the minimum age of 21. Those who knew him well enough to be aware of this also knew what he had been through and how much the chance meant to him, so they looked the other way. As it turns out, around that very time, two privileged Yale University students were making their own choices that would become part of the fabric of the election of 2004—John Kerry signed up with the Navy; George W. Bush joined the Texas National Guard.

Excited as he was about putting on the uniform, the new firefighter began chafing over the authoritarian management style that reigned in Virginia at the time. He'd been fending for himself since his midteens, and he bristled at what he saw as a patronizing work atmosphere; he couldn't abide the guff he got when he questioned things. So he decided to challenge the status quo, using softball games against firefighter teams from places that were more union friendly such as Baltimore and Washington as occasions to pull old-timers aside and seek advice on how to proceed. That led Schaitberger to IAFF headquarters in Washington, which initially was reluctant to help him organize his coworkers because of the formidable legal, political, and cultural obstacles they knew existed in Virginia. But they lost all hesitation once he mentioned that he'd already lined up a pool of several hundred potential union members.

Schaitberger gathered a half-dozen disgruntled Fairfax buddies and set out on a drawn-out drive to organize the department. His young wife received anonymous warnings that her husband shouldn't "get embroiled in this union stuff"—admonitions they ignored. Though easily the youngest of the six activists—more accurately, five, since one turned out to be a plant serving as a conduit to the chief—Schaitberger became the new union's first president. At age 24, still an unschooled hothead, he found himself in charge of northern Virginia's first firefighters' local.

He rose quickly through the ranks to head the state association of firefighters, where he emphasized legislative action to change how local fire departments were managed. Unlike other trades, firefighters had only one employer—government—which made involvement in politics and public policy central to the mission. This was particularly true in a state notoriously hostile toward public employee bargaining rights and their unions.

To increase the clout he could bring to bear, Schaitberger also became president of an activist coalition of firefighters, police officers, and schoolteachers. His governmental focus, and the fact that he was working right across the Potomac River from the nation's capital, brought him to the attention of the president of the international union. During a lengthy conversation between the two men as they drove to the funeral of a firefighter in Richmond, the IAFF chief asked the 30-year-old to head the union's fledgling political effort.

This career path was spurred partly by the personal ambitions of an IAFF insider who, hoping to deter a potential challenge to his job as elected regional vice president for the mid-Atlantic, helped maneuver the up-and-comer into this unglamorous staff job. As it turned out, the new position served as a stepping stone for Schaitberger. From 1976 to 1988, he helped reshape and energize what had been a listless political department. A new union president then asked him to move over to the executive suite as chief of staff, and he spent a second 12-year period running the IAFF's day-to-day operations while learning the organization inside out.

By 2000, pondering a run for union president, Schaitberger gathered a circle of former colleagues from Virginia. Their enthusiasm prompted him to throw his hat into the ring, and though he was unknown publicly, within the IAFF his background and stature were such by this point that he became the first presidential candidate in its eight decades to run unopposed. Schaitberger's priority upon taking office was no surprise—to advance the professional interests of firefighters through legislative and political action. He set up a school for candidates that has helped 425 IAFF members win political office, an idea now being emulated by the umbrella AFL-CIO. He also won a dues increase to fund greater political activity by the IAFF in the future.

This gradualist approach went out the window when, just months after he assumed stewardship of his union, terrorists crashed planes into the nearby Pentagon and the World Trade Center. The evolving demands on the firefighting profession and the inadequate resources reflected in the abysmal communications equipment that contributed to the heavy loss of life among first responders in New York made political action by the union a matter of urgency. There was palpable frustration with the Bush administration, which many firefighters felt was shortchanging them on their role in homeland security. And the heightened public admiration for firefighters provided leverage. The first chance to shape national policies would be the presidential contest of 2004. This was not without risk, given Schaitberger's status as the untested new leader of a somewhat overwhelmed union that suddenly had more on its plate than ever before—and all this in the context of labor's waning political influence and generally weakened position.

With the votes tabulated at Ottumwa's Precinct 10 and another win under his belt, big Rick Kleinman had a single thought: Party time. But where? Usually, after softball everybody knew the destination, but in this new sphere, aware that he would be battling the odds and unwilling to jinx the outcome, he had made no plans. After all, he'd figured third place was the most likely finish—not much to celebrate there—and even that wasn't a guarantee. Now, a startling, come-from-behind victory in hand, he'd have to arrange things on the fly.

He ended up at a local sports tavern, where things were just getting loud when Jack Reed, president of the Iowa state firefighters' union, got a call from an even bigger fish—Schaitberger—inviting them to join him at a party up in Des Moines. It was an hour and a half drive, and Kleinman and his buddies had mulled things over for 45 minutes after Reed left, but the trip turned out to be well worth it. Kleinman, an Army vet, ended up in a lengthy conversation with Kerry's Navy boat operator in Vietnam, and he also exchanged some pleasantries with Kerry's two daughters, though not with the senator, who showed up as well. By the time Kleinman got back to Ottumwa, it was 4:30 a.m.

How had the firefighters gone from acting on the simple desire to just get into the game to attending the victory party in Des Moines?

When the union's top officials had begun brainstorming about how to get involved, the questions far outnumbered any answers. Not only were they inexperienced at national-level politics but they would be out-gunned on every front, starting with their union rivals. This suggested that rather than fighting conventional warfare, battalion on battalion, they had to find a way to engage in asymmetrical battle, using guerilla tactics to mask their weaknesses, exploit their strengths, and catch their foes off guard. They couldn't compete in terms of resources or personnel, mass rallies or other publicity-generating events, bringing in heavy hitters to stir the troops. Any attempt to outdo others on their own terms would merely have exposed the IAFF as an ineffective little upstart.

But the union wasn't completely unarmed: Its chief attribute was the membership itself. Fighting an irregular war that focused on one-to-one engagements with the local population would complement the firefighters' strengths in terms of knowledge of their communities, relationships with the public, and the respect in which they were held. And internally, the membership was distinguished from that of most other unions by its cohesive nature as workers in a single trade, and its ability to function as a team—a skill honed of necessity since it was the only way firefighters could survive on the job.

And so the IAFF's leadership came to realize that its best shot was to harness those traits, get out of the way, and ride the members as far as they could take the effort. The local rank and file, the guys who actually put out fires, would win or lose this thing. And, by a stroke of fortune, Iowa—the first vote in the primary season—appeared hospitable to this approach. For one thing, its rural and small-town demographic made it the kind of place where people tend to know and respect their local firefighters.

Firefighter union officials had no manual to consult, but planning their approach appeared to mean three things in practical terms:

1. *A strategy stressing local autonomy, with the rank and file taking ownership of the process and being accountable for the outcome.* This required placing decision making at the lowest possible levels, with the union's leadership providing guidance and then leaving it to local officials and members to adapt general principles and programs to conditions on the ground. The international's big shots—such as they were—as well as its staff members and activists would be kept largely out of the way. The links between firefighters and the communities of people they served would have to be the lifeblood of the campaign.

2. *An endorsement process going well beyond the routine whereby workers accept a preordained favorite or passively select from a multiple-choice list.* If workers were going to put their heart and soul into the effort—the only way this effort

had a chance of succeeding—they had to believe in it at least as much as their leaders did.

3. *Tactics designed to capitalize on the unique characteristics of the union and its members.* By definition that meant devising maneuvers targeted to this endeavor rather than using labor's generic practices.

And there was an added wrinkle: the IAFF is likely the most Republican of all unions with, astonishingly for a labor organization, more GOP members than Democratic ones—44 versus 40 percent. So not only did a heretofore back-burner union that had been long focused more on professional matters than politics largely determine the outcome of the Democratic nominating process, it was *a Republican-dominated union* that did so! And one that arguably had a bigger effect than all other labor unions combined, even though many of them were long-time influential players in the Democratic Party.

Something unusual was required to ensure that the endorsement would be taken to heart in firehouses in Des Moines, and Nashua, New Hampshire, and Peoria, Illinois. To be sure, this was not entirely a virgin process; given his politically charged background, Schaitberger was no blank slate on the matter. He'd privately concluded by April 2003 that the IAFF should get involved as never before and that it should be on behalf of Kerry. But he was realistic enough to know it wouldn't mean much if it came from the top or even from a formulaic survey of member preferences, which often reflects previously expressed leadership preferences or mere name recognition. So the IAFF started from scratch with a process that included time-consuming exercises and discussions to establish ideal candidate attributes from a firefighter's perspective. That was followed by intensive polling by an independent firm of the union's members and leaders, as well as focus groups and in-depth interviews with candidates to determine who best fit the profile. The process lasted six months, leading to the IAFF's endorsement of Kerry in September 2003. The unprecedented willingness of their union to go out on a limb like this created a buzz among firefighters in Iowa and elsewhere.

This is not meant to sugarcoat the process; it was not entirely smooth sailing internally for the IAFF, nor could it have been given the group's political makeup. Mike, a fire-fighter from Queens, called the Rush Limbaugh radio show to mock the notion that union leaders spoke for the rank and file and to share with the host a mutual disdain for the "bosses of organized labor." Nor was he alone. Some Democratic-lean-ing members wrote Schaitberger that the union was crazy to go out on a limb for Kerry, who was trailing so badly. And then there was the strong support for native son Gephardt in the very geographic area that would be asked to put its shoul-der to this wheel—the Kansas City, Missouri–based region, which oversaw Iowa. Louie Wright, the IAFF's international vice president in the region, put aside his personal feelings—his own local, with a sizable membership of 1,150, had donated to Gephardt's campaign—and managed to get people on board. What helped him was the comprehensive and inclu-sive way the endorsement had been arrived at—and the unam-biguous orders from the Washington headquarters of a union representing a trade in which decisions were obeyed, not debated. That didn't, however, ease the ruffled feathers of other unions on the Missouri AFL-CIO's executive board;

they simply agreed to disagree. But on the whole, the scattered signs of dissent paled before the firefighters' mounting enthusiasm for the battle they were about to undertake in Iowa, in the early primary states, and beyond.

Why, though, *did* they end up in Kerry's corner? Dean, after all, was widely regarded at the time as the probable nominee. Gephardt had been labor's champion in Congress and inspired feelings of loyalty from many trade unionists. North Carolina Senator John Edwards was talking more than anyone else about America's division into the rich and those struggling to get by. If firefighters overwhelmingly wanted Kerry, it was more personal than policy driven—and it stemmed from how the senator had responded to a seminal event in firefighter history four years earlier in the city of Worcester.

Worcester is a surprisingly anonymous place. Few outside Massachusetts can pronounce its name, and fewer still are aware of its status as the state's second-largest city. It's the only location at which Sigmund Freud spoke when he visited the United States in 1909, it jump-started pro basketball's greatest dynasty by sending collegians Bob Cousy and Tommy Heinsohn to the Boston Celtics in the early 1950s, and it boasts a surprising array of universities for its size. Yet throughout its long history, even as the hilly old city became home to a still-thriving community of German-Jewish refugees in the 1930s, it has languished in the shadow of its neighbor just 38 miles to the east: Boston.

But for one tragic moment, Worcester became the center of the universe for America's firefighters. At 6:13 p.m. on December 3, 1999, a Friday evening early in the holiday shopping season, fire broke out in an abandoned warehouse. Two firefighters entered in search of any homeless people who might be trapped inside, only to end up overcome by smoke in the 80-year-old building's confusing maze of dark, windowless rooms. Mayday calls that they were running out of air prompted four other firefighters to charge in, before disappearing themselves as the five-story structure began collapsing around them. What ensued was an eight-day ordeal of recovering bodies—the last to be found, Paul Brotherton, 41, left six children—followed by days of funerals attended by 32,000 firefighters from around the world, the largest IAFF memorial in history.

The instant Kerry learned that a catastrophic fire was raging, he ordered his jet, which was in midflight to a fact-finding mission in Asia, to turn around. The way the supposedly aloof New Englander comforted the widows and children resonates to this day with local firefighters. "He felt our hurt. It's something we've never forgotten," says Frank Raffa, a longtime Worcester firefighter and razor-thin Vietnam veteran whose eyes still redden when he recalls searching on his hands and knees for his coworkers in the wreckage. Raffa, president of Worcester Fire Fighters Local 1009, set up a command center to assist the wives and children of the men trapped inside and to coordinate the rescue-turned-recovery operation. Four years later, Iowa flowed from Worcester's sorrow, which had forged immutable bonds between Kerry and firefighters.

The professional lesson Worcester firefighters took from the Cold Storage Fire was that with the right equipment, such as imaging cameras to let them know conditions inside, things might have turned out differently. Within a couple of months, the IAFF invited Kerry to speak at its annual legislative conference in Washington. That led him, in the weeks after, to open his Senate door to the firefighters and collaborate with them on bills that might help, including the Fire Act. Bonds between Kerry and firefighters were further strengthened after the terrorist attacks of 2001 as he sponsored a series of measures, ranging from the Father Judd Act to the SAFER Act. The former recognized a victim of the World Trade Center who ministered to fallen firefighters; the latter contained $7.8 billion for 75,000 hires over five years—similar to an earlier plan to put 100,000 police on the streets but, like much about firefighting, far less publicized.

Given this background, the IAFF's endorsement, based as it was on criteria well beyond labor's typical reference to voting scores, produced a candidate for whom firefighters' support would be impervious to political roller coasters or disastrous poll figures and that would not be dependent on the exhortations or whims of union leaders. Candidate in hand, the union's leaders focused on how to ensure that this would not be a Washington-run effort. The emphasis was shifted downstream to people in the region, in the first instance to Wright, the Kansas City–based official for Missouri, Iowa, Nebraska, and Kansas and a firefighter since 1972. A wiry stick of energy, Wright began huddling with officials from Iowa's statewide union and then with leaders of firefighter locals to discuss how to translate the international's goals into effective movement on the ground.

Wright recognized the practical challenge of relying on the rank and file. For one thing, Iowa had the second-smallest IAFF membership in his region. Given that, and facing far bigger labor unions whose forces in Iowa were being buttressed substantially by out-of-towners, eschewing outside help was by no means a self-evident choice. But Wright understood that if the firefighters' union was small in Iowa, it was small outside as well, and any efforts to play on that turf would pale in comparison to what other unions could do. Relying primarily on local members, even if it reduced the numbers available, offered at least the chance of sparking a grassroots fire, which just might scramble the playing field enough to change the odds. So Wright sent only two full-time staffers to Iowa to assist with planning and training. To compensate for the lack of resources, he suggested that a visible presence by even a few bearers of the firefighters' trademark gold-and-black at each scheduled Kerry event in Iowa, given the local celebrity that often accrued to them, could spark some useful dialogues while allowing the union members' effort to remain unobtrusive.

The union's Washington officials were not afraid to weigh in at key moments, even if behind the scenes and from a distance. To rally the troops at one low point in December 2003, Schaitberger got leaders of 22 Iowa locals on a conference call. During a 45-minute pep talk, he acknowledged that things looked discouraging and that the union was isolated, but then he appealed to their pride as firefighters accustomed to having their backs to the wall. He stressed the significance of what they were doing for their professional future, and he offered two practical suggestions: the Carloads for Kerry plan and the call for the gold-and-black color scheme to be clearly visible at every caucus site in each of Iowa's 99 counties. The latter was a seemingly innocuous ploy that would pay dividends—capitalizing on the widespread popularity of the firefighter brand, it ensured that anyone in search of a safe haven that evening would have a readily identifiable spot to repair to.

"I really believe that turned the whole thing around," said Ricky Kleinman. "Kerry was down and out; they were saying he was done. That was really our grassroots organization right there, where it all started." By a stroke of fortune, firefighter colors are Iowa's colors as well, notes Vilsack, who was governor of Iowa from 1998 through 2006, when he term-limited himself. By that, he means they are the school colors for the state's biggest sports franchise, the University of Iowa.

Compare the IAFF's approach with that of other unions involved in the caucus, and stark contrasts emerge. Early in the last presidential election cycle, as attention focused on Iowa and its first-in-the-nation contest, the political activities of two groups of unions attracted the lion's share of public attention. The Alliance for Economic Justice consisted of 21 unions with a combined membership of 5 million workers—a third of the American labor movement—including the International Brotherhood of Teamsters, the United Auto Workers (UAW), and the United Steel Workers of America (USWA). Their candidate was Dick Gephardt, son of a Teamster milk truck driver and former law school classmate of Hoffa's. More importantly, as the top congressional Democrat hailing from neighboring Missouri and having previously won the caucus in Iowa, he seemed to have a good shot. In short, backing Gephardt was a no-brainer for a labor union.

Meanwhile, two powerful and savvy unions coalesced around the man with the lead in the polls, the most money, the Internet savvy, and the best line: "I'm Howard Dean, and I'm here to represent the Democratic wing of the Democratic Party." They were the American Federation of State, County and Municipal Employees (AFSCME), with 1.4 million members, and the Service Employees International Union (SEIU), with 1.6 million. AFSCME, led by Gerald McEntee, who also ran the AFL-CIO's political committee and was the federation's political guru, was the biggest union in Iowa. SEIU, the federation's largest and fastest-growing union in the entire country, was the biggest AFL-CIO union in the next primary state, New Hampshire. Its leader, Andrew Stern, is among the country's most ambitious and high-profile labor leaders. In fact, Stern was featured in a prime story on *60 Minutes* in mid-2006, notable at a time when few were paying attention to labor.

Twelve years earlier, McEntee had taken a shine to another small-state governor, Bill Clinton, and employed his union's impressive know-how, connections, and resources to help guide the long-shot candidate through the primaries. As a result, McEntee had acquired a reputation within labor as a kingmaker. This time around, seeking a horse to ride to the nomination, McEntee looked at a number of candidates, including Wesley Clark, Kerry, and Edwards, before settling on Dean, who was enticing on several fronts. Not only was he surging, he offered the prospect of backing another successful outsider—thus repeating a previously successful formula of McEntee's.

For his part, Stern has a strongly independent streak; less than two years later he would be the driving force in forming the rival Change to Win federation, leading his SEIU out of the AFL-CIO. Not surprisingly, he too settled on the maverick Vermont governor in 2004. (To be fair, SEIU does have an endorsement process that engages members more so than many other unions.) Stern waited to see which way McEntee would go, and when it was clear he also favored Dean, the two decided to hold a joint press conference. They believed their organizational muscle and inside-the-Beltway credentials—two major gaps in Dean's campaign—would put him over the top, not just in Iowa but in clinching the nomination. The press conference was well played, with the media serving as willing accomplices, reporting that this more or less sealed the deal because it provided exactly what the insurgent campaign had lacked. It didn't hurt that McEntee and Stern are two of the most visible, accessible, and quotable American labor leaders.

Let's recap: almost two dozen unions were in Gephardt's corner, two giants supported Dean, while about 30-odd unions remained on the sidelines, preferring to see how things sorted themselves out, as did the AFL-CIO itself. And, though few noticed, the firefighters were behind John Kerry. Both major sets of unions—the alliance of old-line, mostly industrial unions and the powerful duo of service and government workers—waged high-powered, visible, and expensive campaigns on behalf of their candidates. AFSCME alone poured in $3 million. They held competing news conferences in and out of Iowa, flew their well-known national leaders to well-publicized events, stocked rallies with large numbers of labor activists, and did all the traditional door-to-door canvassing, phone banks, and everything else unions do in campaigns. And they added some finishing touches: on the eve of the caucuses, Teamsters from as far away as Ohio and Colorado drove seven 18-wheelers into Des Moines and encircled a downtown hotel where a Gephardt rally was taking place, their air horns and engines filling the night with noise in an unmistakable show of power.

While the firefighters' activities were carried out behind the scenes and focused on unglamorous activities such as one-on-one persuasion to painstakingly build up support, it was the other unions that appeared outwardly impressive and that drew the attention. They were, in every way, the opposite of the firefighters, with their resources and their reinforcements from out of state. And they endorsed in unison, based on shared political considerations and on behalf of large conglomerations of workers. Gephardt, on paper anyway, had 5 million union members behind him and Dean 3 million, compared to the 263,000 for Kerry. They were, in short, following labor's political playbook, and they seemed to be on the right track.

But we have seen how this play ends, how things came together for the firefighters and their candidate on caucus night. The other unions' activities bore little fruit and in many ways actually backfired. Their pronouncements and visibility raised the bar for how their candidates were expected to fare in the voting, making the results all the more crushing. And, particularly in the case of Gephardt, with their omnipresent involvement, they didn't so much complement the candidate's campaign as *become* the campaign, to the extent that some of the congressman's aides wondered privately after rallies why there were only steelworkers or auto workers present.

Where are "regular Iowans?" one asked. "Where was the public?" An official with the United Food and Commercial

Workers Union, which endorsed Gephardt, told me afterward that labor should be at most part of a campaign's "foundation, not the whole building." Kerry got targeted assistance from a union, while Gephardt's aides assumed he could rely on labor to stage rallies, build support, and supply votes, the official said. Meanwhile, the public, at least some segment of it, was unimpressed by someone easily branded as the candidate of big labor. Dean's unions, meanwhile, were mocked in some quarters for acting in fact as kingmakers and engaging in calculated outside political manipulation. To cap it off, on caucus night itself much of the supposed strength these unions brought proved illusory because only Iowa residents could actually join in the discussions. The firefighters, who had slipped under the radar screen in part precisely because they were local, certainly could—and did—participate. No one from competing campaigns, trade unionists, or anyone else for that matter could compete with the cohesion, coordination, and efficiency of the firefighters. And the union's work didn't end there.

While Kleinman and hundreds of other Iowa firefighters were toasting the outcome, their colleagues in New Hampshire were preparing for *their* showdown. New Hampshire loomed initially as a stiff challenge for Kerry, even after the success of Iowa. True, Gephardt had dropped out, but he never had been seen as a major factor in New England anyway. Kerry was one of three New Englanders fighting for the state, along with

Dean who had governed neighboring Vermont for eight years, and Connecticut Senator Joe Lieberman. Retired General Wesley Clark, who shared and indeed surpassed Kerry's military background, hoped to make a strong stand in the Granite State. Meanwhile, SEIU was frantically trying to restart Dean's campaign with the help of staffers from headquarters who'd been sent there, though some seemed dazed by what had hit them in Iowa. "Blindsided" was the word one used, comparing it to a tsunami, as he now labored to stem the momentum the firefighters had suddenly given Kerry.

But for a second straight time the firefighters—only marginally larger at 2,800 in New Hampshire—proved to be both the backbone of Kerry's campaign and more than a match for all rivals. As is generally the case with the IAFF in New England, New Hampshire firefighters are entrenched in the state's body politic, with at least a dozen serving in public office at the time, and the union profited from its members' personal appeal and political connections.

Instead of carloads, their staple in New Hampshire was edible—the chili feeds that quickly became an appealing local trademark of Kerry's campaign. During the protracted period before caucus night in Iowa when he was struggling, these events—initiated and run by firefighters—were arguably the only positive feature associated with Kerry's effort. To reinforce the link in people's minds, firefighters held each chili feed at a fire station. Over time, these events became the most visible activities carried out for any candidate in an otherwise gray mass of voter identification efforts and phone banks, door-to-door leaflet drops, and get-out-the-vote drives. Given the more traditional nature of a primary, the firefighters engaged in such activities along with other unions. But they were buttressed by a weapon rivals didn't have: hundreds of uniformed colleagues from throughout New England—where the union has deep historical roots—and from as far away as Arkansas, Florida, New York, and New Jersey. A plumber from Connecticut or a teacher from Rhode Island just wouldn't have had quite the same panache or be as identifiable. The lore of the Cold Storage Fire in nearby Worcester was still potent enough years later so that not just firefighters but management—in the person of the city's chief—journeyed up to New Hampshire to stand in the cold and pass out leaflets for Kerry.

Once again, the firefighters had the good fortune to wage a critical battle in a little state whose small-town demographics, where firefighters are especially well known and trusted, were tailored to their strengths. And this time they benefited from the momentum their brethren in Iowa had provided and the refurbished image it gave Kerry as a winner. After he finished on top in New Hampshire as well, Kerry had a full head of steam. If Iowa had staggered Kerry's opponents, it was the one-two punch that provided the TKO. Just three weeks later, he would win the endorsement of organized labor as a whole and increasingly be seen as unstoppable. The rest of the primary season would soon become anticlimactic.

The endorsement brings us to the second front on which the little IAFF was waging its unlikely fight among giants. Even as the union was campaigning in the primary states to gain voter support, it was maneuvering institutionally within the AFL-CIO, the two efforts complementing one another. In a sense, the IAFF's bureaucratic infighting made it possible for the firefighters to do what they did in Iowa and the early primary states by keeping the AFL-CIO out of the campaign; later that field success would provide leverage, allowing the union to work its will with the AFL-CIO.

The IAFF's first imperative was to avert an early labor endorsement before the primaries even began. In 2003, pressure was mounting from some powerful union presidents who aimed to signal labor's strong opposition to President Bush and ensure that a nominee would emerge relatively unscathed from the primaries and be at full strength in the general campaign. At the time, Kerry was barely a blip on labor's—or anyone's—radar screen, and an AFL-CIO endorsement would almost certainly have gone to Gephardt, longtime leader of the congressional effort against free trade. Using his status as an ally of AFL-CIO president John Sweeney, Schaitberger worked vigorously behind the scenes to ward off what might have been the final blow to Kerry's reeling bid. He had to do this twice; in August and earlier in the spring, Sweeney looked into whether there was "sufficient consensus" for an endorsement. Schaitberger, it should be noted, did not block such action by himself; AFSCME President McEntee, intrigued by Dean's ability to energize the Democratic base and raise huge amounts of money on the Internet, also inveighed against an endorsement.

This was critical because early AFL-CIO backing for Gephardt would have led to a unified labor effort in Iowa on behalf of the congressman, thereby preventing the firefighters from coming to Kerry's rescue. Keeping the federation on the sidelines, on the other hand, gave individual unions room to act independently, making possible the firefighters' all-out thrust in Iowa and beyond. That room to maneuver also provoked the split among larger unions that divided support between Gephardt and Dean, weakening both of them, even as two-thirds of the nation's unions remained neutral. This created the ideal conditions for an unknown but ardently committed and disciplined labor organization like the firefighters to make waves.

Then, once the IAFF-propelled Kerry shot to the front of the pack after Iowa and New Hampshire, Schaitberger—in a total reversal of his original effort to discourage an endorsement—used his widening influence to push for just such action. Getting the AFL-CIO to do so was by no means a foregone conclusion. There were a number of factors working against Kerry at a time when most primaries still lay ahead. The first time the AFL-CIO had taken such action, with former Vice President Mondale in 1984, the results were so counterproductive that the AFL-CIO vowed not to repeat it, holding to that stand for 16 years until Vice President Gore ran. The case for Kerry was decidedly weaker. He had neither served in a Democratic administration nor was he as allied with labor. Moreover, having been embarrassed so recently by events in Iowa and their aftermath, many of labor's political leaders saw no need to jump back into the political ring, preferring instead to let Democratic primary voters decide. And if there was to be an endorsement, of the two remaining major candidates, John Edwards boasted a lifetime pro-labor voting record of 96 percent to Kerry's 91 percent—usually a sacrosanct index for the AFL-CIO.

So Schaitberger, his work cut out for him, wasted no time after Kerry's Monday night win in Iowa. By Wednesday, the firefighters' chief already had spoken with several union presidents, in a delicate undertaking. Schaitberger couldn't push too hard lest he arouse resentment among colleagues he had unexpectedly vanquished in the caucus. So he focused on what was in it for them, striving more to plant the seed than win immediate converts—much as TeKippe had done with the last Gephardt holdout. Schaitberger tried to get others to think about how labor could best exert some influence not only on the race but also on the eventual nominee's outlook.

As Kerry's primary wins mounted over the next few weeks, Schaitberger spoke to wavering union presidents on the general board—the endorsing authority—and stressed that time was of the essence if labor was to be a player. Meanwhile, he put a bug in Sweeney's ear, gently prodding him to do a 180 and urge the board to endorse a candidate. A cautious man, Sweeney was reluctant to press for a vote before he was certain a consensus existed. Once Schaitberger secured diverse support from grocery workers, steelworkers, teachers, communications workers, and construction trades workers, he made a strong pitch to Sweeney. In the end, he helped bring about an outcome that was anything but preordained, even up to the very last minute.

On the morning of Thursday, February 19, 2004, the unusually harsh weather that had been pounding the nation's capital for weeks temporarily broke, providing a reminder that spring was only a few weeks away. The respite was especially welcome to officials at the AFL-CIO, preparing to hold a rally at noon outside their headquarters in downtown Washington. Perhaps the only discordant note was the first song that blared through the loudspeakers, a Rolling Stones' tune seemingly out of place for an event taking place under a huge banner promoting American jobs. As if to compensate, in short order

Bruce Springsteen's "Born in the USA" reverberated down normally staid 16th Street, just a couple of blocks north of the White House.

The mood was festive for this hastily called event, at which the AFL-CIO was poised to announce an endorsement in the presidential sweepstakes. Wary of the lunch hour slipping away, those present suddenly erupted as federation president John Sweeney finally exited the building and walked onto the stage, followed by Senator John Kerry. Behind them was a man recognized by few even in this union-dominated crowd—Harold Schaitberger, president of the International Association of Fire Fighters, trailed by a phalanx of uniformed firefighters.

What was happening today was highly significant for Kerry; just a month after the firefighters had rescued his flagging bid, the AFL-CIO was now clearing his path to the nomination. The federation's move shifted the focus away from intramural Democratic squabbling and toward a general election pitting Kerry against Bush, thereby making the nomination virtually a foregone conclusion at a time when the challenge being mounted by Edwards was still fairly strong. Strong enough, for example, to convince the clothing workers' union (UNITE) to stick with him through New Hampshire and beyond. Labor's decision put its vaunted foot soldiers and war chest at Kerry's disposal for subsequent primaries and more importantly, provided a sense of inevitability, all of which allowed him to conserve remaining resources for the fall.

Though Sweeney told the crowd that the AFL-CIO's leadership had "unanimously voted" to endorse Kerry that morning, this masked the actual internal struggle. In fact, five major unions representing 23 percent of the AFL-CIO's 13 million members had refused to join in the endorsement. They were the UAW, SEIU, International Brotherhood of Electrical Workers, American Federation of Government Employees, and UNITE. Yet despite the lingering hesitancy right up to the moment of endorsing, the IAFF had prevailed in the backroom politicking just as it had among voters. (If you recognize the early signs of labor's eventual split, you're right, for two of those unions would lead the breakaway from the AFL-CIO 19 months later. Interestingly, having lost this political battle, they would leave claiming that the AFL-CIO was overly focused on politics, as opposed to organizing.)

The public, of course, saw none of this infighting. The manner in which the firefighters flexed their newfound muscle inside the AFL-CIO was, to most people, as invisible as their impact at the polls. Unless, that is, someone had happened to play Kremlinologist with photographs of Kerry's victory speeches on Tuesday nights as the various primary states voted and had wondered about the mustachioed man, same size and age if more solidly built, invariably standing next to the candidate on the platform. Or the several men garbed in gold-and-black located somewhere in the background on those occasions.

Discerning listeners might have picked up on Kerry's shifting phraseology as he made his points in words that reflected his gratitude—and debt—to the firefighters. When, for example, Kerry wanted to attack the president's tax cuts, he would compare what a wealthy person and a firefighter would get. Or, questioning Bush's priorities, one line became a staple, even making it into a television advertisement three days before the Boston convention: "We shouldn't be opening firehouses in Baghdad and closing them down in our own communities."

Another clue might have been the presence of firefighters at the February endorsement event. Normally a rare sight at AFL-CIO gatherings, reflecting their lack of an activist role, here they were everywhere. A few uniformed officers on the stage stood solemn and erect, in novel juxtaposition with steelworkers and Teamsters, teachers and laborers and autoworkers, while IAFF staffers in the crowd wore their gold-and-black T-shirts and waved signs.

Or someone might have listened in as Kerry, relaxing momentarily inside the AFL-CIO building after the endorsement, acknowledged privately how essential the role of the firefighters had been from the get-go in his bid for the nomination. "They were fabulous," he told me. "They were the first. They were the spirit of this campaign."[3]

And the secrecy would have been blown in the unlikely event someone read the small print in some labor bulletin three weeks after the February rally and noticed that Sweeney had named Harold Schaitberger cochair of Labor 2004, newly created to lead the AFL-CIO's election efforts. That occurred at the AFL-CIO's annual winter executive council meeting in Bal Harbour, Florida, where labor leaders were pondering how to improve political prospects for the fall and beyond. This was a sensitive matter. A star after he picked Bill Clinton out of a crowded candidates' lineup in the early 1990s, McEntee's political luster had recently dimmed because of his aborted fling with Dean. Having endorsed Dean with much fanfare and plunged right into Iowa and New Hampshire, only to be bested by the smaller firefighters' union, McEntee had abruptly yanked his support from Dean, engaged in a public spat with him, and then hinted at displeasure with the federation's endorsement of Kerry.[4] Naturally the press, which had ignored the firefighters' saga, loved the McEntee-Dean episode, which fit right into the prevailing storyline of an inept labor movement full of inside-the-Beltway intrigue. Conservative commentators in particular relished the image of trade unionists' no longer honoring the notion of loyalty and jumping ship at the first sign of trouble. Rather than embarrass the well-connected and still respected McEntee by removing him from his prized post, Sweeney established the new election panel and placed Schaitberger atop it alongside McEntee—a rather meteoric rise for the president of a small, unknown union.

Let's conclude by looking more closely at why a burly softball pitcher and a modest Navy vet clobbered Hoffa's 18-wheelers, McEntee's millions, and Stern's troops—and what it means.

The element everything revolved around was the individual firefighter and the traits he brought to the battle, particularly knowledge of his local community and its residents, and the respect with which firefighters are regarded. The personal relationships that result from both factors helped firefighters build support over the weeks before the caucuses, persuade residents to ride in the Carloads for Kerry program, and then close the deal on caucus night. Police officers also serve the public, but their main interaction with average citizens is handing out speeding tickets or ending noisy parties. Firefighters rescue people, save homes, and administer emergency medical care. They also tend to participate in community activities such as Little League baseball, charities such as burns foundations, and Big Brothers and Sisters. The IAFF is, for instance, by far the nation's largest contributor to Jerry Lewis's annual muscular dystrophy drive.

The nature of the Iowa caucus provided a good fit, with its communal aspect and premium on personal influence. While voters in other states' primaries cast ballots privately and anonymously behind curtains, participants in a caucus take sides publicly and collectively, after extended efforts to sway one another. That dynamic highlighted personal relationships, credibility, and trust and played right into the hands of people like Kleinman. The IAFF would later shift its tactics in other states, but the momentum had already been built, and its candidate's chief rivals were either diminished or defeated.

Third, the IAFF's strategy of relying on grassroots troops gave the union a chance to exploit its unique strengths, while compensating for the union's vulnerabilities; their tactics wedded those assets to the local environment. Beyond that, the approach tapped into—and took to a new level—a political trend: the gradual shift away from a mass-marketing approach and toward old-fashioned retail politics. In a way, what the firefighters did was to intensify the move away from mass mailings, TV buys, and anonymous tactics by honing and amplifying the personalized approach in a manner that fit both their distinctive traits and those of the caucus system.

The structure and organization of the union and of the trade it represented, elements rarely considered in looking at labor, were critical in a number of ways. The firefighters' ubiquity, as noted, was custom-made for Iowa's caucus because it helped assure that Kerry would get to keep virtually all of his supporters. By necessity, firefighters are found everywhere people live, including the Deep South, where labor tends to be notoriously weak. Meanwhile, the homogeneity of the union in that it represents essentially one profession provided a shared set of concerns and a greater likelihood that a favored candidate would resonate widely among members. Its hierarchical, chain-of-command nature got the plan disseminated, coordinated, and executed. Firefighters are accustomed to functioning in a paramilitary manner.

Buttressing all this is the fact that firefighters belong to perhaps the most highly unionized profession in America, at some 85 percent. And while they are in every community, they are not spread out in a plethora of small shops but rather located in a discrete set of workplaces. Even the schedule of the fire profession, mundane as it might seem, contributed. Most firefighters are on what is sometimes called the *California swing shift*, working a full 24-hour period, followed by a couple of days off. That let the Iowa firefighters focus on campaigning for long stretches in the run-up to the vote. And on caucus day itself, it meant that fully two-thirds—1,600—of Iowa's firefighters were free all day to arrange their carloads, make last-minute adjustments, deliver the riders, and attend the caucuses. More than half did so to the maximum extent. Making use of the union's unusual level of organization, IAFF officials had identified Republican members and urged them to volunteer to work on caucus day. That freed most Democrats for political activity, accounting for the high percentage of those available who actually participated in the car-load program.

The manner of endorsing—based not on overt political cal-culations but geared instead toward finding the candidate who reflected the outlook of firefighters and who saw the world as they did and was therefore someone whom they could believe in—left them personally invested. That explained their zeal and perseverance when things got tough, and this commit-ment applied to the leadership as well. The IAFF was not about to switch horses if things didn't go well. This ran counter to a trend for union endorsements to mean less and less, as evidenced by the "Reagan Democrats" or by George W. Bush's strength in both 2000 and 2004 among white males, including those who belonged to unions. It also differs from the facility with which some unionists, after Iowa, jilted a can-didate as easily as they'd initially sidled up to him. Nor was the IAFF's performance in this instance a one-time thing. In pre-vious local and state races, an average of 64 percent of mem-bers had abided by the union's endorsement—impressive when one considers the partisan divide within the union and the union's willingness to go either way politically. The fire-fighters contribute as high a portion of their money to Republicans as any union.

The combined effect of the thorough endorsement process and the membership cohesion was powerful. Jim Spellane, spokesman for the electrical workers, says that unity was the key to success for the firefighters in Iowa—and to the less-than-stellar performance of some other unions.[5] It's critical, he told me, to "make sure the troops are ready, willing and able, behind you"—especially at a time when the ability of labor leaders to command that workers rally to a political cause has so seriously dissipated. International Brotherhood of Electrical Workers (IBEW) polling showed its members to be all over the lot on the primary field, which was the main reason the union, whose 750,000 members placed it among the half-dozen largest in the AFL-CIO, didn't endorse early and abstained even when the federation made its decision in February.

In a field where several candidates have a claim to labor's support, it seems, one energetic and creative union whose members are devoted to a specific candidate may be more influential than a collection of labor leaders engaging in a more calculated embrace of a candidate. The kind of consensus-driven, lowest-common-denominator mechanism required to achieve the backing of "organized labor"—that is, the AFL-CIO as a whole—might well be a thing of the past, or should be, in any case.

The reputation of the IAFF for working well with office-holders from both parties boosted the credibility of the Kerry endorsement among the union's members and beyond to the citizens they were trying to reach. Mark Ouellette, who helped coordinate Kerry's chili feeds in New Hampshire and is a past president of the state's firefighters, says his work on behalf of local political candidates has benefited immeasurably from voters' perception that "we're not just a one-minded group of unionists." This seems to suggest that less can be more as regards labor and politics; with less partisan engagement translating into more credibility as a spokesperson for the members' and the public's interests. The IAFF's focus on professional matters, its independence, and the perceived lack of political intrigue among its leaders—all factors that had made the union appear an unlikely player—in fact helped it succeed.

It's not as if the IAFF had been politically unengaged, and it benefited greatly from the type of politics it *had* practiced in the past. Though the union long had a low profile, the work it focused on behind the scenes supporting its locals' bargaining and legislative efforts on state, county, municipal, and local levels led it to compile a voluminous data store at headquarters. That information dealt with the resources, characteristics, and needs of communities across the country. "Everything is local here," as one official put it, in a variation of Tip O'Neill's classic quote. From the 1960s on, this knowledge had proven critical time and again when unions negotiated contracts with a given town, city, or county. Now it would serve a new purpose in this national campaign, precisely because of the IAFF's grassroots approach to the primaries. If Kleinman and Post and the other campaigners possessed unparalleled knowledge of their communities, it wasn't solely because of their treks around town or their outgoing personalities. While the international mostly stayed out of the Iowa campaign, providing such data proved invaluable in helping local officials and members proceed.

And though they surprised everyone, in recent years the firefighters had been doing dry runs of a sort. The union had helped elect Arizona's Janet Napolitano as governor in 2002 after 12 years of GOP gubernatorial rule, and rescued Vilsack—as he is the first to grant—from a double-digit deficit in his initial race for the Iowa State House in 1998. Under Schaitberger's lead as political director, the union had quietly built up a respectable political action committee (PAC) and clearly was poised to exert itself on a national level when the opportunity arose.

Finally, the near-invisible nature of the firefighters' campaign in Iowa genuinely contributed to its success. The notion of the squeaky wheel getting the grease fits journalists' coverage of labor, and clearly those wheels belonged to the giant trucks driven into Iowa by the Teamsters on behalf of Gephardt and figuratively, to the two large unions supporting Dean. However, while the anonymity attached to the firefighters in Iowa helped their effort in various ways, it also meant that the public was not made aware of the little union that could.

Nor, it seems, has the labor movement itself absorbed the lessons from what the firefighters accomplished and what other unions didn't. Let's look briefly at two events in Washington that sandwiched Labor Day in September 2006. At the first, AFL-CIO President Sweeney, the political director, a pollster, and others unveiled with great fanfare the federation's campaign plan for November's congressional elections. Nearly everything it trumpeted about its goals and tactics could have been—and was—said two years earlier, or four years earlier, or six years earlier: the same throwing of money at political campaigns, the same worn techniques, all apparently reflecting the belief that the same is good and more of the same is better. Chart after chart, slide after slide, table after table, all showing how successful labor's past political efforts have been in terms of getting union members to the polls and how this one would build on all those performances. Nary a fresh idea or novel approach or self-criticism was voiced.

This would be the AFL-CIO's biggest off-year election effort ever, they all said. Several skeptical reporters asked how that could be, in light of the founding of Change to Win a year earlier, a split that cost the AFL-CIO seven unions. Because, federation officials insisted, the remaining unions would compensate by working harder. After the room had cleared out, I pressed the point with top AFL-CIO political operatives for many minutes—to the eye rolling of nearby communications staffers. I tried to point out that having lost one-third of their membership since the last go-around, to surpass previous efforts they would have to ramp up their spending and efforts per member by more than that amount. They said they would indeed do that. That evening I got a call from a leading AFL-CIO official, indicating that as a matter of fact they had erred: this *wouldn't* approach the biggest effort ever. What they meant, she added, was that the individual unions remaining in the AFL-CIO would beat *their* previous combined efforts. The call came after the wires had already put out a story touting labor's biggest political effort to date.

More important than the communications glitch was the focus on the same old, same old. Labor officials continue to spend more time and resources preaching to the choir, seemingly oblivious to the fact that they're going after a shrinking segment of the population—virtually the polar opposite of the force multipliers pursued by the firefighters in Iowa.

(Note to AFL-CIO: Though the press depicted Iowa as an unmitigated disaster for labor, it wasn't, and not only because of the overlooked firefighters. Some 25 percent of the caucus goers were from labor households, in a state with only 11 percent union membership, meaning union members were well

represented at the caucuses. So all those unions actually succeeded in spurring turnout. And Gephardt pulled 22 percent
of the union vote, compared to only 8 percent of nonunion
voters. There simply weren't enough union members in Iowa,
meaning there were fault lines in focusing exclusively on labor
voters in the first place. This was a double whammy in Iowa,
as Gephardt and even Dean often lost their supporters at a
given precinct because there weren't enough nonunion supporters to allow them to qualify. So trying harder or putting
more money into the same thing—turning out the members—
is throwing good resources after bad. Labor's shortcoming was
not one of execution but of a strategic failure to come to grips
with the implications of labor's overall membership decline.
As organized labor keeps throwing more and more money at
turning out its membership, it ought to keep in mind the definition of *insanity*.)

And no, the success of the Democrats in the November
2006 congressional elections does not mean labor has turned
the corner politically. If anything, these elections represented
a blown opportunity for unions for reasons to be discussed in
Chapter 3. A week after that first session, labor's top leaders
gathered in a Capitol Hill hotel with senior officials from the
Democratic Leadership Council (DLC) to announce the
DLC's support for labor's top legislative priority—a package
of workplace reforms guaranteeing workers the right to
organize a union if they so chose. (As you will see shortly, this
is a right that exists in virtually all industrialized democracies,
but in the United States it is more prominent in theory than
in reality.) Sweeney was there, along with McEntee and—lo
and behold, a woman—Anna Burger, leader of the breakaway

rival Change to Win federation, as were Vilsack, chairman of the DLC, and its executive director, Al From. Labor came perilously close to signing away its independence as a political actor and putting its fate in the Democratic basket, all the more so because, at the session a week earlier, the AFL-CIO had acknowledged that its political endorsements in the congressional elections would be more one sided than ever. Though the process hadn't yet been completed, labor's political officials could name only one Republican they were backing, compared to dozens in past elections.

Recall that a key factor in the firefighters' recent political success has been that they are perceived as honest brokers making decisions based on the merits and on their members' professional interests, not as appendages of a particular party. Recall too that their operational distance from the Kerry campaign in Iowa meant they complemented, rather than became, his campaign.

Stepping back from the details, the reasons for the firefighters' accomplishments in the last presidential primary season boil down to this: they started by tossing out labor's conventional wisdom and cookie-cutter approach. Instead, they critically evaluated the traits of their union and their members, analyzed the electoral environment they were entering, and devised a strategy to connect those two sets of factors. Then they adopted tactics that meshed what they brought to the table and what they needed to achieve. Everything they did was part of that cohesive whole, from an endorsement process that would keep members on board during a tough effort relying on the rank and file, to a coordinated showing of the colors on caucus night to exploit the public persona of firefighters. And all the plan's elements were fashioned with a mind to minimizing the union's considerable weaknesses while maximizing its unique assets.

The specific activities the firefighters chose are not necessarily replicable by other unions engaged in other political situations—but that's precisely the point. A one-size-fits-all program does not work, especially for an institution or movement growing weaker as we speak. The firefighters' formula for success was not any precise set of activities but rather a flexible and adaptive approach. With that approach in hand, they showed that by playing its cards just right, labor can wield surprising influence. There's still life there. A careful look at the recent forays into politics by labor, including the firefighters, indicates not that unions have entirely lost their political clout but rather that a weakened labor movement can no longer simply go through the motions and expect to get anywhere. A creative approach that taps a union's strengths, however, can produce wonders.

And yet, the IAFF—indeed, the whole labor movement, which the firefighters had pulled along—ran into an obstacle down the road as the general election approached. What occurred at that point suggests that even when labor makes spectacular efforts here and there that generate results, the growing frailty of the labor movement as a whole eventually imposes limits. This was a hurdle labor couldn't budge. Before we are introduced to this appealing young obstacle in Chapter 3, we first turn to the other major arena in which labor is struggling to carry out its mission—the workplace. And there we'll meet a group of workers whose efforts were no less significant than the firefighters', who faced equally long odds, and whose struggle offers important lessons of its own—the poor but proud women who skin and fillet and pack the cat-fish of the Mississippi Delta.

As you read, keep in mind the inextricable link—barely sketched yet—among politics, organizing, and the workplace. Until labor sharpens its political act—pushes once again its issues, including labor law reform restoring the right to organize, onto the national agenda—it will continue to shrink in membership. That, in turn, will make it yet harder for unions to have any say on legislation and federal policies that affect both their members' working conditions and their own institutional survival. And labor's downward spiral will con-tinue, with the attendant pulling down we have seen of job security, wages, worker safety, and the like. This nexus is labor's most vexing problem, even if union leaders continue to snipe at one another over whether to focus on politics or organizing as the solution to their woes. Misunderstanding their dilemma serves only to guarantee the continuation of their woes.

CHAPTER 2

DELTA PRIDE

If the case of the Iowa firefighters shows what labor can achieve in the political arena given the proper strategy, the story of Delta Pride illustrates labor's potential in the realm of the workplace and workers' lives, as well as in the broader community—despite declining resources, ebbing strength, and adversaries with influence. This achievement is all the more stunning because it occurred in a state in which the elite has long viewed organized labor as an alien element and in which union membership has represented a scant 5 percent of the workforce.

The sleepy Delta town of Indianola lies in the heart of Mississippi's Sunflower County, an isolated region where change comes slowly, if at all. Grab a counter stool at one of the local eateries, and just as in years past, they'll slide you a plate of fresh local catfish with homemade hush puppies and coleslaw. It's the kind of delicious and inexpensive fare you'd expect to find in the catfish capital of the country, and when you're done, they'll urge you to "Come back and visit us again, y'hear?"—making a first-timer feel almost like an old-timer.

You can get a room at the inn for $40 a night, but unless you book the second floor, you may have to sweep the blackened window clear of crickets simply to peer outside or block the vents with your shoes to keep them out. And try to avoid the little green frogs that every few seasons invade the area and hop all over people. Whites still tend to cluster north of the railroad tracks, where stately homes and some sprawling estates dot the countryside. South of the tracks one finds a world of stark poverty, where blacks live in narrow shacks virtually on top of one another, though in recent years some have been torn down.

The town—population 12,066, hometown of blues singer B.B. King, and birthplace of the White Citizens Council that was formed a half-century ago to defend Jim Crow practices— is midway between Jackson and Memphis and 25 miles east of the Mississippi River that divides the state from Arkansas. It retains a provincial view of the outside world, sometimes startlingly so. On my first visit years ago, a deputy sheriff wearing a fake smile greeted me in mellifluous tones, "How about that—you all the way down here from St. Louis, Kansas, just to visit us." He was, of course, about as genuinely glad to see me as he was geographically literate since my intent was highly subversive: to report on a bitter labor struggle that had racial overtones. But then as now, manners and at least the pretense of hospitality trump sincerity.

Yet some things *have* changed in Indianola over the past decade. Mayor Tommy McWilliams, that icon of the local establishment, is gone, replaced by a black mayor. Turner Arant, an aristocratic yet friendly farmer who reigned over more than a thousand workers as chairman of the board of

Delta Pride, the world's biggest catfish processor, left that post after showing his lavish home to a reporter and explaining how the good Lord had blessed him. It was a faux pas considered all the more egregious given the workers' living conditions. Local law enforcement has changed too, with justice now dispensed in Sunflower County by an elected African-American sheriff. A black inspector now approves buildings, while the levee board is racially mixed for the first time, and surrounding towns have black officials of their own.

And down at the catfish processing plant, where the atmosphere was once thick with hostility and marked by arbitrary firings, grievances have dwindled to a few and are generally worked out casually by both sides. The last formal arbitration took place years ago, and mass firings of workers for "insubordination" or other questionable digressions are also things of the past. A new layer of management, familiar with unions, was brought in from California and instituted ergonomic changes among others. More broadly, many Indianola residents who labor for a living share a belief that they can achieve at least some progress—economic or political—if they stick together.

Each of these is a significant transformation for a remote place largely untouched by the civil rights movement of the 1950s and 1960s; together they are little short of startling. Indianola's path from there to here has had a most unlikely trigger. To a large extent, the changes stem from these same catfish workers, their labor union, and the seminal struggle the two waged in the early 1990s, one whose reverberations are still being felt today. The catfish workers episode suggests some of the key factors that need to be present for labor to realize its potential. The workers who went on strike—some

900 impoverished black women—prevailed despite being entirely out-gunned and facing seemingly insurmountable obstacles. Indeed, it is hard to imagine a more unequal confrontation, or more hostile terrain on which to battle it out. But with their union framing the fight in a way that resonated broadly, unexpectedly out-strategizing the company, and then communicating the message with a shrewdness that usually eludes labor, the workers not only succeeded far beyond their own expectations but have for years been witnessing the enduring effect.

By the 1990s, though the sweet autumn smell of cotton under harvest still permeated the countryside, catfish was nudging it aside as the king crop of the Mississippi Delta. Less dependent on the weather and requiring less space, pond-grown fish proved highly profitable and rapidly grew into a $2 billion industry in Mississippi, one dominated by a relatively new Indianola company called "Delta Pride." Within a decade of its founding in 1981, Delta Pride was handling 40 percent of the world's farm-raised catfish. It provided Sunflower County farmers with a place to sell their fresh fish, and it also allowed them to share in the profits from the ready-for-market product, which was sold to grocery retailers around the country. And supermarkets valued Delta Pride's catfish because it sold so well.

Early morning on any given day in Indianola, you'd see farmers like Joe Oglesby peering into their ponds as they fed the fish or checked the oxygen levels. Even on Sunday, the time-honored traditions of breakfast and church would wait; dawn was the most important time of the day. Catfish is a risky crop, unseen by the farmer until it's harvested and subject to being spoiled at any moment by malodorous algae or a lack of oxygen. While catfish ponds require fewer workers than traditional crop farming, they also require closer inspection. That kind of daily involvement invested farmers personally in the outcome in a way that went well beyond worrying about balance sheets or quarterly profits.

The 180 farmers who ran Delta Pride—each white, each prosperous—had a double bite at the apple. Oglesby, who operated a midsized farm in the Delta and was an original stockholder in the company, would buy fingerlings at three or four inches long, feed them for 18 months, then harvest them at 1½ to 2 pounds. His catfish were trucked live to one of the two Delta Pride plants, where in less than a half hour they were turned into the finished product, which—in light of the care that accompanied every step of the raising and processing—he likened to prime beef. If the farmers didn't need much in the way of a workforce in the first step of the process, they needed plenty when it came to the assembly-line work that went into preparing the fish for sale to customers. That meant keeping labor costs low via brisk and efficient production.[1]

Many of Delta Pride's 1,200 workers had once picked or chopped cotton in the now-mechanized cotton fields, before switching to the catfish industry. Although their jobs had moved inside, they found little difference in terms of the low pay, unhealthy working conditions, and what they deemed constant affronts to their dignity. Under close supervision, they killed, beheaded, de-lunged, filleted, graded, boxed, or froze the fish. Even a matter as personal as bathroom visits was strictly regulated; they were restricted to six a week, none longer than five minutes—including the walk. Violations meant formal "write-ups" and eventual dismissal. Work breaks were so infrequent and their tasks so repetitive that local physicians were finding arthritic problems in workers as young as their early twenties, Dr. Ronald Myers of nearby Tchula, who had treated several of the workers, told me. All this for poverty-level wages.

In a phrase that would become memorable, Ester May Woods, among the older workers at 51 and a veteran of 8 years filleting Delta Pride catfish following a quarter-century in the cotton fields, called it "the plantation mentality brought into the building," as we spoke one evening. "I try not to see it in that light, but my mind focuses back to the old plantation," said Woods, who was 14 when she began in the cotton fields. "This takes the place of the cotton patch. That's the way it seems to me. The wages and the way they work you—they never let up."

As the farmers saw it, they *couldn't* let up. They may have achieved prosperity as a result of their cooperative's well-earned success, but increasingly their backs were against the wall. What the workers viewed as matters of indignity the farmers viewed as economic imperatives. For years Mississippi catfish farmers had been at the forefront of the fledgling industry, but by 1990 they were facing growing competition from copycat operations in surrounding states that had learned from their formula for success. They didn't want to alter workplace practices that had proven fruitful, and with fuel prices rising, the last thing they were willing to do was increase wages in any meaningful way, especially if this was being urged by a brash new union that had recently invaded their plant and their town. The farmers had never worked under union restrictions, and they didn't understand or appreciate the notion of someone telling them how to use their workers.

As contract negotiations neared, the catfish farmers felt morally and economically justified in taking a hard line against the workers' demands, and given the power differential, they were confident about the outcome of any showdown that might result. They held all the traditional cards in a labor-management battle, and as backup, the town's power structure was behind them; the mayor conveniently moonlighted as their attorney. The farmers sat on the board of directors of banks that held the workers' mortgages. The police were their friends. And their prospective adversaries, the ones stirring things up, were a few out-of-town, ragtag union types, outsiders from Tennessee intruding into an area that had virtually no acquaintance with, or sympathy for, the labor movement.

On top of that, the farmers felt that unskilled laborers were lucky to have steady work in the first place. While Oglesby understood that the catfish workers "want to better themselves," he noted that they were virtually all black women with few options and that, as such, the "plant has been a godsend for these people." This was, after all, a town whose population was 60 percent African-American and long had suffered from high unemployment, with about one in six blacks being jobless.

The workers harbored no illusions about what they would be getting into if they fought to improve their conditions, but they also felt they had no choice, if they—or even their children—were to have any chance at a decent future. "Who's to say that Tangelia won't end up at Delta Pride?" Sarah White, 32, asked as her 6-year-old daughter ran outside to play at their public housing development in nearby Moorhead. White had begun picking cotton at age 12, trailing behind her mother and aunt with a small sack. At 16, she left the cotton fields to live with her grandmother in St. Louis, a common migratory path for many black Mississippians. After returning to Indianola, she started at Delta Pride for $3.40 an hour, where she was now in her eighth year as a catfish skinner. Like many of her coworkers, she was a single mother.

Maybe if the workers stood up now, White said, her daughter "won't have to struggle as hard as I did." Whatever the outcome, at least White would be able to look herself in the mirror. "We're going down in history," she predicted, "as black women in Mississippi who tried to do something."

Neither side was prepared to back down. As the first contract talks approached since the plant had been organized by United Food and Commercial Workers Local 1529 in Memphis, the stage was set for a showdown.

The phone rang one morning in the fall of 1990 as I was sitting at my desk in St. Louis, oblivious to what was occurring 400 miles to the south. It was Al Zack, the chief Washington flack for the United Food and Commercial Workers (UFCW), telling me, "There's a great labor story on the Mississippi Delta. Nine hundred women have walked out of a catfish processing facility. It's the biggest strike by black workers in the history of Mississippi, but nobody's writing about it."

The last time I'd heard about catfish, I was a kid and the guy in the pet shop was selling me what would become the bottom-crawling specimen in my prized aquarium. And the Mississippi Delta sounded like another planet. But Zack was far too enthusiastic to ignore, and he pushed all the right buttons. "It's just the type of story you're interested in; it's got race and gender, human drama, and it's David against Goliath. The local papers aren't really covering it, and you guys are the nearest big newspaper. I figured with the *Post-Dispatch*'s Pulitzer tradition, and the platform you guys still run, this might be up your alley," he told me.

Clearly, he hadn't just picked up the phone without doing a little research. Founded in 1878 by Joseph Pulitzer, the newspaper was subsequently edited and published for well over a century by three generations of Joe Pulitzers, and to this day it carries in every edition the statement the first Pulitzer wrote when he retired on April 10, 1907. It reads in part: "I know that my retirement will make no difference in its cardinal principles, that it will . . . never tolerate injustice . . . always oppose privileged classes . . . never lack sympathy with the poor . . . never be afraid to attack wrong . . . ."

If I was innocent about catfish, I shared every journalist's desire to write about things others overlooked, especially if they fell within one's reporting field. In short order, I'd corralled the two top Metro Desk editors to make the case for rushing to the Delta to cover this labor dispute. Both were skeptical that our readers would care about what seemed to be a hopeless effort in a remote area involving some marginal product. That was understandable; most editors are dubious about covering union doings even a block away, so why spend the resources to go out of our way for something like this?

Fortunately, like Zack, I knew my audience. The senior of these two editors, Laszlo Domjan, was steeped in the tradition of the original Joseph Pulitzer, a bearded man who was born in Hungary in April 1847, left as a teenager and made his way to St. Louis, where he founded the *Post-Dispatch* and served as its first editor. Domjan never tired of relating in a dramatic if tongue-in-cheek fashion how he was born in Hungary exactly a century later in April 1947, fled as a youngster, made his way to St. Louis, and became an editor for the *Post-Dispatch*. "Listen guys," I said, looking intently at the bearded and bespectacled fellow who had hired me, "this needs to be covered. And if we don't do it, who will?"

A few days later I was in Indianola, being back-slapped by the deputy sheriff for having cared enough to come "all the way down here from St. Louis, Kansas." But someone *was* sincerely glad to see me—a young man named Neel Lattimore, a freelancer from North Carolina whom the union brought in to facilitate coverage. In retrospect, that was the first clue that this would be a most unusual labor campaign. He was available to help with problems big and small the entire time I was in Indianola, a proactive notion almost unheard of in a labor struggle. Lattimore, incidentally, was sharp enough that First Lady Hillary Clinton would soon recruit him to serve as her press secretary in the White House.

The catfish workers had walked out after rejecting Delta Pride's three-year contract offer by a resounding vote of 410 to 5, embittered by a proposed raise of a nickel an hour they said would leave many near minimum wage. To the owners' contention that the company's profits had dipped the past couple of years, they countered that the plants were key to Mississippi's lucrative catfish industry, serving as a market for the farmers and a processor for their fish, and so they shouldn't be considered in isolation.

The town, which had long hidden its conflicts, now was visibly on edge as a result of this labor confrontation, emotions further roiled by the black-white undertones. Almost immediately, violence exploded when new hires and some veteran workers crossed the picket lines. Both sides contributed, as bricks were hurled, windshields were broken, nails were thrown in the street, replacement workers tangled with pickets, and police, reacting to their first strike, arrested 17 people. Police beat at least one striking worker after she shouted at a replacement worker. The FBI launched an investigation into possible civil rights violations, even as the company obtained an injunction that limited the picketing. Within a few days, police were patrolling the plant 24 hours a day, but at every shift change the tension was palpable. Throughout the town, once-muted labor and racial divides erupted in the smallest encounters. A man sitting next to me one night at a tavern north of the tracks, upon finding out that I'd just arrived from Missouri, remarked: "You're lucky you don't have them uppity n----rs up there." His tone was casual, as if this was a normal and unobjectionable sentiment.

Yet amid the rising acrimony, I observed something else as well. At every turn, there were signs of a subtle, multipronged, and sophisticated union campaign; one so divergent from labor's typical practices that it would have been notable anywhere, let alone in an out-of-the way place with as minimal a labor imprint as Sunflower County. Snapshots of the effort cropped up in a variety of ways.

Behind the scenes, union officials were doing strategic research on two levels. One involved examining Delta Pride's corporate practices, markets, and business ties in search of vulnerabilities so that the union could effectively apply pressure. The other track focused on unraveling an interlocking nexus of power in Indianola that buttressed the company's hard stance vis-à-vis the workers, in hopes of somehow weakening those links. As a union official commented to me, "When you have an entire community infrastructure, from the mayor to the police to the finance company that holds notes on cars, bringing pressure on individuals, then you really don't have the freedom that we think we have as Americans."

One morning I watched as two white men and three striking Delta Pride female workers marched into the Peoples Bank of the Delta. Startled bank employees looked up from their stations to see the intruders politely but firmly demand to see the bank's president. Southern etiquette being what it is, the group quickly found itself in the office of Bill Ainsworth, the first time the three women ever had met a bank president. One of the men, Jeff Fiedler, had been painstakingly probing the links among business, politics, economics, and law enforcement in Indianola. Fiedler, from the AFL-CIO's staff in Washington, told Ainsworth that the union knew several key Delta Pride stockholders doubled as bank directors, a potential conflict of interest. He also warned that the union was aware of the credit pressure being exerted on the striking workers, which it regarded as improper coercion, and it had filed a complaint with the National Labor Relations Board. Ainsworth, a genteel man clearly taken aback by this rude beginning to his day, agreed to consider the visitors' request to sign a pledge not to stop credit because of the strike.[2]

Meanwhile, hoping to strike a public chord, the union tried to cast the workers' cause as something more transcendent than a narrow bid by a group of employees for higher wages, indeed as bigger than a labor-management dispute. Their first rally featured Aaron Henry, the longtime president of the Mississippi NAACP who decades earlier had cochaired with Fannie Lou Hamer the Mississippi Freedom Democratic delegation at the 1964 National Democratic Party convention in New Jersey. Henry rigged up a sound truck on the side of the road near the main Delta Pride plant, where some 600 workers joined him and soon moved onto the nearby cotton field. When Henry finished talking, the women began singing "We Shall Overcome." It set the tone for much of what would follow in the weeks ahead.

The union quickly prevailed upon people from around the South, often hallowed names from past civil rights struggles, to bring their message to Indianola. The Reverend Joseph Lowery of the Southern Christian Leadership Conference told workers at one rally that the Delta Pride strike was where poor workers must take a stand. "God may just have chosen Indianola in the nineties, as he chose Birmingham and Selma in the sixties, to be the watershed that turns this country around," Lowery said. If the reverend was somewhat overstating the case, he certainly put the town and employer on notice that this would not be business as usual, while also boosting the spirit of the workers.

The themes expressed at these rallies were brought to life on the picket lines by workers who had powerful stories to tell and memorable ways of telling them—and who made themselves available day and night, outside the plant and at home, to do so. From these women, one heard little of the usual union strike talk of specific contractual items, and much about dehumanizing work conditions, oppressive poverty that had lasted over generations, and the need to stand up to the powerful. "Now is the time to fight," Verdell German, a fillet-trimmer, said quietly one afternoon as she paused from reading her Bible on the picket line, early in the strike when the lack of discernible progress had left many workers discouraged. "If we don't fight now, we'll go back into slavery. We'll be working for nothing all our lives."

The union's transformation of the strike into a quasi-spiritual undertaking, which was critical to broadening support for the workers and paving the way for subsequent labor actions that would prove decisive, almost didn't occur. To stop the growing campaign, the company had reached out to black ministers to try to lower community support for the strike by convincing them the workers had no legitimate cause and that their action should be denounced. A number of local ministers were wavering, but the union, having anticipated this, tapped Charley Hhorn among others. Hhorn, who was the political director of the Mississippi AFL-CIO, worked with key ministers to convince them not to denounce the strike, which would have hurt the union's goal of infusing the message with moral overtones. Hhorn had spent nearly three decades in the labor movement and knew almost everyone who mattered in the state, and he used all his contacts in the Mississippi Baptist Association. (Hhorn later parlayed this episode into a second career in politics. After helping Bennie Thompson get elected as the

Democratic congressman from the area, Hhorn was hired as district director for Thompson, who in 2007 became chairman of the House Homeland Security Committee. In an example of labor's oft-unnoticed impact, the election of the staunchly pro-union Thompson was facilitated by the local political stirrings the catfish workers' campaign had set in motion; his ascent, in turn, helped deepen the long-term regional impact of the strike.)

Union leaders tried to put the farmers on the defensive by connecting their views to a retrograde past. Delta Pride's unyielding posture was attributed to its ownership by local farmers with strong attitudes about the place of their workers. Joe Price, of the regional office in Atlanta, said, "They've switched them from the cotton fields to the catfish plant, and they still regard them as field hands. It's been the plight of the blacks here for 300 years."

To offset Delta Pride's built-in advantages, the union looked for any missteps on the part of the owners it could exploit. If the small-town setting magnified the crosscutting social, political, and economic clout the company enjoyed, it also heightened the public shame that could be visited upon the wealthy owners. No sooner was it reported that Turner Arant had taken a journalist to his 7,600-acre farm and talked about how he felt "blessed by the Lord" than the union made that part of its narrative. The union had the good fortune to be focusing on a central and symbolic figure at Delta Pride; not only was he chairman of the board but the company's brochures featured a recipe from his wife, Sybil, for catfish baked with cheese and almonds. In addition, Arant had helped found the Catfish Farmers of America and was a former Mississippi Farmer of the Year. He was in many ways the public face of the industry. So when people learned of Arant's escapade just as they were hearing how Delta's workers had allegedly been treated over the years and now were getting by on a $60 weekly union strike stipend along with a donated bag of groceries, there was a good deal of head shaking around town. And then Tommy McWilliams quit his position as general counsel to the company after complaints that those duties conflicted with his other job as mayor.

But even though the union was gathering sympathetic attention for the catfish workers and their efforts, the dispute was dragging on with no resolution in sight. That, of course, favored deep-pocketed Delta Pride, whose owners had few worries about feeding their families, unlike the single mothers huddling near the fires being lit nightly on the picket lines. About 200 workers eventually returned to the job in order to survive, taking their place alongside those few who had felt they couldn't afford to leave in the first place. They, plus the replacement workers being hired, allowed the company to continue to process catfish, hence retaining the market for the farmers' raw product, which in turn was sold to retailers around the country. Union leaders knew that public interest would begin to wane, and media coverage was still, at best, regional.

It was time, the union knew, to enlarge the battlefield, just as the issues already had been broadened. In a straight, one-on-one local conflict, pitting the workers against the company, the catfish processors might come across as the good guys, but they were unlikely to prevail where it mattered—getting an improved contract. Fortunately, from its perspective, the union had laid the groundwork by its strategic research and behind-the-scenes work, and now it could try to capitalize on the empathy it had achieved for the catfish workers. Having brought the strike into the public consciousness and plumbed Delta Pride's weaknesses, the union was ready to take the next step.

A month into the struggle, the food workers union called for a nationwide boycott by consumers, hoping to force Delta Pride to retreat from its tough negotiating stance. This was a daring move, one that could easily have been interpreted as a sign of desperation. Under the best of circumstances, a boycott is extremely difficult to pull off. It requires that the public be aware of the action, conversant with the issues, and supportive of the workers. Each of these is problematic in large measure because of the media's lack of interest in such matters as well as labor's own inability to effectively promote its message. Even when there is public interest, efforts to build consumer involvement encounter myriad factors driving consumption habits and decisions from value to personal taste, family preference to convenience, and the availability of alternatives. And even when a boycott manages to get off the ground, there still is no guarantee of success. To have an impact, enough people must participate for long enough to affect the company's bottom line, but attention and commitment often wane over time.

Pulling this off has grown more difficult over the years because labor's shrinking numbers have reduced the natural base of support for such actions. This suggests labor's dilemma in a broader sense: its weakening state puts it in a defensive position where it has a greater need to call on its biggest weapons—strikes, boycotts, and the like—but its weakness makes such tactics more problematic. This Catch-22 will be discussed in the next few chapters; for now suffice it to say that under these circumstances boycotts are not only difficult to win, they are a risk to even try because they can easily blow up in the union's face. A failed boycott is a major setback for a labor campaign because it reveals a lack of public support to both the employer and the workers. In light of all this, it's no surprise that boycotts are uncommon and successful ones even more so.

Such premises were reasonable, well founded, and, as it turned out, utterly irrelevant in this case. The very day the union issued its call, one of the three leading supermarket chains in St. Louis—Dierbergs Markets—jumped in on its own, not even waiting for its customers to vote with their wallets or for protests to materialize outside their stores. Instead, Dierbergs seized the initiative, declaring that it would immediately expand the selection of catfish in its 14 local stores to "prepare for a boycott."

Within 24 hours, not only had Dierbergs gone ahead and switched to another brand, so had St. Louis's biggest local chain, Schnuck Markets, with 59 stores. And two days later, the other major chain in town, National Supermarkets, changed to a new supplier for its 57 outlets. This clean sweep of the St. Louis area was a major coup for the Indianola workers because a substantial amount of catfish was sold there—3 million pounds a year—and the three chains accounted for more than half of it.

Two factors were connected to the lightning-fast hat trick in St. Louis. One related to the racial makeup of St. Louis because it was a city evenly split between blacks and whites, where the virtual absence of other ethnic groups had led to the framing of issue after issue in stark racial terms. In that context, a grocery executive spoke privately of the local sentiment toward the apparent mistreatment of Mississippi's catfish workers. "With the black worker in that environment," he told me, "it's a very sensitive, volatile issue for us."[3]

Then the Congressional Black Caucus, at the behest of Rep. William L. Clay, a veteran St. Louis Democrat, decided to investigate the dispute it called "both a civil rights and labor issue." The caucus cited "rampant allegations of police brutality and intimidation," and it contended that "many other local businesses in the [Indianola] area are asserting pressure on the strikers by cutting off credit and retaliating against family members." As the UFCW's Zack said, "I think the chains realize that this very definitely is a civil rights problem as much if not more than a labor issue. Supermarket chains have always shown much more responsiveness to civil rights issues than to labor issues."

The second factor, though, did relate directly to labor; it was difficult for the markets to ignore the fact that the same international union representing the catfish workers, the United Food and Commercial Workers, dominated the St. Louis grocery industry as well. Moreover, UFCW Local 655 was the largest and most powerful of any union in St. Louis, raising the stakes for the supermarkets. And so, even if done in understated midwestern fashion, it had an impact when Local 655 President Bill Campey prodded each of the three chains behind the scenes "to please purchase from one of the other union companies that supply these products during these trials and tribulations down there."

Within the next few days as the news spread, average St. Louis residents got involved. Edward Kaletta, 74, planning a quiet weekend of golf, was forced to change his plans after his wife, Glad, 72, was moved by press accounts of the plight of the striking catfish workers. "Honey," she told him, "we have to go to Indianola, Mississippi." How would they locate the catfish workers, he asked. "We'll find them," was her response. And so they did. Following a 400-mile drive, they pulled into Indianola and asked a woman washing windows on the main street if she knew about the strike. The woman dropped her rag immediately and drove to the house of a striking worker who was penniless and about to be admitted to the hospital. The Kalettas gave her $50. The worker proceeded to serve as a guide for the four hours they spent in Indianola. The couple, who owned a candle company in St. Louis, handed a check for $250 to the union to buy hot meals for the workers. Neither of the Kalettas had previously been an activist for civil rights or labor causes. "When we were having all those civil rights marches in the 1960s, I was raising eight children," Glad Kaletta told me. "I didn't get to go out and help, and I've regretted it ever since. . . . I feel so good about [helping the Delta Pride workers]."

Back in St. Louis, the issue gained momentum. There was one instance in which about 100 St. Louisans rallied for the striking workers at a Baptist church. Visiting St. Louis to solidify the growing support, a Delta Pride worker spoke to the group, which raised more than $800 to help the catfish workers pay their bills.

Behind its firm front, Delta Pride was feeling the pinch. Three weeks after the boycott began, a father and son who were stockholders in Delta Pride were indicted on a charge of bribing a union negotiator to try to quash the strike. A federal grand jury in Oxford, Mississippi, found cause to believe the two had offered a union negotiator $5,000 "to betray her friends for money." The charges included four counts of attempted bribery and one count each of attempted extortion and conspiracy. Despite Delta Pride's public denials that the boycott was hurting business, the indictment said that in offering money to the union official, one of the alleged conspirators had told her that even before the boycott began, mere talk of it already had cost the company $1.5 million.

Things would only worsen for the firm as the boycott spread beyond St. Louis. More than 30 supermarket chains joined in the effort. Memphis-based Local 1529 began sending striking catfish workers to picket stores in various areas still selling Delta Pride products, imploring customers not to buy the items and pressing stores to drop them. Many of these workers had barely left the Delta before, let alone Mississippi. Now, encouraged by a union that was purposefully taking a back seat to make workers the story and having already undergone a local baptism by fire relating their personal stories on the picket line in Indianola, they moved rather seamlessly into this new role.

The boycott hit the company particularly hard in Atlanta, Detroit, Houston, and St. Louis, with St. Louis being the most affected market. Media coverage of the labor actions grew, and on a single day reporters from the *New York Times*, *Newsweek*, and the *Philadelphia Inquirer* showed up in Indianola to chronicle the struggle. The Boston City Council passed a resolution asking city institutions to cut off all orders of Delta Pride catfish.

And then, suddenly, three months after the strike began, just as Indianola braced for a rally drawing supporters from throughout the South, 48 hours of negotiations produced a tentative settlement.[4] The company's proposed contract included raises of 20 percent along with hefty premiums for skilled work, with some salaries to rise by close to 50 percent. A joint union-management safety committee would be set up to combat repetitive movement injuries, and union officials would have unlimited access to work areas to investigate grievances. There would be no limits on bathroom breaks, other work rules seen as onerous would be eliminated, and supervisors would be prohibited from asking personal questions. Moreover, Delta Pride would hire back the striking workers. This outcome was more than the workers had dared hope for.

In an exultant, gospel-style meeting at a black church south of the railroad tracks, the striking catfish processors approved the new contract by a vote of 479 to 1. As one of their advisers, the Reverend Michael W. Freeman put it: "We had hoped for respect and dignity, and we got it—all over the nation." Then he exhorted the workers to return with renewed enthusiasm to their jobs. "Now that we got some money," he said, his voice rising, "we got to sell some catfish!"

So it came to pass that, against overwhelming odds, an unimposing group of poor and unskilled workers beat a world-class company with everything going for it, including the tangible backing of the community's power structure. In the blink of an eye, these women saw a foreboding wall of banks, politicians, police, and businesses rise up against them, as if the wealthy farmers and their cooperative needed a boost. Yet, in relatively short order, the company caved and the wall crumbled before these eminently replaceable workers and their upstart union. This turnabout would have been notable anywhere, but these women made their stand in a small southern town rife with vicious anti-labor sentiment situated in a right-to-work state.

The saga of the catfish workers tells us a good deal about labor's latent power, and what it takes to realize it. In retrospect, what labor did here seems simple, as do many successful efforts after the fact. By finding creative ways to marshal the moral authority of its members and appeal to the larger community, by piecing together a strategy that probed at the employer's soft points, and by using the media to its own advantage, the union scored a most improbable victory.

The first key was the realization by union leaders that, given their relative weakness compared to their adversaries, they could not go toe to toe and slug it out in a straight-up fight waged on conventional turf. The workers, subsisting on 50 pounds of rice, beans, flour, and peas given every other week by the union, would not be able to outlast their prosperous employers in an economic struggle. So the war needed to be moved to a different plane, one that transcended the conventional labor-management terrain, and, hopefully, one that would inspire people not directly involved to side with the workers. Given the circumstances, the way to bring this about was to link the conflict to the locally evocative issues of civil rights and human dignity. By tackling head on what was most difficult—issues of race, power, and venue—they hoped not only to negate but to turn those factors to their advantage. And the most effective messengers would likely be the individual workers themselves, provided that their inherent credibility could outweigh their lack of polish or experience.

Second, given the advantages the employers started with, including their own resources, backed by the community's political, legal, economic, and law-enforcement power, the union had to fashion a tactical approach equal to the challenge. Every attribute the workers and the union brought to the fight needed to be harnessed and coordinated while the company and its backers were probed for vulnerabilities. Even if the union was to stay largely in the background while the workers told their story—indeed, became the story—it had to be clicking on all gears, with the local, regional, and international levels of the union each contributing its most salient skills to the mix. What that translated into was the Washington headquarters supplying analytical and communications expertise, the Atlanta regional office providing civil rights veterans from across the South, and the Memphis local bringing in its activists to attend to the picket lines, the food distribution, and other practical matters.

Finally, in a radical departure from most union undertakings, a communications plan was recognized as indispensable. The media had to be brought into the equation to serve as the union's force multiplier. The typical picket-line leafleting or dueling talking heads in the local newspapers and on television would not inspire the public involvement union leaders knew was critical. Labor leaders generally suspicious of journalists and highly protective of the union's message had to relinquish those concerns and take the risk of not only allowing but encouraging unfettered media access to the campaign. Beyond that, they had to trust unschooled workers to present the issues in a way that would resonate in the public's mind, while hoping that the media would not exploit them or make them look incompetent.

These various factors laid the groundwork for what proved to be the decisive tactic in the struggle: the boycott. It would not have had the support or impact it did had it not been intentionally linked to the broader story of the South and its racial history and had it not been told through the voices of workers. The union's strategic analysis of the company was pivotal in determining when and how to act and whether this was the avenue to pursue. As a one-trick pony in terms of product, and a perishable one at that, Delta Pride was highly susceptible to the pressure stemming from reduced sales. And the communications element was indispensable in terms of getting out the word about the struggle, building public support, and putting Delta Pride on the defensive—all of which made the chances for a successful boycott realistic.

These separate elements worked hand in hand; for example, the union's research showed which cities were large markets for the company's products and also might be prone to supporting the workers—and the media strategy was geared from the start toward raising awareness specifically in those key locales. Meanwhile, centering coverage on the catfish workers themselves prepared them to be spokespeople in other areas where they were able to personalize and humanize the strike, elevating it there into something beyond a union-management spat, as was done in Indianola. That also helped to further its impact, well after the strike had ended. For example, the catfish skinner concerned about her young daughter's future adapted so quickly to the role of a spokeswoman for the strike and boycott that she was later chosen by the union to run its Indianola branch. She also became president of the new Mississippi Workers' Center for Human Rights, which helps workers deal with workplace problems including discrimination, sexual harassment, and other concerns. In a state where 95 percent of workers are not organized and either lack access to a union or won't approach one for fear of losing their job, the center performs a vital function and assures that the strike's ripples are still being felt.[5]

The public support that developed for the workers was not inevitable; remember that the farmers, who put their heart and their sweat into this particular crop, had their own compelling stories to tell. But they were so quickly overwhelmed by the union's blizzard of activity that they never managed to take the offensive. This, of course, is a sharp reversal of the momentum that usually occurs in labor disputes.

Because the union's dealings with the media were so central to the outcome and so unusual for labor, it's worth looking into them in detail. In this sphere, as in all aspects of the union's stewardship of the workers' action, nothing was done randomly or left to chance, despite the seemingly spontaneous unfolding of the strike's public face.

Let's start with the union's opening salvo on the PR front—the telephone call from Al Zack advising me of the developing labor action. It would be an understatement to say that reporters tend to be amenable to having their egos stroked; it's surely not the paycheck that brings us to the profession. (Some 70 years ago, when bylines were starting to come into usage, Heywood Broun, founder of The Newspaper Guild, railed against them, to the consternation of journalists who relished their newfound recognition. Heywood retorted that reporters would end up trading the glamour for real remuneration. He lost the battle, but he turned out to be on target, at least for the world of print.) But Zack's call was a calculated action undertaken because the local audience and market in question fit neatly into the careful evaluation the union was doing even before—especially before—the strike began.

St. Louis was, for a variety of reasons, highly relevant to the UFCW and its looming showdown in Indianola. It had a large number of people who traced their ancestry to Mississippi, given St. Louis's status as perhaps the nearest nonsouthern metropolis. That meant that news of the strike would resonate among the area's residents and that any eventual call for public engagement might generate a positive response. The racial composition of the city reinforced these points. Additionally, St. Louis not only has a strong labor history, it also has a strong labor present. Its unionization rate of 22 percent is nearly double the national average and among the highest of any major American city. Partly as a result, the weekly *St. Louis/Southern Illinois Labor Tribune* has the top circulation of any local labor newspaper in the country, further assuring that strike-related activities would be well publicized in the region.

Beyond the prospect of public support, the city offered a high-profile grocery sector bearing some distinctive features. It was dominated by three large firms, which means that the decisions of just a few executives can have an inordinate impact. As noted, those companies accounted for more than half of the substantial amount of catfish sold annually in the city, and because the families involved tended to be active participants in local civil and social life, management at each firm was attuned to and solicitous of public sentiment, and highly protective of its community image. Bucking the national trend of chain dominance, St. Louis supermarkets are not faceless commercial entities but are mostly homegrown. The family names are on the stores, their namesakes are individually known, founding fathers still watch over their progeny, and business is more than a matter of dollars and cents for them. The city is just small and parochial enough that reputation and standing and being perceived as doing the right thing truly matter to those who live there.

As noted, Missouri's largest union, UFCW Local 655 in St. Louis, 17,000 members strong, represented virtually all employees at those three supermarket companies. Given the labor solidarity with a sister local in the same international, it was inevitable that Local 655 would urge the grocery chains to take action on behalf of the catfish workers. As a result, the supermarkets had more at stake in the boycott than merely maintaining their public image or meeting their customers' wishes. The companies' own labor-management relations—keeping their workers happy, not antagonizing the union and boosting the odds of smooth contract negotiations the next time around—were also at risk.

And St. Louis had something on top of the presence of an active labor movement, the likelihood of public support, and the fortuitous structure of the grocery industry. The icing on the cake was that St. Louisans, it so happens, eat a heap of catfish along with their prized pork steaks. As stated, given geography and historic migration patterns, St. Louis's population includes a healthy slice of people with Mississippi roots, and, frequently, they have relatives who are still living in the Magnolia State. That helps make catfish a popular item in St. Louis, raising Delta Pride's exposure to any impact the boycott might have on consumption patterns there, while also boosting the level of public interest in the strike.

All of these factors, the UCFW knew, would almost certainly predispose the local newspaper to leap right into coverage of the strike, especially if its editors felt they were leading the way on this particular story. The interest, empathy, and perhaps even action this would produce among readers would sustain that coverage, thereby raising the issue's local profile to the advantage of the union and workers.

With that foundation in place, two predictable things indeed occurred: local coverage expanded and so did the boycott in the area, each intensifying the other. As the UFCW had anticipated, those developments spurred media and consumer interest in other urban areas possessing at least some similar traits—a large black population, a robust labor movement, a history of migration from Mississippi, and a shared connection to the South or to the civil rights movement. This was a domino theory that actually panned out.

Union leaders believed that a finely honed communications plan integrated into this kind of scheme would be far more likely to achieve the union's goals than, for instance, generic press releases targeting national media outlets in larger metropolitan areas. Pushing the effort forward required not a big one-time media splash but rather consistent, wall-to-wall coverage in targeted areas. It was more critical to the campaign's success that consumer behavior and community conversation in a St. Louis or Atlanta be influenced rather than briefly intriguing readers in a Manhattan or Los Angeles who, aside from other differences, were deemed unlikely to be routinely clamoring for fresh catfish at their supermarket counters. And a midsized, regional paper might be more enamored of being ahead of the curve on a dynamite story, and therefore expend resources to stick with it, than a national paper used to such status and committed to covering the world. Just how much all this contrasts with typical union thinking—or lack thereof—about how use of the media might fit into an overall strategy will be examined in more depth in Chapter 5.

With that kind of forethought going into the strike, it is clear in retrospect that however uneven this labor-management confrontation appeared from the outside, if anyone was overmatched, it was actually Delta Pride. That said, a broader question arises: What here is transferable to other workplace situations in which labor might be involved? Not every labor conflict, after all, unfolds in a place with the richly textured history of the Mississippi Delta, contains the stark moral storylines of the cotton pickers-turned-catfish processors, or fits into the larger mosaic of the civil rights movement.

Stepping back from the specifics, the union did several basic things. Rather than taking a cookie-cutter approach—batting offers and demands back and forth until the stronger side prevailed—it carefully assessed the situation on the ground and determined how this particular fight could best be waged. In turn, the union put the local workers out front, making them the centerpiece of the struggle, while receding into the background and providing structure and resources as needed. And it adopted tactics that maximized labor's strengths in this encounter, while minimizing its weaknesses.

In essence, it did exactly what a different union—the firefighters—in an entirely different situation, would later do, while adding the media component. And both unions achieved rather startling victories that on paper should have been beyond their reach.

The catfish workers' campaign shows that labor can not only win in the most difficult workplace situations but also that its actions can have profound and lasting impact. It also suggests that the chances of success can be increased when labor develops an innovative strategy geared to the task at hand, instead of going through the motions and relying on time-worn approaches that worked back when the playing field was more or less even. Yet in so doing, the catfish story, like the firefighters' in the political realm, suggests what type of extraordinary effort is required to win.

And it is clearly an anomaly. If this triumph shows what labor can accomplish by maximizing union and worker strengths and capturing the public imagination, it is nonetheless an exception in a growing tide of union ineptitude that has concrete consequences for workers, union or not. Far more common are those instances in which labor falls flat on its face or, worse, shies away from even attempting what it knows will be a losing fight—be it in organizing, defending workers' rights on the job, or contractual battles—that would only expose its weakness.

Even in those latter instances, however, labor remains highly relevant. Whether we're talking about a rare victorious outcome, such as the catfish workers, or the more typical failure, the level of labor's strength and skills has real consequences for the conditions of workers. If labor's pertinence is evident in Indianola, it's no less so in the more frequent cases when it loses; it's just that then the effect goes in the other direction.

Often, labor's impact occurs without the public's even realizing its involvement in the first place. This flows largely from media indifference and is one reason for the mounting consensus that unions have become irrelevant. Indeed, that is the case in several recent episodes that captured a great deal of attention, even if the union role was essentially overlooked. But they demonstrate just how much the labor movement's remaining influence, or lack thereof, still matters.

Hurricane Katrina evokes a host of powerful memories for most Americans: a hurricane slamming into the Gulf Coast with ferocious winds and drenching rain in late August 2005. Rushing water that topped the levees and inundated much of New Orleans. People on rooftops frantically waving to would-be rescuers. Residents growing testier by the day as conditions worsened in the Superdome with no help on the way. Overwrought local police officers torn between their families' needs and their jobs. Federal agency heads seemingly unaware of how dire the situation was. Official praise bestowed on clearly hapless officials. A spiraling blame game as those in various points in the chain of command—whether local, state, or national—pointed fingers at one another. The onset of widespread public doubts about the administration's competence, which soon morphed into sharp questioning of Iraq policy and execution as conditions there deteriorated—all of this combining to drive down President George W. Bush's ratings and then drown the Republicans in the 2006 midterm elections.

The combination of a riveting story with the exigencies of round-the-clock cable programming led to saturation coverage, much of it overwrought. The instant the levee breech occurred, virtually everything that followed was reported and filmed with great detail, analysis, and color, whether the water's destructive path, the loss of human lives, the flight of the survivors, the rescues and tragedies, the breakdown of law and order, the economic cost, the political infighting, and the rebuilding. And it seemed every presidential utterance, action, and inaction, was exhaustively covered as well, particularly once it became evident that President Bush was strangely disconnected from what was transpiring, to the point of strumming an air guitar as he flew to the West Coast while New Orleans was being submerged. He soon topped that with the unforgettable, "Brownie, you're doing a heck of a job." The cameras and microphones and notepads were there for everything the president did, whether belatedly acknowledging the lagging federal response, trying to recover from PR blunders by making several trips to New Orleans in the weeks after, or making solemn pledges about the city's future.

It was all endlessly hashed over and dissected—almost all, that is. Missing was one of the most remarkable parts of the entire Katrina tale. For Bush did something far more provocative than strum a guitar or make an offhand remark to an aide; *he made the decision to suspend normal pay rates for the thousands of construction workers who would be rebuilding the Gulf Coast in the storm's wake.* The 1931 Davis-Bacon Act sets a minimum pay scale for workers on federal contracts by requiring contractors to pay the prevailing or average pay in the region. The rationale was that Americans' tax dollars shouldn't subsidize employers who offer their employees substandard wages. In issuing his presidential proclamation on September 8, barely a week after the storm struck, Bush not only took an action that risked harming workers in several states already reeling from the devastation, he showed himself willing to brush aside one of labor's prized tenets. It was a double smack in labor's face because hourly wages in the affected right-to-work states—including parts of Louisiana, Alabama, and Mississippi—already were so low: $9.84 for a pipe layer in Louisiana, for example, and $7.67 for a backhoe operator or $6.14 for a truck driver in Mississippi.

Given the pro-business leaning of the administration, it is not surprising that it would look favorably on a measure that would lower costs for contractors in this instance and send a broader signal to business, while also weakening organized labor. (And, in fairness, that would stretch federal dollars further.) However, what is noteworthy—and telling—is that a president who was already wounded by his initial inattentiveness to the catastrophe and who was fending off a national outcry about the cleavages that had been revealed between the haves and have-nots would feel confident enough to act on his ideological predisposition. It says less about the president than about the perceived weakness of the labor movement that he was willing to risk labor's wrath over an issue so critical for it at such a delicate moment.

It's also instructive that his unwitting accomplices here were the media, which devoted scant attention to what was a fascinating sidebar to the main story. That clearly did not stem from a desire to protect the president's flank on Katrina since he was being hauled to the woodshed on so many other hurricane-related fronts. Rather, it reflected the media's instinctive downplaying or flat ignoring of anything to do with labor. Labor, however, was outraged and argued vehemently—in letters to the president and by applying political pressure through various religious and community leaders, as well as a few legislators—that the main effect would be lower pay for workers at a time of great vulnerability. Faced with those mounting appeals, which were on top of the more public outcry about the response to the storm itself, Bush reluctantly rescinded his order on October 26. He had issued it just 10 days after the storm hit the Gulf; it took 48 days to lift it.

This case goes a good way toward rebutting the notion that labor's weakness renders it irrelevant in today's America. What its undeniable weakness in fact does, of course, is something quite different: it exposes workers to forces they cannot hope to ward off individually. The economic toll the prevailing wage decision risked exacting on a large group of workers, and the mere fact that it could be taken in these extraordinary circumstances, shows just how much labor's decline matters. At the same time, the abrogation of Davis-Bacon did not stand because labor's decline is not the linear descent into insignifi-cance often depicted. And so, given the reservoir of strength the labor movement was able to muster here, the very same Katrina case showed—from both ends of the equation, weak-ness and resilience—the continuing relevance of labor.

The devastation and uprooting caused by Katrina still loomed high in the public consciousness when, in January 2006, another tragedy gripped the nation and consumed the media. An explosion at the Sago Mine in West Virginia killed 12 miners—presaging what would turn into a tragic year in America's coal mines. The dramatic rescue attempts, the rais-ing and dashing of hopes, the prayerful local reaction, and finally, the tragic ending all captivated the public. Once again, there was wall-to-wall coverage of virtually every imaginable aspect of the story, from whether the company had delayed getting the information out, to the lone survivor's lengthy recovery, the explosion's cause, to the impact on the commu-nity. As with Katrina, the media became part of the story and engaged in a good deal of self-examination—this time on erroneous news reports that the miners had been rescued, sparking a roller-coaster ride for waiting families. And there was one more similarity: the role of labor was almost com-pletely absent from the reporting and commentary.

If labor should have been an intriguing sidelight to Katrina reporting, here it cried out to be front and center, because the most cursory analysis would suggest that labor was an integral factor, for better or worse, in the Sago disaster and ensuing developments. In Katrina, labor's weakness had nothing to do with the flooding but threatened workers' wages after the fact; in the coal mines, the inability of unions to fulfill their most basic function of protecting workers on the job played a role in allowing the tragedies to occur in the first place.

Unions fill a critical function in achieving and promoting workplace safety in two distinct yet related ways. On the national level, a robust labor movement can help craft legislation and push to update laws and regulations that govern safety procedures across various industries. It can help select, or at least veto, key appointees who will oversee those statutes, while also using its political influence with legislators to assure that vigorous enforcement will take place. On the level of the work site, unions can make sure that necessary steps are actually being carried out in terms of equipment, training, and practice, and that management is not gambling with safety to save money or boost productivity. Local unions also provide a mechanism for workers to raise safety concerns and to have contractual protection when they do so. Ideally, these two processes reinforce one another, with labor nationally using its clout to get laws with teeth in them and the workplace unit guaranteeing local compliance by the company.

Weak unions, of course, have just the opposite effect on safety, especially since well-funded and organized industry associations and business groups will rarely fail to fight for the rights of their members to compete unencumbered by costly and unwieldy oversight. Similarly, on the plant level companies will inevitably take advantage of the absence of an assertive union or of any union at all, to trim costs. That doesn't make them bad apples, unless this is carried to an extreme or laws are clearly flouted; it simply means they are acting in a rational fashion on behalf of their own goals as employers.

And so it was that labor's inability to protect workers' safety either locally or nationally had practical consequences for Sago miners. On a federal level, given its ideological gulf from the administration, coupled with its waning institutional strength, labor provided virtually no input into legislation, regulation, or enforcement. As a result, the White House had the leeway it wanted in appointing mining industry insiders to critical posts. No sooner did the Bush administration take office in early 2001 than it chose a former mining executive named David Lauriski to run the Labor Department's Mine Safety and Health Administration (MSHA). In his stint at MSHA, Lauriski oversaw the reduction of the number of inspectors by well over 100—about 15 percent of the total— and the trimming of fines on coal operators. In fairness to Lauriski, some of these changes reflected administration policies and funding priorities, as well as mine closings, more than his own initiatives. At the same time, he withdrew 17 proposed regulations affecting mine safety, while hiring a variety of former coal-mining executives and lobbyists. The number of mine rescue teams also dropped, reflecting a trend that preceded Lauriski and the Bush administration. Federal law requires two such teams for each mine, but by 2004 there was only one team for every four mines.

After he resigned in 2004 to work for a mine industry consulting firm, amid accusations of irregularities—by subordinates, not him—with his agency's granting of contracts, Lauriski's federal post remained unfilled for two years, meaning that at the time Sago occurred, the mine safety agency was without a permanent director. Even more damning, the Labor Department official who filled in lacked experience in mine safety issues. The Sago mine was cited for 208 violations in 2005, leading up to the explosion. According to a state report done for West Virginia Governor Joe Manchin, some of those violations were serious and might have contributed to the tragedy, such as failures to control methane and coal-dust accumulation, or to properly shore up shafts against collapse, and deficiencies in emergency planning and escape routes. The accident rate for Sago, which was bought in 2005 by the International Coal Group, was nearly triple the national average, yet fines on the company totaled less than $30,000, with some as low as $60 apiece. Those 208 violations marked a threefold increase from the mine's 68 in 2004. The importance of proper federal safety measures, regulation, and enforcement was made clear by the fact that most of the dead miners survived initial explosions but perished because they lacked adequate oxygen supplies and slowly suffocated from carbon monoxide poisoning.[6]

As labor stood by helplessly on the national level, unable to influence legislation, presidential rulings, or appointments to key posts, its ability to compensate by riding herd at the other end—through practical vigilance and pressure in the Sago mines—was equally nil. Sago was a nonunion operation. This status reflected the declining unionization of America's coal mines, a figure that stood between 85 and 90 percent in the 1950s and 1960s, dipped slightly to between 75 and 80 percent into the 1970s, but now is 32 percent and dropping.[7] At coal mines represented by the United Mine Workers of America (UMWA), union safety committees are part of the contract and participate in inspections when federal officials show up. Miners have the right to withdraw from work in any area deemed unsafe by the committee until the problem is fixed, and the safety committee can call in federal inspectors at any time. Workers exercising any of these rights are shielded from punitive repercussions. In nonunion operations, if a miner complains of danger and a foreman says it looks safe to him, in practice the miner may end up with the choice of going into the shaft or going home. In this context, the much-publicized failure of the company to notify MSHA of the explosion for two hours, despite the agency's immediate notification rule, is perhaps less surprising.

Dramatic as it was, Sago was merely the table-setter for an unrelenting series of mining tragedies over the course of the year. It was followed the same month by a fire at the Aracoma Alma Mine that killed two West Virginia miners. In May, five Kentucky coal miners perished in an explosion at the Darby Mine. By the end of 2006, 47 coal miners had died in mining accidents—the highest in more than a decade and more than double the previous year's toll.

Yet, while the Sago incident drew an extraordinary amount of media and public attention, and the next few mining tragedies rode that tailwind of publicity, subsequent fatalities went increasingly unnoticed, when just the opposite should have occurred. Rather than people becoming numb to what seemed repetitive developments, it should have been clear that something systemic, and therefore more alarming than a simple twist of fate, was occurring. But, absent an understanding of the broader labor-management context and the underlying themes, the deaths in the nation's mines appeared to be sad yet unrelated accidents and attention gradually waned, even as the toll mounted. There was some regional coverage, particularly among three or four newspapers in West Virginia and Kentucky, about lax enforcement and questionable appointments, but there was little focus on what had allowed this to happen: labor's growing inability to perform functions it had carried out for decades.

One simple fact suggests the role unions can play at the local level even when their national political strength is ebbing: of the 47 mine workers killed, only 5 were UMWA members.[8] And each of those 5 was killed in a single accident involving that one fatality alone, not in a broader mine failure. At year's end, a state report on Alma, for example, showed that the company had failed to take a host of precautions: water wasn't available to fight the fire because it had been turned off; hose couplings didn't fit; carbon monoxide monitors were not installed; and ventilation controls were not maintained. Nor, in the absence of union oversight, had federal enforcement identified or fixed *any* of these problems. On the federal level, some of the discarded regulations, such as one mandating nonflammable conveyer belts in mines, might well have prevented some of the disasters.

Much like with Katrina, though too late to save lives already lost, labor ultimately marshaled some strength, in this instance helping push through Congress in the summer of 2006 the MINER Act, which mandated more oxygen supplies underground, greater availability of emergency breathing devices, two-way communication throughout a mine, and better training for evacuation, while also establishing a single telephone number mine operators must call within 15 minutes of an accident. Lawmakers were pressed to act as a result of strong testimony and personal lobbying from both the mine workers' union and families of miners who had died; some observers saw it at best a halfway measure.

The story, however, does not end there. Despite everything that had transpired in the mines, the president felt confident enough about labor's vulnerability to act in the same fashion he had with his prevailing wage order after Katrina. Here, he used a backdoor maneuver to unilaterally put through his nominee for director of MSHA without Senate approval. Since the fall of 2005, Bush had been seeking the confirmation of Richard Stickler, who spent 30 years as an industry executive for mine operators in West Virginia and Pennsylvania before a stint as a mine safety official in Pennsylvania. But shortly after Bush nominated him, concerns over mine safety raised by Sago forced the Republican Senate leadership to put off votes on Stickler twice in two months for lack of support, most notably among legislators from coal-mining states. Then, with the focus on mines abating over the course of the year, rather than choose another nominee, the president took advantage of the closing of the Senate shortly before the November congressional elections to install Stickler via a recess appointment.[9]

The third in this trio of developments, known as "Kentucky River," occurred in the fall of 2006. Despite its moniker, unlike the other two it was not a sudden natural catastrophe or series of disasters but rather a long-anticipated legal decision, and it understandably commanded far less public attention. Yet its consequences are potentially far reaching both for labor, because it threatens to cut short a rare success story in terms of organizing new workers, and for the public at large.

On October 2, 2006, the National Labor Relations Board ruled that nurses with some supervisory responsibilities on their hospital shifts could be considered supervisors and thus be exempted from forming unions or even from union protections. In addition, even nurses who worked supervisory shifts only on a rotating basis might be ineligible, depending on how regular such assignments were.

The NLRB case stemmed from efforts to clarify supervisory questions in a case a few years earlier that involved Kentucky River Community Care, Inc. The majority opinion was led by the board's chairman, Robert J. Battista, who was the former attorney for the Detroit newspapers during the city's protracted and bitter newspaper strike and lockout and who critics say had moved the NLRB sharply rightward. A board member wrote in a dissenting view that the ruling "threatens to create a new class of workers under federal labor law; workers who have neither the genuine prerogatives of management nor the statutory rights of ordinary employees."

Unsurprisingly, the decision was hailed by the U.S. Chamber of Commerce for offering "a good, clear standard" on supervisory matters, while AFL-CIO President John Sweeney complained that it allowed employers "to strip millions of workers of their right to have a union, by reclassifying them as supervisors in name only." The three-to-two vote was along party lines, with Republican board members in the majority and the Democrats opposed.

Though it received only brief one-day coverage from the news media, the ruling is significant for three reasons. In the most direct sense, it will hinder organizing efforts among nurses, who have constituted one of the few growth sectors for unions in recent years, with tens of thousands of new members. Much of that organizing has been done by the California

Nurses Association, which has expanded from California to a variety of states, reflecting the widening field of interested nurses. The group is just one element in what has quietly become a nationwide phenomenon. A few months before the NLRB's ruling, leaders from unions representing more than 200,000 registered nurses launched an alliance, dubbed "RNs Working Together," to focus on organizing and improving patient care. Among them were the American Federation of Teachers, American Federation of Government Employees, Communications Workers of America, United Steel Workers of America, United Auto Workers, and United Nurses of America/American Federation of State, County and Municipal Employees. As the nurses saw it, Kentucky River was a bid by a conservative board to stem this surprising momentum by the upstart members of their profession because it jeopardized the push toward making hospitals corporate profit centers.

At its July 2005 national convention, the AFL-CIO proposed encouraging unions with members in the same field to set up an industry coordinating committee to increase worker effectiveness. Within a half-year the nurses became the first to do so, hoping to mobilize against the impending legal effort to diminish their right to organize. As the anticipated ruling neared, they escalated their efforts to raise public alarm. In August, several hundred nurses protested at the American Hospital Association in Chicago, claiming that hospital executives and business associations were pushing the NLRB toward a decision that would be detrimental for the entire health-care industry. Despite a dramatic scene that included nurses blocking entrances, there was scant media coverage.

More broadly, because federal law bars such employees from forming unions, the precedent stands to affect workers in any trade, industry, or profession by creating a new category of supervisors. On construction sites, in the local auto repair shop, in assembly plants, at newspapers, or in schools, experienced workers who have risen to a certain level, yet are not seen—or remunerated—as supervisors, often have some responsibility for or control over newer employees. If the reasoning behind Kentucky River leads to such workers' being removed from existing unions or excluded from forming new ones, a new structural hurdle would be created for an already struggling labor movement, and a host of employers would be freed at least partly from dealing with troublesome unions. Even worse, management could nudge that process along by bestowing certain new responsibilities on groups of workers, thus making them ineligible to join collective bargaining units.

Finally, the general public, or at least anyone who finds himself or herself being treated in a hospital, stands to be affected in terms of the care and attention provided because nurses would be deterred from acting as patient advocates. As the health-care sector has shifted away from consisting of independent community facilities that provide treatment to those who need it toward larger regional facilities (and as the industry becomes more profit oriented), nurses have found themselves increasingly embattled. Staff reductions aimed at cost cutting have raised patient-to-nurse ratios even as greater demands are placed on remaining nurses, allowing them less time and flexibility to care for their patients and attend to their specific needs and requests. Since nurses tend to work closely with patients, decreasing the time they can spend with individual patients has a multiplier effect in terms of diminishing the overall care provided by doctors and other hospital caregivers.

It is in the face of these trends that nurses have increasingly pushed for better staffing levels and patient care. That has led them to turn to unions for two reasons: the collective power that would help them fight for those improved guidelines and the ability of individual nurses on a daily basis to advocate for their particular patients without fear of being reprimanded or fired. If they are no longer protected by a union contract, nurses say, they would hesitate to go to bat for a patient, knowing it would likely be less effective and could even cost them their jobs.

Given the potential ramifications of the Kentucky River decision on a variety of levels, the labor movement has sought to make its overturning a priority. But if the ruling threatens to make organizing even more difficult, thus exacerbating the movement's institutional decline, labor's political weakness reduces the likelihood of any success in the effort since it has scant input in any appointments relevant to labor rulings.

In a strange twist, the catfish workers' case, even though it occurred more than a decade before Kentucky River, played an indirect role in the ruling. When the farmers' cooperative was forced to back down to the workers' demands in Indianola, the state's business community had no choice but to accept that outcome. But it got a chance to settle the score in 2002 in Magnolia, where management at a metal plant labeled a number of workers as supervisors, the case becoming one of the three that led to the NLRB's eventual Kentucky River decision. That suggests how unions and labor issues permeate much of what goes on in the workplace, even when they draw little notice, and how interconnected labor's battles and workers' conditions on the job often are, however peripheral labor's flagging status appears to make it.

Even though they are largely about union frailty, these three recent episodes indicate not labor's irrelevance but just the opposite, by depicting in practical terms the importance of its ability or inability to fulfill its role. When labor is unable to carry out its end of the bargain by providing workers a voice on the job and protecting their safety on the job, it affects a broad swath of workers, union or not—and perhaps, as well, a wider community. Even as the nation vows to rebuild New Orleans and narrow the economic and racial gulf so tragically exposed, labor's perceived vulnerability threatened to condemn thousands of laborers, at their time of greatest need, to ply their trades for substandard wages. Coal miners die in part because their union has yielded its grip on America's coal fields and because the labor movement as a whole has largely lost its influence over the federal regulations and enforcement that affect the very people whom labor is supposed to represent. As the health-care industry changes in ways that put the bottom line ahead of medical care in many instances, the efforts of nurses to fight back collectively to protect their patients is compromised because labor's political futility has robbed it of its ability to influence appointments to labor boards.

To assert that labor has suddenly lost its relevance because it is now so weak and unable to affect events is to erroneously conflate the inability to fill a role with the lack of that role. It is as naïve to think that work-related conflicts and unsolved labor-management problems no longer exist in a postindustrial age as it was to believe that after the fall of communism all ideological tensions would vanish from the international scene. Labor continues to have a very real impact; its flagging capacities and influence simply tilt the results in management's favor, thereby skewing the tripartite industrial relations model—management, labor, government—that has served the United States well for over a century.

Katrina, Sago, and Kentucky River demonstrate something else: the extent to which labor- and work-related topics are missing from the national discourse. Much of what happened here was possible only because few knew what was happening. That, in turn, reflects two separate but related conditions already noted—the dismal state of labor coverage in this country and the inability of trade unionists to craft and communicate a coherent message. The causes of labor's public invisibility and how it could be remedied will be addressed more fully later in this book. But for now, consider the following: if people knew what was being planned for Gulf Coast workers or why mine safety suddenly veered southward, might not that engender a rethinking of the notion that labor's slippage is inconsequential? Of the assumption that unions no longer are of any significance in twenty-first-century America? Wouldn't the Kentucky River case, properly explained, show the range—and importance—of the issues at stake in labor's many battles, and why a reinvigorated labor movement just might be a much-needed counterbalancing force in a variety of arenas? Even the catfish workers' tale, while a union success story, raises this question: if this is the first you have heard of it, has labor not missed a golden and rare opportunity? And can it afford not to laud—and to learn from—such dramatic successes, especially one that simultaneously depicts the need for unions, what they can accomplish, and the sustained impact they can have?

Finally, each of these instances brings home the importance of the political realm for labor and the way it intrudes into workplace-related struggles. They show the clear link between labor's ability to represent workers on the job and its level of influence in the legislative or political spheres. Labor can't safeguard workers' rights on the job if it is politically marginal, or is so perceived by those in power, because decrees and appointments and rulings done without labor's input are likely to hurt workers. That, in turn, undermines labor's credibility among its constituency and limits its ability to organize new workers, both by making it seem less salient or, in a more formal sense, by actually removing classes of employees from the purview of unions, further weakening any remaining clout on the federal level.

Put more concretely, if labor can't exercise any control over who is appointed to the boards that make decisions like Kentucky River or to the agencies that oversee mine safety, it will be increasingly unable to deliver on the job. The result will be declining worker respect and dwindling membership that exacerbate labor's lack of political influence, making it ever harder for unions to turn the situation around. Thus we begin to see the downward cycle in which unions are gripped.

Labor's workplace woes and its political futility are inextricably linked, and unions won't make real inroads on protecting
or organizing workers until they begin to change the environment in which those activities take place.

It won't be easy. An anti-labor stance is one of the few matters—low taxes are another—that unify social and economic
conservatives. And on the other side of the political ledger,
Democrats take labor for granted, both during elections and
beyond. The lack of political influence has contributed mightily to labor's steadily downhill trajectory; that won't change
until labor becomes an integral player in elections, affecting
both the outcome and, equally important, the debate, especially, as we will see in the next chapter, in presidential contests. The firefighters' example demonstrated that when it
engages in a strategically deft way, labor can move mountains
in the political arena.

CHAPTER 3

HEARTLAND VALUES

The presence of the National Football Hall of Fame makes the welcoming little city of Canton, Ohio, a mecca to millions of gridiron fans everywhere. During the 2004 presidential race, it occupied another perch as well. With late-October polls showing Ohio evenly split, it was drawing political volunteers by the busloads as the Bush and Kerry campaigns fiercely contested every last household in the blue-collar city. While it falls on the smaller end of Ohio's 'C list' of cities—which also includes Cleveland, Columbus, and Cincinnati—both sides deemed Canton pivotal, winnable, and manageable in terms of size and required resources. George W. Bush had taken the city in 2000, but now, given the steel industry's problems and a local unemployment rate hovering at around 10 percent, yard signs bespoke palpable dissatisfaction with the status quo. History suggested the stakes were huge; a Republican had never won the White House without capturing Ohio.

This frenetic political activity was taking place against the backdrop of an economic recovery that appeared to be a jobless one, and Bush risked becoming the first president since Herbert Hoover to preside over a net loss of jobs. Free trade, championed by the Republicans and their business allies, was clearly not proving cost free to people whose livelihoods had long depended on making things that now were increasingly being made in low-wage countries that, not coincidentally, generally lacked labor unions. And along with job insecurity came a trail of other concerns, health coverage high among them.

In rust belt states like Ohio, whose 232,000 lost jobs since 2000 included 170,000 good-paying manufacturing positions—and all the more in a place like Canton, long dependent on the increasingly vulnerable steel industry—conditions were ripe for a focus on bread-and-butter issues. Some 1.4 million Ohio residents lacked medical insurance, a number that had grown by 114,000 in Bush's first term. An Ohio Republican Party strategist told me as Election Day neared, "This is a Republican-leaning state, but the economy and the loss of manufacturing jobs have hit Ohio harder than most states, and it's sort of evened up the score."

I had the good fortune to be roaming the critical, up-for-grab states of Ohio and Pennsylvania in the fascinating run-up to the election. Their electoral importance was indicated by the constant attention being paid by the Bush-Cheney and Kerry-Edwards tickets; scarcely a day passed without at least one of the four candidates visiting one or both states. In Ohio, my assignment was to cover efforts by both the Bush and Kerry campaigns to get voters to the polls. Just across the border in the old mill and mining towns of southwestern Pennsylvania, I was looking at things from the opposite perspective: examining the thinking of conflicted steelworkers and miners as they grappled with the cultural pull of the Republicans versus the economic appeal of the Democrats. Both states were full of such people, who often are labeled "Reagan Democrats" or "NASCAR dads," "gun lovers," or "blue-collar conservatives." Whatever the moniker, they have become swing voters in swing states. They were widely seen as holding the key to this particular outcome not only in their states but even in the over-all election. And among the midwestern or border battle-ground states, Pennsylvania and Ohio were the largest prizes, with 21 and 20 electoral votes, respectively. Two states, replete with hard-hit industries and economic malaise everywhere one turned, full of ambivalent blue-collar voters, many of them union members—and what seemed startling was what *wasn't* happening in the campaign and what *wasn't* being said.

Canton, an urban area with a small-town feel, was a perfect prism through which to view the preelection tumult and the prospect for change. The timing and territory seemed tailor-made for electoral inroads by labor and its Democratic allies, and indeed, union members in Canton were busily engaged in efforts to capture voters. Through door-to-door canvassing and nonstop leafleting, they sought to energize their base and peel away those who had sided with the GOP the last time around. Evenings, in old-fashioned union halls or community buildings, hundreds crowded in for strategy sessions. If ever there were an environment for a spirited public discussion about the deindustrialization of America or the dumping of cheap foreign products, about how corporate decisions made far away alter life for local residents or about the toll that reduced benefits take on struggling families, this was it. But that debate never took place, of course. Sue Williams, helped by a thousand like her and abetted by a curiously compliant labor movement, saw to that.

Williams, a pleasant young Canton mother venturing for the first time into politics as a phone bank captain for the Bush campaign, was an unlikely protagonist in this drama, but by now she was fully engaged. With the election approaching, she had recently doubled her political workday. On a Friday afternoon just four days before the vote, she was making calls from her cubicle in the local campaign headquarters as her two homeschooled children, a boy and a girl, played around her feet. This was all new to her, and she was not prone to dissecting policy nuances. That, however, proved to be no problem, for Sue Williams had her finger squarely on the local pulse and manipulated it effectively. In fact, she rendered nuances irrelevant and even basic issues marginal at best. She did that by tossing away her script and speaking from the heart to residents, or at least to their answering machines on this workday in a working town, and her instincts would prove to be correct: the president's faith was what mattered, not the residents' jobs.

"I'm here to remind you that the president honors God, and that by voting for the president, you will honor God as well," she informed one household after another, proceeding to stress values, values, values. None of those values dealt with the importance of employers' keeping their word on providing pensions earned over a lifetime of work or figuring out how to keep jobs in small towns so the Midwest could retain its character. Instead, they dealt with restricting gay marriage or reproductive choices. Asked by a reporter whether health care for families or a livable wage for workers also involved values, she demurred. Those, she said, were political issues unrelated to religion or morality; they revealed little about a candidate's character and hence were not suitable for her electoral pitch.

Did the message she was delivering mean that the president's opponent, Senator John Kerry, was against God? Sadly, it did, she said, in understated fashion and with no trace of glee. She added that this was not a partisan matter; she was open to supporting a Democratic candidate in the future if only she could find one who was on God's side. "I'm not a Bible thumper," she explained. "I'm not aligned with the pro-life people. I do support a ban on abortion, but I think they're too *activist*. I call myself pro-Christ." In the eight-hour span she worked that day, some 520,000 phone calls, many broadly similar to hers if a tad more subtle, were made by GOP volunteers in Canton and across Ohio.

Less than 24 hours later in downtown Columbus, the capital of Ohio and its largest city, a politically savvy GOP volunteer named Ken Mowbray was knocking on doors in the old ethnic neighborhood of German Village. He had hoped for an assignment closer to his suburban home, but now Mowbray and his wife struggled good-naturedly to find the house numbers to match their list. It was a tidy middle-class section of town packed with small brick homes, cobblestone streets, and large dogs; largely Democratic and a tough area for Bush, said Mowbray, who was targeting what he called "soft Republicans" who might not vote unless urged to do so.

Ohio State Buckeye signs and flags competed for prominence with political ones. When knocks on doors went unanswered, Mowbray tucked brochures under welcome mats. Homeowners who were around weren't always encouraging. One said in brusque fashion that he didn't care for the president's tort reform initiative because as a conservative, he believed in accountability and didn't want to "let big business off the hook for bad things, weaken the notion of responsibility, or dilute the rights of individuals." Rather than debate, Mowbray changed the subject to President Bush's strong leadership, apparently a mutually more acceptable topic. As we walked away, I asked Mowbray why he hadn't challenged the fellow on tort reform. Surprisingly, Mowbray said he thought there was merit in the man's comments.

At the next house, the owner, a general contractor, expressed misgivings over a different matter, this time the war in Iraq. "I can understand Afghanistan," the man said, "but Iraq totally eludes me." As before, there was no direct rebuttal from Mowbray. As we walked on, I wondered about the Iraq criticism. Again, Mowbray said he couldn't disagree. Puzzled, I stopped Mowbray and his wife on the sidewalk and asked why he was expending so much effort on Bush's behalf, since he seemed rather critical of a number of key administration policies. The answer, rapid and unambiguous, seemed at first to explain little, but on reflection it explained everything: "I'm a Christian. I see him as being more in line with my morals and values."

So there it was. Just as with Williams, the issues—as traditionally defined anyway—didn't matter to Mowbray. More accurately, they didn't exist for Williams, while for Mowbray they played a distant second fiddle to something far more transcendent that could scarcely be countered by normal political argument. It drowned out anything labor might have tried to bring to the discussion. And this was on top of what I had just experienced in southwestern Pennsylvania, where people like Harry McCree, a 48-year-old steelworker, were wrestling with what they labeled—helped by the media and omnipresent political commentators—as their core values on one hand and campaign issues on the other. Health care and Social Security, along with party loyalty, were pushing McCree toward Kerry, but values were working in Bush's favor.

McCree said he was "a reasonable person, so I try to weigh things," and he certainly appeared to be, but why, I wondered, did he see himself as being in the position of weighing two such uneven concepts, apples and oranges as it were? Why was he juggling something as lofty as "values"—moral princi-ples—against what seemed by comparison a rather mundane and even selfish focus on material "issues"? And in any case, why was he considering voting against what he acknowledged were his own best interests? The mental gymnastics McCree was engaged in mattered greatly because he was a typical sol-dier in a million-person army of hunters in Pennsylvania, many of them blue-collar workers or even members of the 900,000-strong Pennsylvania AFL-CIO.[1]

What was going on here? This is the Heartland, home of level-headed and clear-eyed people with their feet firmly on the ground. What kind of political debate is this, where prac-tical, bread-and-butter issues like job security and pensions are so easily brushed aside or minimized by the people most affected by them? How could such concerns have been ren-dered almost unworthy of serious consideration? Admittedly,

I did have some inkling, having just read Tom Frank's insightful book *What's the Matter with Kansas*[2] about how conservatives have managed to substitute cultural populism for the genuine economic article, thereby prompting many working people throughout the Midwest to vote against their own pocketbooks. Besides, it's all a ruse, he says. Voters are led to believe they're putting an end to outrages such as the ranting of leftwing professors at state-funded universities; once elected, however, these candidates forget all about those loony academics. Why? Because they're too busy lowering taxes for the wealthy or reducing regulations for business, thereby hurting the very people who put them in office. (Later, I'd read David Sirota's 2006 book *Hostile Takeover*[3] which complements Frank's work by focusing on the extent of the economic changes being made by officials who have seized political power in this manner.)

So what was transpiring here in Canton and Columbus and outside Pittsburgh, and by extension around the region, wasn't a total mystery to me. But what's not discussed in the books, and what I couldn't understand from what I was seeing around me, is why no one was fighting back. Where was the rebuttal? When did protecting guns and not protecting gays become exalted values that could dominate a campaign, as health care and a good job were reduced to mere temporal issues and notions of economic justice became, well, invisible. Strangely, this was playing out among people who were actually living their "family values" and yet appeared willing to set aside policies—and politicians—who would help them take care of those families, in favor of largely symbolic goals that probably wouldn't be accomplished anyway. So why wasn't someone engaging these voters, trying to refute such notions? Where, in particular, was labor's voice in all this since it was their agenda that was being displaced, their constituents who were being targeted, and their movement that was being decimated?

It was, in fact, nowhere to be heard on this particular terrain, and so the effort worked among enough of these key voters to sway the election. Williams and the others reflected attitudes, behaviors, and scenes that repeated themselves throughout the country, especially in the battleground states of the Midwest, as values trumped all other considerations. Polling showed that in key state after key state, moral and cultural concerns carried the day, both in getting people to the polls and then in influencing their vote. Tangible issues were swept away in a tide of righteous indignation about the war supposedly being waged on Christianity or on traditional marriage. Or in anger about blasphemous art that somehow stirred people who had never seen it, or about flag burning that never occurs, even as those same people found themselves unable to assign responsibility over the fact that suddenly their jobs were being shipped overseas. Labor's issues were drowned out in all this—not that it tried particularly hard to press them.

Nor was any of this a dramatic departure from the recent past. For years, Democrats and their labor allies, who in this instance would lose Ohio and thereby the election, had been befuddled by the Sue Williamses of the world. They have captured the battlefield of values—defining this critical turf in cultural and moral terms that give the GOP an inherent edge, even as they exclude troublesome economic matters—thus rendering irrelevant those concrete concerns that once resonated in these parts. In the process, proponents of this cultural populism manage to paint its foes as elitist snobs who revel in telling regular working folks how to live, even as it serves the interests of the nation's true elite, the corporate powers that exercise real control over people's lives.

Populism, originally based on the working person's grievances against the avarice of the wealthy class who kept him or her in his or her place, has been subsumed by a false populism that fires people up against some obscure professor's ranting or gay couple's intentions while ignoring the ever-tighter squeeze on average Americans. It would be difficult to overstate the consequences of this trend, which by and large excludes from the national political dialogue any real examination of specific economic, industrial, and corporate policies, let alone broader matters such as economic fairness or community survival. As a result, it leaves largely unexamined potential questions about what those with economic power are doing with that power. It also leaves the values field to those who define it in religious, moral, and cultural terms, thereby skewing the electoral debate, influencing the selection of candidates, and affecting the outcome. And it marginalizes the labor movement by removing or at least downplaying the very issues that have been labor's staple and that long made unions part of a powerful electoral coalition. All this at the very time that such matters logically should be examined as never before, with the rise in economic insecurity and income disparity affecting ever-growing numbers of working- and middle-class Americans.

But wait, you might reasonably say, what about the congressional election of 2006: Wasn't a corner turned, with Democrats sweeping to victory after benefiting from substantial help from labor? Doesn't this mean that labor finally managed to get across its message, that it is once again flexing its political muscles, and that labor's resurgence is just a matter of time?

As a matter of fact, it wasn't and it doesn't. Granted, labor backed the winning side in the elections, and union leaders now get their telephone calls to majority staffers in the Senate and House returned. Yes, they have enlisted the help of key lawmakers such as Edward Kennedy and Nancy Pelosi in efforts to raise the federal minimum wage and to support a few of their other issues. House Democrats even changed the name of the Committee on Education and the Workforce to the Committee on Education and Labor. If the whiff of recent success has buoyed trade unionists about the movement's prospects, it's understandable given the political desert in which they have wandered for years. "For the first time in a decade, we're on the offense," an AFL-CIO spokesman exulted in late January 2007, as he pressed me to attend the executive council session to be held shortly in Las Vegas. (Remember Hoffa? These days, continuingly dwindling labor coverage translates into virtual pleading aimed at those reporters still on the beat.)

What, I inquired, was behind the notion that labor is on the move? "The congressional elections," he replied without missing a beat. And yet this reflects a basic misreading, a hazardous one at that, of what has occurred. Labor's self-congratulatory mood over the results of these elections, and its stated goal of carrying that effort forward to the 2008 presidential contest, amount to a recipe for continued political insignificance—and for perpetuating the movement's overall decline.

If this sounds counterintuitive, that's precisely why it's so important that it be understood, most of all by labor itself.

In fairness, what labor did leading up to the November 2006 elections should first be acknowledged. It ought to come by now as scant surprise that labor's efforts were largely overlooked both by the press and political pundits. But while few noticed, the AFL-CIO put together its most expensive midterm election effort ever, spending some $40 million. The 32 battleground states it got heavily involved in were the most it had targeted in any election, including presidential contests. And that was by no means the whole story. Individual affiliates of the AFL-CIO undertook their own campaigns, led by Gerald McEntee's American Federation of State, County and Municipal Employees (AFSCME), which poured $35 million by itself into the effort. Andrew Stern's Service Employees International Union (SEIU) of the rival Change to Win federation expended another $35 million. Throw in the various other unions in both federations and labor spent upward of $150 million, engaging in heavy doses of phone banks, leafleting, and door-to-door canvassing.

And for its money and effort, labor generated some tangible results. In the wake of its get-out-the-vote push, about one-quarter of all those who went to the polls were from union households, a figure not much above labor's past efforts but nonetheless relatively impressive when one considers its shrinking share of the workforce and the way labor has been written off. (Not, however, quite as impressive as labor's breathless rendering of this statistic would indicate; taking two-adult households, and figuring one union adult per family, that makes one in eight voters, or 12.5 percent—precisely the portion of union members in the workforce). And these voters did more than just turn out—they overwhelmingly voted as union leaders wanted. Some 74 percent of union voters chose labor-endorsed candidates—virtually all Democrats—for the House and 76 percent chose labor-endorsed candidates for the Senate. The combination of those two factors—turnout and ballot choice—meant that labor was instrumental in providing the winning edge in the election. Among union households, Democrats enjoyed a startling 50 percent margin, versus a mere 2 percent margin among nonunion households. So without labor's role, rather than the "thumping" Republicans received, the election would have been a squeaker, with House control up for grabs and the Senate almost certainly remaining in GOP hands.[4]

So, clearly, labor reestablished itself as a key political ally in a Democratic congressional victory. Yet, despite that, 2006 represents a missed political opportunity for the American labor movement, which chose to focus on tactical operations aimed at getting out the vote among union members rather than raising its issues in the public marketplace. To the extent labor addressed these issues, it did so as it preached—quietly, privately—to its own choir, and a shrinking one at that. Rather than seeking to shape or even influence the public debate—let alone change anyone's mind—labor defined its role as motivating its members and then getting them to the polls. Labor leaders will gladly discuss the figures of volunteers and phone calls, leaflets, and turnout, but don't ask them how and where they actually influenced the discussion.

It's no surprise that when the votes had been cast, exit poll after exit poll showed the election was primarily about the public's frustration over a mismanaged war, followed by perceived administration incompetence and congressional corruption. Even New York Senator Chuck Schumer, who spearheaded the Democratic Senate campaign effort in 2006, acknowledges in his book *Positively American* that his party won by virtue of Republican failures and still lacks a positive message for average Americans.[5] Analysts of all persuasions agree that the Democrats succeeded in nationalizing the election, turning it essentially into a referendum on Bush and Iraq; what it wasn't about was the growing economic imbalance or the assault on working Americans, let alone labor's specific agenda.

Raise your hands, anyone who heard the slightest discussion during the election of a rise in workplace fatalities. Or an analysis of the link among the slew of coal-mining tragedies, the deunionization of America's mines, and federal decisions on safety policy and appointment of oversight personnel. Who remembers, amid the frequent reiterations of failures surrounding Katrina and its aftermath, anything about the administration's effort to deny construction workers their normal wages as they rebuilt devastated areas? Wouldn't that have dovetailed nicely with all the concerns expressed about the socioeconomic and racial chasms revealed by the storm, as well as the supposed back-of-the-hand treatment the administration was giving those affected? How much dialogue did labor spark about the fact that the wage share of the gross domestic product (GDP) is near a record low while the share of profits is the highest in a half-century?[6] Can anyone recall a single syllable being uttered about how restrictive labor laws, compounded by lax enforcement, have curtailed the ability of unions to organize and allowed employers to block, stall, or derail legitimate efforts to do so—and how that relates to the wage stagnation experienced by working Americans? Or, indeed, how the attack on labor has facilitated the various policies affecting the status of the middle class, which so many are decrying without exploring the roots?

In a campaign that for a while was filled with discussion about stem cell research, Michael J. Fox, and Rush Limbaugh, where was the talk of what might befall hospital patients because of a labor board ruling that could compromise the ability of nurses to advocate for better care? How much conversation was there about the impact of free-trade agreements with authoritarian governments that pay their workers pennies and ban labor unions, forcing American workers to compete with the impoverished of the Third World in a race to the bottom? These and all other labor issues put together—with the singular exception of minimum wage, largely a symbolic matter for unionized workers and even for most workers in general—didn't capture one day's worth of the debate or coverage related to Congressman Mark Foley's e-mails to congressional pages. The media obviously had a lot to say about this, but blaming them entirely for the absence from the national discussion of these matters would be far too facile, as we'll discuss in the next couple of chapters.

Though the moment to raise such issues was so opportune—given the public's well-documented if vague sense of unease about no-bid contracts and secretly written energy policy and tax breaks for the wealthy, as average people cope with competitive market forces—labor didn't even attempt to shape the debate. The wind was blowing in their favor, but unions declined to get onto the playing field. With average Americans indicating pessimism about their children's economic future for the first time in history, labor was content to let the elections turn almost entirely on the administration's war policy and the GOP's internal difficulties. In other words, had Donald Rumsfeld heeded the prewar advice of Army Chief of Staff General Eric Shinseki to send an invading force to Iraq big enough to win the peace, or had Foley not taken a shine to congressional pages, the election might well have turned out differently. While it's true that labor's political calculations that such GOP missteps would suffice to put the Democrats over the top proved correct, in a more profound sense labor missed the boat. At a time when its foes were highly vulnerable on a set of issues related to the economic dislocation facing working people, labor failed to seize a rare opportunity to put its message on the public radar. Compounding all this was how servile labor's involvement was in the 2006 campaign, with the labor movement exercising less independence than ever. With one or two exceptions, labor exclusively endorsed Democrats, a marked contrast with past elections when it supported a couple of dozen Republicans. So in every sense, labor was an appendix to the Democratic campaign effort.

Labor's focus on turning out its members, as opposed to a broader and more ambitious game plan of devising a coherent message and potentially shaping the mandate, isn't new. Unions have long been about the nuts-and-bolts activities at election time. What makes this problematic now for labor is that the context has so drastically changed. Decades ago, when unions represented upwards of one-third of workers, labor's message resonated far more forcefully into the broader population. In addition, with labor an integral part of the

Democrats' New Deal coalition, work-related topics were inherently part and parcel of the national discussion. Finally, the advent of a moralistic populism had not yet stripped the values terrain clear of bread-and-butter concerns.

So the bottom line was that labor worked harder than ever in the 2006 election, devoted more resources, and helped the Democrats succeed—yet its message remains unheard, its survival remains in doubt, and its raison d'être is as little understood as ever. Labor's "success," even though it occurred at an optimal time for it to achieve a breakthrough, likely compelled not one more single American to sign on to its agenda or even to better understand work-related matters.

There's a second reason why the 2006 elections mark less of a turnaround for labor than its leaders believe: in matters related to organized labor and the workplace, presidential power has proven to be far more decisive than congressional authority. That's not the case in many other areas of government policy—defense or transportation, for example—where the key is money, which makes congressional appropriations and authorization processes critical. For workplace and labor issues, however, spending levels and legislation in general often take a back seat to executive decisions, particularly ones that receive little scrutiny. It is the president who appoints federal mediation as well as labor relations boards that rule on grievances affecting specific workers while setting far-reaching precedents. It is from the White House that orders are issued that dictate whether prevailing wages will be paid or union jurisdiction at job sites altered. The administration fills enforcement positions that will either regulate industries to ensure compliance with safety rules, or conversely reduce red tape and then wink as employers save money and cut corners. And it determines the details of trade pacts, then appoints trade representatives whose work is critical to the ability of U.S. workers to compete or, conversely, see their jobs and even entire industries go abroad. The president or vice president or cabinet members determine which groups will be invited to help fashion public policy in given areas of the economy, and whether labor will be at the table or instead find itself reacting to decisions made by the people at that table.

It's no coincidence that labor's sharp decline began with one of President Ronald Reagan's earliest decisions—to confront the air traffic controllers union—even as Democrat Tip O'Neill reigned as the most powerful man in Congress. That not only led to the destruction of the Professional Air Traffic Controllers Organization (PATCO), it more importantly sent a message to employers that it was open season on unions, and the symbolism was widely received and heeded. Perhaps in only one other entreaty—"Tear down that wall"—would Reagan prove so successful. Nor is it mere chance that as labor's woes have mounted, by January 2009 the White House will have been, from a union perspective, in hostile hands for 20 of the past 28 years. The vacillation of congressional control over that period has meant little. Even the lone interruption to a GOP White House, Bill Clinton's presidency, buttresses the point that when labor fails to help shape the national dialogue, its most important issues can easily be shunted aside. Despite labor's considerable help in both of Clinton's campaigns, he vigorously opposed labor on its most important issue of the time: the signing of international trade pacts that hastened the exporting of manufacturing jobs.

Not only are the stakes higher for labor in presidential contests, it's also the case that the challenges are more daunting
because it's easier for values to obscure economic issues.
Appeals to values and character and morality dominate more
readily in national elections pitting two individuals against
each other than in a patchwork of contests that often turn at
least partly on local issues. In fact, the congressional elections
of 2006 make it more—not less—likely that cultural values
will rebound in 2008, depending, of course, on who is nominated by the parties. The ascent to power of liberal
Democratic lawmakers from places like San Francisco and
Boston may provide ready-made targets on these grounds.
Moreover, the failure of the national security issues as Iraq
falls apart makes the other Republican strength of recent
years—traditional values of morality, virtue, and character,
buttressed by social wedge issues—potentially all the more
important. And recall, as Schumer and other Democrats
acknowledge, that their side didn't so much puncture the
Republican hold on values as manage to sidestep them because
of self-inflicted GOP wounds. Looking forward, the potential
upside for labor is that if it finds its voice and prepares a message that resonates, in presidential contests outside groups
have far more of a say in helping select a candidate in the first
place and setting the electoral agenda.

But the problem of labor's missing voice transcends politics.
If the union message is muted during electoral season, it's positively absent and unaccounted for the rest of the year. Given
labor's inability and often its unwillingness—both apply, as we
will see in Chapter 5—to communicate its views and aspirations and accomplishments, compounded by the media's indif-

ference to workers and their unions, labor's story is missing from the daily public conversation. At times it seems as if labor is the only topic *not* discussed in the United States. The national dialogue is filled to the breaking point with complex and weighty matters, ranging from the true nature of Islam to the validity of global warming. On the other end, it's replete with Hollywood's newest couples and the latest scandals. And then there's everything that fits between the truly serious and the merely distracting—whether steroids in sports or the merits of organic foods. Virtually the only verboten topic is anything that touches on American workers or the organizations that represent and fight for them. Labor leaders and their issues are almost entirely absent from the evening news shows or the Sunday morning talk shows, with the rare exceptions generally occurring during high-profile strikes, events that, given labor's mounting weakness, are rarer than ever.[7]

What's puzzling about labor's failure to deliver its message is that most people agree with almost all of its policy goals. Whether it's keeping jobs in America, better safety enforcement, or assuring that trade deals don't kowtow to regimes that oppress their own workers, polls—and common sense—suggest widespread public agreement with labor's stances on each of these specific issues. But if labor isn't making clear why these things aren't happening or what the underlying forces at play are, that public sentiment means little in practical terms for the well-being of workers or the rejuvenation of the union movement. And it won't gain traction if people don't connect the declining strength of the labor movement with the increasingly embattled status of American workers. How many people know that the period of labor's greatest strength, the late 1940s to the mid-1970s, was also the period in American history when the economy worked best for all levels of society? Or that labor's decline over the past quarter century has gone hand in hand with a rising discrepancy between how the top economic strata fares compared to average Americans? Or why these trends are not coincidental? How much thought is given to what would likely happen to average Americans' wages and benefits—and to the growing economic disparity—if unions simply faded away? Why aren't these the starting points for a discussion about economic concerns and labor's role and how to improve conditions for average Americans?

The lack of an effective voice has had three far-reaching consequences for labor: it has skewed public policies related to workers, the workplace, and union rights; it has created a vacuum in terms of public perception that allows labor's adversaries to define it in negative ways; and, as a result, it has jeopardized labor's survival. And these factors constantly exacerbate one another, pushing labor downward toward declining numbers, reduced clout in the workplace, and a sense of irrelevance and inevitable decline.

The most obvious consequences flowing from labor's lack of a powerful voice relate to policy. Because labor doesn't make its agenda front and center, topics such as the relationship among trade agreements, worker oppression overseas, and the loss of American manufacturing jobs and its impact on the middle class don't get seriously addressed by policymakers. Every detail of a Social Security crisis that might occur decades down the line is sliced and diced while concern over the crisis of millions of good-paying jobs already going overseas in a trend abetted by government policies is simply dismissed. This occurs whatever the political mix of the government; over the past quarter century plus, labor's woes have grown through Democratic control of the White House and Congress, Republican control of both branches, Democratic executive control and Republican legislative dominance, and Republican presidents coupled with Democratic lawmakers. If that doesn't show labor that its approach to elections is lacking, it's hard to know what would. Little-noticed executive branch decisions limit worker rights and hurt labor, and labor's inability to prevent them—or to shine a public spotlight on the most egregious when they occur, such as those surrounding the Sago mines—does untold damage to unions and their members. Labor's virtual invisibility compromises its ability to generate public or political support for its objectives while allowing its adversaries to tilt the playing field.

Labor's silence also means that its enemies get to define what unions are all about and what they supposedly seek, creating a damaging discordance between the public's generally positive view on the issues relevant to workers and the popular perception of the sole institution fighting for those outcomes. Hence, the common images of autocratic union bosses who spend members' money in ways contrary to their political interests, when, that is, they aren't flat-out corrupt and simply stealing the money. Of pinky-ring labor leaders who loll on golf courses and run thuggish or violent unions, even when the source of much of those images, the International Brotherhood of Teamsters, has over the last decade undergone a most remarkable, if underappreciated (and underreported), transformation. Or of unions that make outlandish demands of employers who simply wish to remain competitive, thereby costing jobs because of sheer greed. In that regard, it is mind-boggling that labor hasn't made the story of Cleveland's Mr. Coffee plant a tale known to every household in America.

Mr. Coffee, made famous years ago when baseball legend Joe DiMaggio hawked the products in advertisements, employed 390 workers at its suburban plant outside Cleveland to produce 5,000 coffeemakers a day. It was an American success story in more ways than one; most of the workers were African-American women, and many had landed there from the welfare-to-work program under welfare reform. The workers earned modest salaries, from $8 to $10 an hour, with no pension plan, and the plant was efficient and profitable. But after buying it, the Sunbeam Corporation of Boca Raton, Florida, decided in 1998 that it could make still more money by moving production to Mexico. The Teamsters union, which represented the workers, fought back, hiring investigators and traveling to Mexico to expose the working conditions and wages there. Also facing an aroused coalition of community and religious activists in a strong labor town, the company withdrew its plans, but two years later, benefiting from trade agreement provisions and a worn-out workforce, it shipped the work to Mexico and Mississippi and later to China. The 390 employees joined the tens of thousands of Ohio workers who had seen their jobs exported, often not for economic imperatives but simply because employers could increase their profit margins. Talk of thousands of jobs puts people to sleep. Why doesn't labor tell the story of Joe DiMaggio and Mr. Coffee, the welfare-to-work women, the corporate moves, the Chinese workers slaving away for pennies on the hour, and what's happened to the little Ohio community? Why doesn't labor tell this story every day and twice a day before elections? Certainly it has all the elements to resonate around the country.

Finally, labor's inability to avert these policies and alter these perceptions inflicts profound institutional damage on the union movement because they help shrink the membership and weaken labor in its collective bargaining and other battles with employers, while feeding the sense that labor is outmoded. If labor can't protect workers' interests or even retain its share of the workforce, it's natural that it would be seen as little more than a relic.

A concrete example of how these factors have converged to put labor on the brink is found in the obstacles unions increasingly encounter in trying to organize a workplace. Forming a union would appear to be a black-and-white matter since American labor law sets forth a relatively straightforward process by which workers can decide whether or not to have a union. The fact that workers seem at face value to be opting against doing so carries a double whammy for labor: it not only weakens unions by shrinking their base, but it also reinforces the perception that labor has lost its relevance since it suggests that workers have simply decided that forming a union isn't in their best interests.

Tell that to Lori Gay, a registered nurse with 20 years on the job who, along with some of her coworkers, has long been trying to organize the Salt Lake Regional Medical Center in hopes of improving staffing levels and patient care. The hospital's nearly 200 nurses demonstrated sufficient support to legally mandate an election on forming a union. It was held in May 2002—but five years later the nurses, and everyone else, had yet to learn the result. Before the votes could even be counted, the ballots were impounded because the hospital asserted that some nurses shouldn't have been eligible to vote since part of their chores involved supervisory tasks. A few months later, the Denver regional office of the National Labor Relations Board ruled that the nurses were indeed eligible to be part of a bargaining unit, but a second appeal by the hospital sent the case to NLRB headquarters in Washington for a ruling, where it sat for years. In the fall of 2006, following the Kentucky River decision, the matter was returned to the Denver NLRB to be adjudicated based on examination of that ruling. In February 2007, the regional board ruled that some of the nurses had been ineligible to vote, putting the ball back in the court of the United American Nurses (UAN), the union involved, to decide whether to ask the NLRB in Washington to review that decision. Not only would the regional ruling eliminate the votes of the specific nurses in question, it might also void the entire election because management could argue that their mere participation in the campaign had influenced the votes of others. In May 2007 the board accepted the union's request to review the matter.

Gay never anticipated that five years would pass without the results, good or bad, ever being known. "I did not, but I think I was naive at the time," she says now, "reading about other cases where it's pretty common. It's a process that's allowed to happen, appeals and delays without ever getting a resolution, and employers hoping that in the delay process there'll either

be a lack of interest among new employees or people dismantling themselves and not staying organized. That's against our
whole system; if you vote for a president or anybody else, your
ballots are opened in a timely manner."

In fact, half of the original Salt Lake City nurses have
moved on; even if it turns out that the nurses did vote for a
union back in 2002, it's unclear whether the turnover means
that a new election would have to be held and the whole
process begin anew. This could be why many employers find
it worthwhile to delay the outcome of a union vote, hoping
a lack of interest or disillusionment will set in, a rollover of
staff will void the election, or that the extra time will allow
management to work its will with employees. It's a viable
strategy because of the inadequate staffing and resources
provided to the NLRB, which makes for a time-consuming
process in the best of instances. This is only exacerbated by
the employer-friendly nature of the board should a case
wend its way to the top.

But that's merely the tip of the iceberg. Employer resistance
to American workers exercising their right to unionize doesn't
begin when the employees vote; companies often seek to avert
an election right from the get-go. The most egregious actions
typically occur in the period leading up to a vote, as companies pull out all the stops to dissuade employees from even
going down that road. Mandatory meetings where supervisors
warn workers about the harm a union would bring, harassment or surveillance of employees, and threats to close or
move the business if a union is formed are all illegal and all
often deployed. So too is disciplining or firing workers pushing for a union vote. Such actions serve a dual purpose: they

silence or remove troublesome activists and have a chilling effect on the rest of the workforce.

From a cost-benefit analysis, such employers have made a rational decision that their chances of being targeted in timely fashion by federal labor officials are small. That's borne out by the facts; in a recent year the median time between workers' filing an unfair labor practice charge and a ruling by the NLRB was 889 days. Even should a decision eventually go against employers, they often calculate it as an affordable cost of doing business—with any modest penalties incurred in delaying, disrupting, or destroying unionization drives deemed well worth the ultimate savings in wages and in retaining management prerogatives. They have a point since unionized workers, on the average, earn about 30 percent more, are 28 percent more likely to have employer-provided health insurance, have 28 percent more days of paid vacation, and are 54 percent more likely to have guaranteed pensions, according to Department of Labor figures. Penalties for unfairly discharging workers typically amount to paying back wages, minus whatever the worker earned in the interim, and posting a notice that the company will abide by labor law in the future. This flips the notion of a victimless crime on its head; it is probably as close to a punishment-free infraction as one will encounter.

A burly Ohio forklift driver named Bill Lawhorn knows that story all too well. At the very time Lori Gay was pushing for a vote at her hospital in the spring of 2002, Lawhorn was doing the same at Consolidated Biscuit Co. in McComb, an hour south of Toledo. As he carried out his job transporting products to the plant's various production lines, Lawhorn had been noticing an increase in abusive treatment by supervisors, and he began talking with coworkers about forming a union. In short order, some 75 percent of the more than 800 employees signed cards calling for an election for representation by the Bakery, Confectionery, Tobacco Workers and Grain Millers International Union (BCTGM). That compelled a vote, but it also infuriated management. Employees were warned that if they continued the drive they would miss out on promised promotions, see their wages and benefits slashed, encounter tougher discipline, and perhaps even find the plant closed. Some Hispanic workers allege that particular emphasis was placed on warning their group, which was initially among the most fervent backers of the prospective union, that they would lose their jobs. This was no small threat since Consolidated was the biggest employer in the area.

On a weekend three days before the August 2002 vote, Lawhorn was in the garage of his rural home, making "Vote Union" signs with some coworkers. One of his supervisors drove up and told the 11-year veteran point-blank that if the vote failed, he would immediately be fired; the unspoken implication being that if the union effort fell through, employees would be unprotected from reprisals. A stubborn man, Lawhorn immediately resumed making the signs, but on a broader level the intimidation succeeded. The same workforce that had so overwhelmingly supported the idea of a union voted it down by a 60-to-40 ratio. The very next day, Lawhorn was indeed the first one fired—in dramatic fashion meant to leave no doubt about the company's resolve. Three security guards escorted Lawhorn outside, where a police officer called by the company waited for him. That kicked off a succession of rapid-fire dismissals of pro-union workers over the next few weeks.

Five months later, the regional NLRB in Cleveland issued a complaint containing 43 allegations of unfair labor practices against the company and ordered a new election. It also determined that Lawhorn had been fired for his union activity and ordered the company to reinstate him with back pay. A board trial ensued, and an administrative law judge agreed in January 2004 that there had been egregious and widespread violations of the workers' fundamental right to form a union. The company was again ordered to return Lawhorn and others to work with full back pay within 14 days. That prompted a company appeal to the national board, which, two and a half years later, in May 2006, found that some of the violations had indeed occurred and yet again ordered that Lawhorn be reinstated. It also threw out the results of the election, ordered a new one, and told the company to post a notice that it would not violate labor statutes. Five years after it began, the matter was still pending. To get enforcement power in the case, the NLRB was preparing to go before the Sixth Circuit Court.

The circumstances in McComb and Salt Lake City differed, as did the intensity of management's tactics, but the common feature is how effective they were. More than half a decade after legally held elections, Gay was still wondering what the results were, and Lawhorn was still waiting for a fair election and—on a personal level—to be rehired and to receive the first penny owed him. To get by, the 50-year-old Lawhorn has been borrowing money from his three children. "Parents don't borrow from their children, they loan to them," he says. "It's something that really gets to me. This isn't the American way." He's also been hauling garbage in a truck they gave him, putting to use a small compactor he already owned. Ironically, a number of his former supervisors, evidently aware of his work ethic, are paying him to pick up trash at their homes.

These are not rare instances artfully selected to make a point, nor are they by any means among the most severe cases of unionization drives being thwarted by something other than individual decisions of workers. Instead, they are shockingly typical. According to the NLRB itself, 31,358 American workers were awarded back pay as a result of having been illegally fired or otherwise disciplined in 2005, the last year for which such figures are available, often for trying to form a collective bargaining unit at their place of work. That is up sharply from an average of 22,000 to 24,000 the previous dozen years. In the NLRB General Counsel's Summary of Operations for Fiscal Year 2006, General Counsel Ronald Meisburg lists recovery of $111 million for employees, mostly in back pay, a steep rise from the $85 million employees lost in 2005.

Pro-labor organizations use these figures to contend that an American worker is fired, disciplined, or retaliated against for exercising the right to have a union *every 23 minutes*. It can reasonably be argued that labor and some of its allies tend to interpret complex statistics here in somewhat simplistic fashion, lumping together various employer actions as all aimed at union activity and then drawing broad inferences that buttress labor's position. Anti-union groups such as the Center for Union Facts indeed make this argument, one not entirely lacking in merit. But these groups tend to crunch the numbers in overly restrictive fashion and, unsurprisingly, reach conclusions that support *their* perspective. For its part, the NLRB takes no sides, saying its role is simply to compile and report data, not to evaluate it because it does not seek to be an advocate for any point of view. But beyond the ideological tug underlying these differences, what is clear is that the numbers are significant, and that they are growing. In the 1950s, when trade unions were stronger and the labor-management playing field more even, the comparable figures for back pay awarded workers for employer transgressions were under 1,000 a year. And even if labor tends to be generous in ascribing virtually of the recorded cases of employer violations to union-related activity, it is likely, given the nature of such governmental studies, that many such incidents go unreported in the first place.[8]

Earlier this decade, research by Kate Bronfenbrenner of Cornell University's School of Industrial and Labor Relations found that 80 percent of employers facing an organizing campaign put workers through one-on-one sessions meant to intimidate them against supporting the advent of a union in their workplace, often by threatening to move the plant. Fifty-two percent of employers with immigrant workers threaten to call immigration officials during organization drives. Fifty-one percent of companies threaten to close the plant if the union vote succeeds; only 1 percent actually does so, suggesting that this is a tactic to ward off a union rather than a reflection of real economic consequences.

An entire multi-billion-dollar cottage industry of consultants and lawyers has sprung up to meet the employer demand for help in quelling union aspirations among workers. A study in

2006 by the University of Illinois determined that anti-union activities against employees looking into organizing are "both pervasive and effective." Even in Chicago, a heavily unionized city where public officials tend to be pro-labor, the study found that 82 percent of employers hired anti-union consultants, and 30 percent of businesses fired some of their workers involved in organizing. Though by definition a majority of workers favored a union in virtually all cases where an election was called, a union was formed only 31 percent of the time. Just as often, the campaign evaporated in face of an employer onslaught even before workers got to express their preferences in a vote, while in the other third of cases workers changed their minds and voted it down. Another study, this one in 2007 by John Schmitt and Ben Zipperer of a Washington think tank, the Center for Economic and Policy Research (CEPR), found that one in five active union supporters is fired illegally as a result of union organizing, a figure that has risen as the number of successful union elections has declined.

And even when a vote occurs and workers approve a union, that's not the end of it. Employers get a third crack at thwarting or stalling the process by refusing to negotiate the first contract, leading to yet another round with the NLRB. According to the Federal Mediation & Conciliation Service (FMCS), 45 percent of workers who form a new union still don't have a collective bargaining agreement with their employer two years later. And more than a third of all employers never end up agreeing to a contract after workers form a union under legal guidelines. When employers hire anti-union consultants, the prospect of a first contract is almost three times lower.

In reality, the legal system set up to protect workers' rights has grown so unbalanced that when labor uses its waning strength to gain a rare victory in the traditional areas of collective bargaining or strikes, management sometimes retreats to the behind-the-scenes world of labor law to regain its footing. In Mississippi, for instance, after absorbing the defeat inflicted on them by the catfish workers, and unable to retaliate given the public support the workers and their union had generated, the Mississippi business community bided its time. When workers at a metal plant in Magnolia undertook an organizing campaign and held a vote on union representation on May 9, 2001, the employer—taking a page from the argument hospitals were using vis-à-vis nurses—challenged it on the basis that some of the workers had supervisory responsibilities. The ballots were impounded, stored at the NLRB office in New Orleans, and the matter eventually became part of the Kentucky River case. "The workers have been sitting there for years, wondering if they've got a union, and the ballots have not been counted," says Robert Shaffer, president of the Mississippi AFL-CIO. "Hell, they probably floated out to the ocean with Katrina."[9] Actually, they proved to be high and dry; after the Kentucky River decision the ballots were ordered tallied. As it turned out, the workers had overwhelmingly voted 246 to 37 for a union back in 2001; a mere five and a half years later they—at least those still employed there—finally were being represented by the Kansas-based International Brotherhood of Boilermakers as it sought to negotiate their first union contract.

As Human Rights Watch wrote in a report on American workers' freedom to form unions and bargain collectively,

"Our findings are disturbing, to say the least. Loophole-ridden laws, paralyzing delays, and feeble enforcement have led to a culture of impunity in many areas of U.S. labor law and practice. Legal obstacles tilt the playing field so steeply against workers' freedom of association that the United States is in violation of international human rights standards for workers." And that was in September 2000; things have only worsened since.[10]

Compare this situation with some statements most Americans, and public officials, would readily subscribe to, and which the nation already has accepted in a legal and moral sense: "Everyone has the right to form and to join trade unions for the protection of his interests"—from the 1948 Universal Declaration of Human Rights by the United Nations. "All member countries have an obligation . . . to respect, to promote, and to realize the principles concerning the fundamental rights which are the subject of these Conventions, namely: freedom of association and the effective recognition of the right to collective bargaining"—United Nations International Labor Organization (ILO). This 1998 ILO Declaration on Fundamental Principles and Rights at Work was adopted with the unanimous support of all U.S. delegates. Finally, "Employees shall have the right to self-organization, to form, join, or assist labor organizations, to bargain collectively through representatives of their own choosing, and to engage in other mutual aid or protection"—National Labor Relations Act, passed by Congress in 1935.

Such grand principles notwithstanding, the facts on the ground make clear why the employer activity described above is taking place, and at an increasing rate. A January 2007 poll by Peter D. Hart Research Associates showed that among *nonunion workers*, a majority of 53 percent against 42 percent said they would vote to have a union tomorrow, given a free choice, which translates to about 60 million workers. (Among all workers, including those already in a union, the figure jumps to 58 percent.) If even one-quarter of those 60 million workers actually formed unions, the size of the labor movement would double overnight. As economic disparities have grown, as corporations have become more emboldened, and as anti-union activities have become more prevalent, the level of unorganized workers favoring a union has edged steadily upward over the past two decades. It stood at 30 percent in 1984, 39 percent in 1993, and 42 percent in 2001.[11]

This helps explain why employers have aggressively fought to prevent unionization campaigns, but it does more than that: it also debunks the notion that plummeting membership neatly reflects a lack of worker interest in unions. Employers' quashing of workplace union drives, facilitated by the inability or unwillingness of federal boards to act in timely fashion, is part of a one-two punch to unions already hit by the exporting of union manufacturing jobs and increasingly of white-collar work as well. Lacking the political or economic clout to curb that latter trend, the only way unions could keep their ranks relatively strong would be to organize new work sites. Instead, they are depleted at both ends—by unionized industries leaving and by organizing obstacles being put in their way at nonunion plants.

Without public outrage or political pressure, things don't change. A Hart poll found that 77 percent of Americans believe workers should be able to make their own choices about whether to have a union in their workplace, without pressure from anyone else. So people widely believe in that right; *they just don't know how often it's violated or what jeopardy it is in*—let alone the impact this is having on labor and workers. The public is not rejecting labor's message as much as it is not hearing that message in the first place—not surprising since it is barely audible. In the end, it's public indifference more than public hostility that is hurting union efforts to cope with the structural challenges of a changing economy and the actions of emboldened corporate adversaries.

The consequences of these trends are proving deadly for the union movement. From the 1950s to today, labor's share of the workforce has tumbled by more than two-thirds, and now stands at its lowest percentage—12.5—in more than 60 years. This is both cause and effect of labor's decline. How many institutions could take that kind of blow and sustain any type of viability over time? The falling numbers, fewer strikes, and rarer successes in collective bargaining all point to labor's institutional fragility at a time when growing corporate power and a rapidly evolving economy leave workers ever more in need of a strong advocate. Workers and unions have faced tough battles before. Aggressive employers, hostile laws, unfriendly federal officials, or difficult economic conditions are nothing new. Indeed, such challenges have led to some of labor's most memorable battles and most significant achievements because it is precisely in such times that unions are most needed. But this time around, faced with another multipronged assault on American workers, labor is hindered in fighting back, asserting its interests, and defending its members by its own internal weaknesses and the external perceptions of its irrelevance.

As we've seen, labor is still capable of generating results when it plays its cards right, as in Indianola and Iowa, but it's growing too weak for such Herculean efforts to be anything other than an exception. On a more routine basis, labor is proving incapable of defending worker interests, stemming from its institutional frailty and from its inability to stir a serious public discussion of issues of safety, pensions, or job security. Generating such a discussion is more critical to labor's survival than winning a given election because labor's weakness on all fronts stems largely from its inability to make its agenda part of the national discourse.

Faced with all this, what is labor doing to turn the situation around? What is it doing to protect workers while warding off its own demise? What is labor's strategy to defend its constituents and its principles? The right of workers to organize, the aspirations of a decent job with some security so they can care for their families, the goals of affordable health care or a community's survival—those weren't the types of values discussed at the outset of this chapter, but aren't they values too? Aren't they, in fact, family values? So why do the moral values of Sue Williams resonate as they do while those of Lori Gay are muted? Don't the values of Bill Lawhorn merit equal billing with those of Ken Mowbray, however one eventually comes out on their respective merits? Having finally, if belatedly, recognized the dire straits they're in, what are labor leaders doing to fight for their values and thereby for their very existence? The answer is not encouraging from labor's perspective, but answers may lie in what we have seen labor *not* doing in terms of making its voice heard.

CHAPTER 4

FROM DIALOGUE
TO DIVISION

Finally, after so many years of denial, a gathering on
December 2 and 3, 2004, billed as *Labor at the Crossroads*,
reflected the readiness of trade unionists to admit that organized labor was in dire need of an overhaul.[1] For far too long,
the labor movement had been impervious to self-questioning,
its leaders unwilling to scrutinize their own judgments and
performance, determined to conceal any vulnerabilities from
corporate and political adversaries. They had insisted that
labor was still a vital force and was doing as well as could be
expected given factors beyond their control, but such denial
was becoming tougher to maintain in the face of sinking membership. Labor's representation in the private workforce was
not quite one in a dozen workers, meaning that less than 8
percent now carried a union card.

Just a month earlier labor leaders had been jolted by the
results of the 2004 presidential election, which had put an
exclamation point even they couldn't miss on the state of the

unions. Having pulled out all the stops for its candidate, labor was unable to defeat an incumbent, even one who was mired in an increasingly unpopular war abroad and presiding over a jobless economic recovery at home. The reelection of George W. Bush, considered by many trade unionists to be the most anti-union president in American history, was a slap in the face that jarred them from their complacency.

And here it was, reckoning day. Not yet eight o'clock on a chilly Thursday morning, as throngs of people—including a few journalists, myself among them—filed purposefully into the City University of New York Graduate Center at 365 Fifth Avenue to brainstorm about the future of their labor movement, to posit ideas and debate about the changes needed for labor to once again flourish. The sense of purpose within the crowd was electric. "The topic is hot for two reasons," Kate Bronfenbrenner, director of labor education research at Cornell University, told me as she prepared for her presentation. "It's hot because labor is in a crisis, and it's hot because labor is really thinking about fundamental changes that could revitalize it."

No longer able to pretend they were merely going through a tough stretch, the presence of 565 participants acknowledged labor's critical plight and, more importantly, their readiness to do something about it. And the mix of attendees augured well.

There were veterans with richly textured backgrounds like Mark Dudzic, a former sanitation worker who had been active in the Oil, Chemical and Atomic Workers International Union (OCAW) since the late 1960s, once heading an OCAW local in New Jersey. Dudzic's search to give workers a voice had more recently led him to the position of national organizer for the Labor Party, formed in 1998 as a political alternative for workers. There was a smattering of fresh faces like Rachel Yanda, who was hoping efforts like this might help give labor a future she could be a part of. The New Mexico native had become fascinated after taking a labor law course at Sarah Lawrence College, from which she would be graduating in a few months, and already had participated in several union and social justice campaigns. Taking some time off from preparing for her semester finals, she was slated to be on a panel Thursday afternoon titled, "Passion for Justice: Youth Organizing and the Labor Movement." At that same hour, Dudzic would be a panelist on "Regaining the Right to Organize: A Debate on Strategy."

The debates were intense, wide ranging, and at times passionate, with a dizzying array of ideas proposed—such as a renewed emphasis on organizing and a focus on changing labor laws that helped businesses combat union drives. There were calls for more aggressive political engagement, sparking counterarguments from a few who wanted to wean unions from the Democratic Party, which they felt took them for granted, while the close ties between the two prevented labor from articulating its own agenda. Some wanted to merge unions, the result being that corporations would have fewer but more powerful adversaries, internal competition among unions would be reduced, and administrative costs cut, freeing up resources for other purposes. That was the heart of a proposal titled "Unite to Win" that had been circulated over the past month by the Service Employees International Union (SEIU). The proposal was met with resistance from some who worried that small unions, often attuned to their own members' needs, would find themselves gobbled up by larger entities.

There also was some talk, if fleeting, of promoting greater democracy in unions and getting the rank and file more involved as a way of making unions more attractive to unorganized workers. An idea was floated to promote a tougher union stance vis-à-vis employers by guaranteeing at least $200 a week in strike pay from the AFL-CIO for every striking worker. Others suggested improving labor's negotiating skills in hopes of winning better collective bargaining agreements that would satisfy current members while appealing to potential ones. Emphasizing that point, Gregory Junemann, president of an engineering union representing Boeing aerospace employees among others, argued that weakened bargaining power had led to a decline in health-care benefits for his members—at this point provided by 56 percent of employers but on the decline. "As soon as that gets below 50 percent, we have a major problem on our hands," he said, "because if I'm dealing with Boeing or Lockheed Martin, they're going to say, 'Why am I the only one in town providing health-care benefits? Maybe it's time to discontinue it.'" Left unstated was that this, in turn, would further reduce the value of union membership, sending figures still lower, which suggests how labor's various problems compound one another.

The leading proposals focused on organizing, politics, and collective bargaining drew labor's key officials to plenary sessions in the auditorium, while others deemed less central, such as boosting union democracy or increasing alliances with community groups, were relegated to breakout sessions in small rooms, sometimes several floors away. While this made logistical sense, it limited the resonance of some of the most provocative suggestions and follow-up discussions—particularly since those smaller gatherings often spilled out into the hallways, where participants couldn't hear.

Still, this was all new and the tone was refreshing. At the end of the two-day event, top union officials unapologetically pinpointed labor's shortcomings and the dangers they posed to unions and workers. Larry Cohen, then the executive vice president of the Communications Workers of America (CWA) and now its president, conceded that labor's feebleness was damaging its ability to take on employers in the type of negotiating that had long helped boost workers' wages and benefits. "We have seen collective bargaining rights virtually destroyed on our watch," he said in a rather extraordinary admission. "We have to go back to those roots." Stewart Acuff, organizing director of the AFL-CIO, outlining the mix of factors that were thwarting union drives, didn't spare union leaders he said had failed to make it a priority. Bruce Raynor, president of the newly merged textile and hotel workers union known as UNITE HERE, said labor needed to be the spokesman for working America, and he was blunt in his assessment: "I think we've failed in that." Labor's voice had grown so faint, he acknowledged, as to allow pensions promised to workers over decades to be stripped away "without any comment in American society."

The freewheeling and quasi-public nature of the debate was unparalleled for organized labor, Dudzic said. "I've never seen it in my lifetime, this type of open debate among labor," he said. (Nor had I, and it was hard not to recall where I'd been 15 years earlier, almost to the day: in East Germany, during the tense weeks in the autumn of 1989 before the Berlin Wall fell, not registered officially as a reporter, I was surreptitiously observing developments as everyday East Germans began to speak tentatively, still fearful but anxious to test what was permissible.) There was no denying the heady, even liberating atmosphere that reigned as so many disparate elements came together openly over labor's future. For many years the trade union movement had, with some justification, been accused of stifling dissent to present a strong and unified front, which in fact inhibited progress and real strength. And that culture of uniformity extended beyond the sensitive area of self-criticism into what should be normal discourse. When John Sweeney challenged incumbent AFL-CIO president Tom Donahue in 1995, it was, incredibly, the *first, and still only, contested election* in the history of the labor federation.

In that context, the tone of the New York event was sufficiently daring and novel that SEIU executive vice president Gerald Hudson felt compelled to simultaneously praise the open dialogue while urging that there be no recriminations. "There ought to be honest discussion," he told the participants. "It ought to be deep, and it ought to go broad—and nobody ought to be penalized for participating." The mere fact that he made this statement says something. It was delivered after a questioner didn't get a direct response when he asked panelists at a plenary discussion to agree that no union staff member would be fired for posting critical comments on a Web site created to discuss reform proposals, and that dissidents would be encouraged to add suggestions.

As the 21 hours of scheduled discussion unfolded, with dozens of impromptu evening get-togethers in between, it was unsurprising that no consensus emerged about labor's course, given the number of proposals that were tossed about. But there was a buzz throughout the proceedings, hallways were continually filled with energetic conversation, and many participants left late Friday buoyed about what this airing of labor's options might mean for its future.

If the New York event marked the kick-off—indeed the public high point—of labor's introspection, it came on the heels of a somewhat smaller session that had been held three weeks earlier in the nation's capital. There, dozens of trade union activists and labor communicators gathered at the Washington Court Hotel for an event organized by the International Labor Communications Association (ILCA).[2] The discussions focused on how journalists report—or don't—on unions, the role of the labor media, and how the labor movement could improve the coverage it gets. While the focus in Washington was narrower than New York's, the gathering sparked a good deal of attention on a single issue central to labor's survival: communications.

Sadly, these efforts were short lived. Less than a year later, following months of mounting recriminations among labor's top leaders, the movement unraveled with the formation in St. Louis of a rival federation to Sweeney's AFL-CIO. The move was led by Andrew Stern's SEIU, whose original Unite to Win platform eventually morphed into the new federation called "Change to Win" in a tactic that could have been dubbed "Divide to Win." But the question remains if anyone won.

Although labor had finally admitted it was fighting for its very survival, it voluntarily sacrificed one of the few attributes it still possessed: its unity—something even labor's foes had not been able to destroy. At the worst possible moment, *solidarity forever* gave way to *squabbling now*. Granted, things hadn't exactly been functioning optimally, or this entire process of self-examination wouldn't have been launched in the first place. But for a strapped labor movement, the breakup of the AFL-CIO was structurally detrimental in several ways. It created internal rivalries within an institution that already had its hands full dealing with aggressive employers, hostile federal agencies, and powerful forces such as globalization. It wasted scarce resources by creating redundancies within labor in terms of personnel, programs, and real estate. It further blurred and confused labor's message, which was already unclear. And even when the competing federations or individual unions cooperate on a given effort, as they have managed to do on occasion, this requires planning and coordination for something that previously was automatic.

In short order, labor's path had sharply veered from the upbeat mood of New York. "I hoped the debate would continue and would deepen throughout the labor movement," Dudzic says, looking back. Yanda, now a year-plus into a job as a strategic researcher with a large local based in New York, adds that she had no idea how quickly the exhilaration of the conference would become a thing of the past—though in retrospect it was inevitable, she adds. "At that point, I didn't know the extent to which people had reached a wall with each other, with this conversation about labor's future. I didn't think it would come to this point."[3]

It was a play in four parts: a march from the hopefulness of New York to the separation in St. Louis. In almost cyclical fashion, with intervals of approximately 100 days between them, the discussion on Fifth Avenue degenerated into dissension in Las Vegas, disunity in Chicago, and formal division in St. Louis.

With the groundwork laid and various proposals articulated, the AFL-CIO's springtime 2005 executive council meeting in Las Vegas seemed poised for a serious debate about how to go forward. Instead, the leaders of the AFL-CIO and its affiliated unions had barely arrived there in early March when disagreements exploded into angry shouting behind closed doors. The acrimony that spilled into hotel hallways— reflecting the clash of two rapidly hardening positions involving a focus on politics versus an emphasis on organizing, as well as a spat between unions competing to organize a specific workforce in Illinois—was a harbinger of things to come over the course of the year.

Andy Stern's SEIU and Jim Hoffa's Teamsters led a coalition of five unions that also included the United Food and Commercial Workers, UNITE HERE, and the Laborers' International Union of North America. Though few in number, collectively they represented some 5 million workers. That meant they collected a substantial portion of labor's dues, the lifeblood of the union movement, with a share of every dollar going to the AFL-CIO.

In a sign of the shifting alliances that would mark labor's convoluted maneuvering over this period, Hoffa and Stern had months earlier been at odds after Stern said that labor might benefit if John Kerry lost the presidential election, drawing a brusque retort—"ridiculous"—from the Teamster chief. Stern wanted to refocus labor's attention away from politics and toward his plan to restructure labor through mergers. He knew that labor hadn't flourished under the Clinton presidency, and he worried that a Democratic win might diminish labor's sense of urgency about making fundamental changes. Still, his remarks caused consternation among many labor leaders. They thought the movement's future rested heavily on defeating President Bush and that another four years of Bush would be devastating for unions.

But now Stern and Hoffa, leaders respectively of the AFL-CIO's biggest union and its most storied union, found common cause against Sweeney, partly over their desire to devote more of the federation's resources to organizing. Their coalition wanted half of all dues paid to the AFL-CIO returned to individual unions, a proposal that was backed by 40 percent of council members. That indicated rising support for the rebels and trouble—if still manageable—for Sweeney, who sought instead to increase the amount of money spent on politics by $47 million. Those favoring an emphasis on organizing tended to lead unions that included large numbers of low-wage workers consisting heavily of women, minorities, and immigrants. Further, these workers were in industries that had traditionally been unorganized, often worked under dangerous conditions, and tended to do jobs not readily susceptible to outsourcing, such as in hotels or restaurants, nursing homes or menial tasks in hospitals, digging ditches, or transporting hazardous material. Consequently, Stern and Hoffa argued, labor's fate might well hinge on its ability to organize these large pools of workers and dramatically raise their salaries and improve their job conditions, much as labor had done decades earlier for manufacturing workers.

Sweeney's supporters, who represented unions composed largely of manufacturing workers, government employees, and white-collar workers, didn't dismiss the importance of organizing. But they felt that it, along with everything else critical to labor, rested on winning elections. Once that happened, then public policies and labor laws could be reformed, thereby helping organizing efforts and bolstering union rolls.

One of Sweeney's closest allies, AFSCME's Gerald McEntee, the political guru of the AFL-CIO, summed it all up in a position paper[4] in which he said that everything, from workers' living standards and retirement security to the ability of unions to organize, flows from politics. "Winning or losing in politics is what will make the difference in whether our members and all working families have health insurance, good jobs, and a secure environment. Just as important, winning in politics has everything to do with whether the labor movement grows, and that must be our greatest priority."

The differences were exacerbated by generational factors and personal ambition, with several of labor's rising stars, including Stern, chafing under the septuagenarian Sweeney's intention to seek another four-year term in the summer. This was in some ways an incestuous struggle. Both men had come out of the SEIU, which Sweeney had led before being elected 10 years earlier to head the AFL-CIO. His successor was Stern. To be fair, Stern did have years of successful expansion of the SEIU under his belt, having built it into not only the AFL-CIO's largest union but its fastest growing, and genuinely felt his plan was labor's best chance. In Hoffa's case, organizing may simply have been in his blood. Seventy years earlier his father had first made his mark in street-level organizing in Detroit. Quite bravely, I might add. Though physically short, he was fearless. His entire pay consisted of a small share of the dues payments of each member he recruited. So at age 20, Hoffa Sr. would cruise the highways leading out of Detroit, pull alongside sleeping truck drivers and wake them, hoping to talk up the union. Some, armed with tire irons, took him for a bum or a thief; other times a band of anti-union company thugs armed with billy clubs, lying in wait to teach him a lesson, would spill out of the truck. In one year alone he was beaten up more than two dozen times and had his scalp laid open six times; but he ended up organizing the previously resistant truck and car-hauler sector in Detroit.[5]

Any hope for reconciliation was soon quashed as the AFL-CIO prepared to hold its convention in Chicago in late July. Instead, the competing proposals calcified into a struggle among warring labor factions. In June, five dissident unions—SEIU, the Teamsters, the UFCW, the Laborers, and UNITE HERE—set up an informal coalition geared toward promoting organizing, thereby raising the specter of a potential split. Noting that the decline of organized labor had occurred "through both Republican and Democratic administrations," Hoffa argued, "We cannot wait for a ripe political climate to rebuild our movement."

Civility was thrown to the wind. Objecting to the idea of forced union mergers, the AFL-CIO leadership castigated the rebels as fundamentally undemocratic and equated them with childish spoilsports. In turn, the insurgents painted the incumbents as out-of-touch bureaucrats, simply intent on hanging onto power. The stakes were raised when, meeting in the Windy City a few days prior to the federation's gathering, members of the Teamsters' executive board gave the union's leaders the authority to leave the AFL-CIO if they couldn't wrest enough concessions from Sweeney. Officials from three other dissident unions considered a similar move.

It was unclear whether these were serious threats or just bargaining chips, but any doubts were answered almost overnight. Four of the rebel unions decided to boycott the convention, and then, on its first day, Stern and Hoffa pulled their unions out of the labor federation—a move Sweeney labeled a "grievous insult" to workers already buffeted by global economic trends and by the Republican-led congressional hostility to unions. Sweeney won reelection, in the uncontested tradition of the AFL-CIO, but it was a hollow victory because he now headed an organization that suddenly had shrunk by 5 million members.

And so it was that in late September, a season when St. Louis is usually focused on local baseball and hometown Budweiser, residents watched Teamsters, farm workers, textile workers, and others pour into St. Louis. Stern and Hoffa led a total of seven unions—the original five plus the United Farm

Workers and the United Brotherhood of Carpenters—in forming the rival Change to Win federation. They could be accused of many things but not of undue modesty or setting their sights too low. In rhetoric matching the name of the edifice hosting their convention—the Renaissance St. Louis Grand Hotel—newly elected federation chairwoman Anna Burger said: "May the history books record that on the 27th day of September 2005, in St. Louis, 460 delegates gathered and chose to change not just their unions, but their country. Working men and women everywhere are counting on us."

They made it all sound impressively simple. "We are going to put our money into organizing, and we will succeed," Hoffa said, promising "a lean, mean organizing machine." Unamused, Sweeney claimed the rebels had "chosen a path which divided union members at a time when working people are under attack as never before." He admonished them for not having stayed in the AFL-CIO to fight for change within existing labor structures. But their plans left little room for compromise. Not only did they want to pour 75 percent of their resources into organizing, they had vastly different political plans than the AFL-CIO. Instead of donating millions of dollars to the campaign funds of political candidates, they would encourage their own members to run for office while lending grassroots support to anyone who favored pro-worker policies. And they would be far more independent, no longer serving as the election apparatus of the Democratic Party. "That ends now," John Wilhelm, president of the hotel workers' union, told applauding delegates.

And so, in one fell stroke, labor did to itself something business could only have dreamed of accomplishing—*peeling away a major chunk of the AFL-CIO's membership.* That reversed an action taken a half-century earlier, at labor's zenith, when the American Federation of Labor and the Congress of Industrial Organizations had joined forces, making labor even stronger. Now, at its nadir, unions were pulling apart, further dismantling the labor movement.

The action was not without its ironic elements. An insurgency that had urgently called for mergers of small unions within the AFL-CIO to reduce redundant structures had spawned the ultimate redundancy—two labor federations, each with its own administrative layers, organizing centers, communications efforts, and so on. And to those who followed labor closely, the stated belief in unionizing as labor's path to salvation strained credibility. It was a recently acquired article of faith for most of the rebel unions, with only SEIU standing out for its organizing prowess the past few years. Meanwhile, Hoffa was following in his father's footsteps in a second way; almost 40 years earlier the Teamsters had been thrown out of the AFL-CIO for corruption, only to be readmitted in 1987, but they were now once again parting company, albeit this time voluntarily.

The media generally described the split as resulting from competing approaches to saving the labor movement. This handy prism through which to view the unfolding drama suggested that the debate in fact revolved around divergent yet coherent strategies about how to cure labor's ills. But more broadly, labor's relatively brief period of self-appraisal was marked by a series of power struggles, transitory allegiances, personal conflicts, and contrasting proposals—a process facilitated by the absence of even one idea people could rally around as offering a reasonable chance of success. As closer examination shows, there was little coherent about any of the proposals put on the table.

It may seem odd that an exercise begun with such hope fell apart so quickly and then ended in fragmentation at the very moment labor was recognizing what kind of peril it was in. In fact, this was the inevitable result of deliberations that were flawed from the start.

While the proposals to salvage the movement's future were all over the lot, there was one common feature: they generally amounted to little more than pedestrian and predictable calls to focus on one or another of labor's specific roles, be it organizing, politics, collective bargaining, or something else. Each was touted by its advocates as the silver bullet that would revitalize labor, if only enough effort and money and brainpower were shifted to that particular task. For the most part, of course, each conveniently mirrored its advocates' long-favored type of activity and so would allow them to keep doing what they were doing, with the rest of the labor movement hopefully following their lead. But in settling for what amounted to choosing from among its traditional goals, labor was seemingly oblivious to the fact that by now it was too weak to make inroads in any of them.

As I noted earlier, while labor faces innumerable challenges, its overarching dilemma is that its many problems are inextricably linked, and as a result it can't meaningfully advance in any given area. Weaknesses in one area hold back progress in another. Labor's tumbling membership numbers, its lack of real political clout, its defensive posture vis-à-vis employers, its inability to overcome often-inequitable federal laws and rulings—it is the way these and other factors reinforce one another that makes labor's precipitous decline so difficult to slow down, let alone reverse. And it is also what has made labor's self-examination an academic exercise with little prospect of yielding practical results and an adjunct to the personal conflicts that are roiling the trade union movement.

If labor is stymied in organizing enough new members to retain its share of an expanding workforce, it's not because it hasn't trained its organizers properly, spent enough money, or discovered the right organizing formula. Rather, it's that in today's environment the odds are so utterly stacked against it. U.S. industrial policies that encourage the exporting of jobs and negotiated trade pacts that don't give American workers a realistic chance to compete with low-wage earners overseas provide systemic hurdles to boosting union membership. Labor organized 400,000 new members in a recent year, but it suffered a net loss of 200,000 members because 600,000 union jobs were lost as a result of company relocations or closings.[6] Union efforts to compensate for vanishing jobs by enlisting new members at unorganized plants are hampered by the weak labor laws and the labor board rulings that help employers thwart union workplace drives. So labor can't expect to gain members just by organizing more intelligently—it has to change the various policies, laws, and appointments that hinder its efforts and put it in a hole before it starts.

Doing that would require a forceful political presence, but there's the rub: labor's shrinking numbers have diminished its influence in that arena. And so *labor is trapped in a Catch-22*: it can't organize because it can't change the policies and laws; it can't change the policies and laws because it can't organize. As for focusing on effective collective bargaining as a way to appeal to workers as a whole, that too is stymied. With the pendulum having swung so far toward employers, labor's clout at the negotiating table is severely undermined, which makes unions unappealing to workers. One result is that labor is less able to reach the type of contractual agreements that would keep union jobs here and membership steady . . . and on and on in a downward trend. The numbers continue to dwindle and labor's institutional strength ebbs, compounding everything, and putting its very survival in jeopardy.

Compounding this dilemma is the public perception of labor as an ineffectual movement—an image that both stems from and exacerbates labor's other problems. If unions are viewed as barely hanging on, as no longer having much of a role to play, why should anyone—whether political candidates or legislators, potential members or employers, reporters or the public—pay much heed to them? Once again, problems beget problems. On this count, the session held in Washington on communications, while addressing a critical issue for labor, provided few solutions. Its main thrust was twofold: because the media do an abysmal job covering labor, the union movement should consider setting up its own news outlets to get across information about workers' issues. But doing so would actually worsen labor's plight by further marginalizing it from the mainstream news media, also raising questions of the credibility and objectivity of any information conveyed.

So labor finds itself in a conundrum from which it has no idea of how to escape. If union leaders and activists and commentators had stepped back at any point from the hoopla of the position papers, power struggles, and dramatic pronouncements, they might have realized that it didn't matter whether Sweeney's or Stern's or Hoffa's path prevailed. Pursuing organizing, politicking, or collective bargaining more energetically or more cleverly won't resolve the dilemma. Labor's problem is that it can't succeed in *any* of its traditional tasks because they are *all* interdependent, and unions are too weak to jump in at any one point and reverse the momentum. The one proposal that would have been within labor's grasp to accomplish because it is a wholly internal reform—restructuring unions into fewer and larger ones—would at best produce marginal benefits. And even that is now water under the bridge, given labor's split into competing federations. Seen in this light, labor's period of self-examination has been far too timid, narrow, and conventional to have any chance of rejuvenating the movement; in fact, it has been a prescription for failure.

It is hardly shocking, therefore, that labor's long overdue period of exploration—as well intended as it may have been—ended in a series of sophomoric spats and quarreling coalitions. In its supposed fight for its future, labor isn't merely rearranging the deck chairs; it's wasting time and energy arguing about which chair should be first in the row. Absent any genuinely hopeful options that labor could rally around, what could have been a chance to forge a new path instead disintegrated into the spectacle of jousting factions pushing this or that traditional mission. The result has torn apart an already reeling labor movement.

Given the vicious cycle labor is caught in, the only chance it has to emerge from its doldrums is to change the equation, to reshuffle the cards. Labor needs to reinvent itself, not refine the way it operates or fiddle around the edge. Reallocating resources or restructuring unions won't save labor at this point, any more than whining about the media will gain it better play. With labor's traditional roles rendered virtually impossible by the obstacles it faces, it must change the equation by finding a broad mission that is not only achievable but that could actually revitalize the movement.

The irony is that labor is letting a golden opportunity slip by because the country hungers for what the labor movement, uniquely, could offer. With corporate interests verging toward unbridled power while workplace and social gains of the past century are under steady assault, average Americans need an advocate to join the debate and help restore some equilibrium. The delivery of promised pensions and job security, of safe workplaces and accessible health care, are larger than union goals or members' benefits—*they evoke values that affect workers as a whole and the communities in which they live.* But that battle, waged relentlessly by one side of the economic divide, has yet to be joined in any meaningful way.

Meanwhile, in the political arena, the debate over values remains equally one sided; otherwise, Sue Williams and Ken Mowbray would have felt obligated to add some explanation to their simple declarative sentences. As discussed, the topic of values has come to occupy a preeminent place in electoral politics, most noticeably over the past two presidential cycles. Here too, as with job-related issues, the battle has been highly skewed, with ascendant conservative and Republican forces having the field essentially to themselves. It's not that their values have prevailed over competing ones but rather that they have managed to define the terms of the battle—with the acquiescence of everyone else—as their "values" versus the mundane "issues" offered by others. Or, equally devastating: as their values versus the *lack* of values of their opponents, who have simply failed to engage them on this terrain. This, as much as any actual merit of those values, has allowed them to have the moral field essentially to themselves as they run roughshod over their opponents in a manner that has reshaped the political arena. And so the values puzzle—how to best address these matters and win back traditional supporters without compromising its principles, or alienating its base— has preoccupied a baffled Democratic Party in a discussion that is, *but should not be*, quite separate from labor's internal debate.

At the end of the day, the Democrats' concern is the extent to which "values" are making inroads in blue-collar communities and influencing people on whose votes they once could count. Voters on whom, by economic status and often even by economic views, they *still* should be able to count. This problem has by no means suddenly disappeared just because a poorly planned war and a poorly supervised intern program torpedoed Republicans in the 2006 congressional elections. The contrary is more likely, as McEntee said in the summer of 2006, after AFSCME had just held in Chicago what he termed "the largest town hall meeting in the history of the American labor movement."[7]

"I think they'll try and do it, play the values, because they don't have many other things to play. They've got to carry on their backs the programs and policies of George Bush, and candidates will be running away from him," McEntee told me.

In their deliberations, Democrats are perplexed not only in understanding the values phenomenon but, on a practical level, knowing what to do about it. Should they enter the fray, seeking to talk about the sanctity of the unborn and traditional marriage and the like, or ignore the talk about morality and continue to focus on the typical political issues that worked for them in the past? Either choice entails risks: if they engage the debate, what do they say as they enter the discussion on turf defined by their opponents? Unless they're rebutting the Republican stance on God and gays and guns—and how promising would that be?—what exactly would the alternative Democratic values be? And if they instead abstain from entering this debate, aren't they simply ceding the values agenda, and all that it signifies about character and principles, to the other side?

Aside from *what* they'd say, also problematic for Democrats and progressive political forces is the question of *who* is best suited to make the argument. How can any individual running for office, or even a bevy of candidates, counter the unrelenting, 24/7 efforts in community after community by thousands of ministers and social activists and pro-family groups? The political success such values have enjoyed isn't attributable solely—or even primarily—to wisdom spouted by a candidate every four years. Rather, the conservative hold on values flows from the grassroots work of a multitude of local voices around the country, many unaffiliated with the party, preaching and proselytizing and persuading people they know personally. The cumulative effect of this nonstop exhortation by respected local figures allows national GOP candidates to tap into a receptive environment they didn't have to create—indeed *couldn't* have created on their own and on the spot.

This campaign for hearts and minds, which is stubbornly independent of the periodic political race and which in fact often drives—rather than follows—the agenda, has been waged over years where people live, by trusted neighbors and friends and authority figures. At election time, the work is not begun from scratch but merely ratcheted up, with subtle or not-so-subtle suggestions as to which candidate best reflects already-familiar formulations. It involves at that point, literally, preaching to the converted.

If Sue Williams was successful without being particularly persuasive on a personal level, it's because she benefited from groundwork that had already been laid, so she merely had to raise the topic to get heads nodding. And she was speaking to people she knew personally or at least knew something about, unlike her Democratic counterparts, often students or activists flown in from "safe" states such as California to try to turn a swing state. By defining the terms of the debate on values, and by having the troops of local people like Sue Williams, advocates of cultural morality have assured in advance that they will begin with the upper hand, no matter how smart their opponents are or whom they nominate. They have managed to define not only the terms of the debate but the nature of both participants—upholders of traditional morality and family values versus the elitist, know-it-all, permissive liberals who disdain both common folks and God. Good luck, Democrats!

As noted, the substitution of cultural values for economic interests has been explored by observers such as Thomas Frank, who focuses on how it works and the consequences in terms of policy outcomes. He describes a charade in which working people are spurred to base their votes on moral concerns and in return unwittingly elect candidates who provide tax breaks for the rich while helping corporations send these very voters' jobs overseas. The cultural focus serves a dual purpose; it not only excludes economics from the discussion, it also tends to divide workers on the social issues. But the analysis stops there. What has not been addressed is what can be done: How can this brand of "false populism" be denuded in the public mind? And who can fill the void by adding the missing economic element—both the cost to average people of the policies enacted as a result of getting them to focus on cultural values, as well as the very real values that could be linked to job issues? Who can expose the actual impact on working people and their communities of this cultural populism, while introducing into the debate a set of principles related to work and fair play and opportunity? Well, as today's Democratic Party elite, composed of lawyers and multimillionaires and Washington insiders, ponders how to compete on this foreign turf, and as the labor movement seeks a mission that could turn its fortunes around, the most appropriate reaction might be my eight-year-old's favorite expression of the moment: "Duh!"

While a political candidate here and there cannot hope to compete with the tidal wave of well-organized, fervent, and ubiquitous morality advocates, what would happen if tens of thousands of locally respected steelworkers and teachers, miners and nurses, and firefighters and carpenters were to enlist in the battle? Local union workers would have instant credibility in expanding the discussion to include economic and social values like decent pay for an honest day's work, having a voice on the job, accessible health care for families, and keeping good-paying jobs in America so communities can survive and prosper. Whether it's talking to neighbors about the impact of distant corporate decisions or national trade policies on the places where they live or asking their friends what it is they're getting for their morality-based votes or simply focusing on the corporate elite and political power brokers who actually run today's America and who are dismembering small towns and family farms while engaging in distracting talk about largely symbolic issues, unions can use the same grassroots approach that has served the values and morality advocates so well.

By adding the economic subtext, and concerns related to the role and dignity of work, concerns that in this instance—unlike cultural populism—would actually be related to specific policy proposals, workers could help broaden the national discourse and make it more serious. This would assure no particular position's victory on any given issue—nor is it meant to—but it *would* set the stage for a genuine dialogue about what is happening to people's livelihoods and towns, who is responsible, and what kind of country Americans want. It would also enable the open exploration of the impact corporate practices have on people and communities, and how public policies intersect with those practices and those consequences.

The public interest would be served by having those debates meaningfully joined. It would force those who have made a career of pushing values to make room at the table for others whose sense of values—including family values—is equally strong, simply more community-based than personal in nature, more related to work than to sexuality. Ending the cultural populists' free ride by engaging them would not negate moral values, but it would compel supporters to actually make their arguments and not merely assert their superiority. Meanwhile, advocates of the prevailing corporate perspective would have to sharpen their arguments—explaining, for example, how the benefits of free trade outweigh the impact on real people and real communities, rather than simply treating globalism as a fact of nature and dismissing those who question it as out-of-touch protectionists.

As for labor's own institutional survival, there is much merit in making one of its top priorities the carrying throughout the country of the message of work-related values and how they tie in to the lives of families and communities, serving in essence as the spokesperson for the American worker. Unlike labor's fruitless argument over emphasizing politics versus organizing, this is an endeavor in which unions could actually make inroads. And unlike the reasonable but largely peripheral call by some for shuffling boxes on an organizational chart, it is an endeavor where success would make a major difference. Labor's voice would once again become part of the national conversation, as opposed to fighting for an incremental—and self-interested—change in this policy or that labor board ruling.

This shift in focus would not be without trade-offs. Because it would assume a good deal of time and energy, even though it would be largely carried out by the rank and file, much of labor's inside work would be downplayed. Deemphasizing issues like job-site jurisdiction or equally arcane matters would be less of a sacrifice than labor leaders might think since no one outside of unions gives a hoot about those issues. In fact, such struggles are seen as dull and pointless by many workers, and even when successful, labor's pursuit of resolution of these issues helps labor's foes paint it as a narrowly focused, special-interest organization. To the nearly 90 percent of workers not in unions, let alone to the general population, unions often appear to be waging insular battles with little universal import or appeal. That can—and *must*—change.

Rallying people around the values of respect for hard work and support for the community and the public policies those require could resonate among large segments of the population, creating a more receptive and positive environment in which people might actually listen to what labor had to say. If unions came to be seen as embodying values and causes and policies that matter to the lives of millions of working- and middle-class Americans, those tasks now largely beyond it— organizing new members, shaping election debate, and bargaining effectively—would be facilitated.

At election time, the contrast in labor's behavior would be particularly noticeable as it helped supply the economic content that has been so conspicuously absent in recent campaigns, showing how it relates to the lives of ordinary people and their communities, to their values, and to competing public policy suggestions. That would replace labor's current role as a highly partisan, get-out-the-vote mechanism for the Democratic Party. This has the potential of resolving a trio of labor's most basic political quandaries. As we have discussed, even on those (rare) occasions when labor wins, its focus on turnout and other tactics means that it fails to make its message integral to the campaign, to influence public opinion, or to shape the mandate. At most, elected officials owe it a favor or two once installed in office and they throw it a legislative bone here and there, but labor's efforts typically have changed no outlooks, added no understanding that wasn't there before. By serving as the voice of the American worker, by broadening the political and public discussion to include work-related values, and discussing how such practical concerns as safety and job security relate to government actions or inaction, labor could emerge a winner whatever the outcome of a given race. Labor would be doing no more than its social conservative counterparts; helping set the agenda and making its principles part of the campaign discussion.

Second, the dynamics of labor's ties to the Democratic Party would be altered, reducing the images of a subservient labor movement and a beholden political party, to the benefit of each. Currently, when unions visibly get behind a political candidate, that candidate is typically tagged as the favorite of big labor. As a result, labor often is forced to proceed gingerly since its support risks backfiring, particularly in a national race. It is no accident that the AFL-CIO has so rarely engaged in an early endorsement of a presidential hopeful, having seen the damage it did to Walter Mondale. If it changed from pulling out all the stops to frenetically push this or that Democratic candidate, labor would avoid this delicate dance that, no matter how skillfully carried out, means alienating half the population, and many workers, right off the bat.

Finally, labor would also free itself from the persistent, and damaging, charge that it uses its members' mandatory dues for highly partisan purposes with which many members would disagree if given a chance. Backing one Democrat after another bolsters that accusation in a way that giving voice to job-related and economic values would not. And this would have a beneficial impact within unions as well since at least one-third of union members overall, significantly more in some unions, are Republicans and yet others are independents. While the cultural populist onslaught has managed to divide workers who feel compelled to choose between their economic interests and their values, a focus on working values would help unite them.

In their recent debate, labor leaders acted as if their choices were either aggressively backing favored candidates or abandoning politics altogether. Sweeney and his allies who favored a political emphasis said that lessening labor's role in elections would be self-destructive; Stern and other critics countered that what was counterproductive was to be so closely tied to one party, particularly in a secondary role. Moving toward more of an agenda-setting role would simultaneously boost labor's political significance while mitigating many of the current negatives associated with its campaign activities.

But for the labor movement to do this, or indeed to succeed in any other new mission or other change it eventually settles on, it has to learn how to effectively communicate. As simple and even mundane as that may sound, few things would mark more of a radical shift for labor—or have a bigger impact— than if it figured out what it wants to say and how to get it across in a way that resonates within the general population.

Labor's most overriding dilemma, the one touching every aspect of its problems, may be the fact that its voice is not heard. If labor's stories were told, the way in which it is perceived by the public, including by potential members, stands to be dramatically affected.

This reflects another failing of labor's deliberations. While it spent a good deal of time pondering and debating its most appropriate role and mission before the split, and indeed some such conversation has continued at a quieter level within several unions since then, what it didn't do was take a self-critical look at how well it performs the day-to-day tasks that can make or break any organization. High on that list should have been, and still should be, communications.

Shrinking or not, now divided or not, a membership of 15 million people is nothing to sneer at, and it is astonishing that so little is heard about labor *from* labor. A large part of that clearly involves a dysfunctional relationship with the media, with plenty of blame to go around. Labor and its supporters spend a good deal of time complaining about the media's faults—talk about low-hanging fruit—but far too little thinking about how *they* contribute to the virtual news blackout surrounding unions and workers. As difficult as it may be for them to believe, trade unionists themselves are in no small measure responsible for the muzzling of the American worker—and if they were willing to take a hard look at themselves, they could do something about it.

CHAPTER 5

UP ON THE ROOF (OR SILENCING THE WORKING CLASS)

The roof is suddenly getting too small. A handful of beefy, T-shirted autoworkers are jostling me closer and closer to the edge.

This isn't what I expected on my first—and last?—day in San Diego. I had arrived in town just a few hours ago to attend their national convention, and showing up at the union's rooftop reception at the hotel on this Saturday afternoon had seemed like the logical thing to do.

But then this group of guys in a clearly foul mood spotted me, and now I'm more concerned with making an escape than making contacts—especially because we're uncomfortably distanced from the rest of the party. I have known for a while that some of the delegates were mad at me—although until now I hadn't realized quite how angry—but at this moment I don't know how far they're going to take this.

Fortunately, before I find out, the senior union official from the Midwest walks by. He has no use for me, and he hasn't taken my phone calls for years, but he greets me by name and the men back off. I waste no time making my way from the roof down to my room, where I shrug it off as probably just a few guys whose bravado got enhanced at the party. But as I'm crossing the street the next day, another delegate loudly threatens to push me in front of an oncoming bus if I don't agree on the spot to curb my reporting. And when I finally make it into the convention hall, I'm greeted by some raucous boos.

Their gripe was that I'd been writing for several years about a fellow named Jerry Tucker, a former United Auto Workers (UAW) regional official who'd fallen out of favor with the union's leaders because he decided they were too eager to collaborate with the Big Three automakers. A bearded working-class intellectual, he wanted the UAW to return to its militant roots, and toward that end, he had formed the New Directions Movement within the union. The UAW's hierarchy didn't take kindly to this. Despite its progressive stance on social and economic policy, the union had a distaste for internal challenges or criticism, which was a tendency rooted in founder Walter Reuther's efforts to keep communist elements away from the levers of power during the McCarthy era. That had led to the establishment of a so-called administrative caucus within the UAW, which after the legitimate threat of the Red Menace had abated, evolved into a mechanism for stifling dissent and discrediting challenges to authority.[1] Having the temerity to chronicle Tucker, and particularly to frame the episode in this historical context, placed me squarely on the union's enemy list. So the power structure and its supporters, especially those in the five-state Midwest region, already disliked me intensely. Those feelings had been ratcheted up a few notches at this convention because Tucker had decided to run for international president against the incumbent—which was the first major opposition to an incumbent UAW president in four decades.

And that was just the tablesetter. My real offense, or at least the most recent one, was that shortly before coming out here, I'd been tipped off that union officials were booking thousands of delegates into a dozen nonunion hotels. That raised the specter of picketing by local hotel workers against the United Auto Workers union and its convention—about as embarrassing as it gets in the world of labor. Remember that this was the same UAW that had waged several high-profile national campaigns seeking to persuade Americans to buy union-made American cars instead of imports. When I had sought comment on the hotel flap from Solidarity House, as the UAW headquarters in Detroit is known, I was informed that I'd be smart to drop the whole matter. No one would care about this, UAW flacks had helpfully counseled, adding that writing about it would likely end my access to top union officials. What access, I had politely inquired before filing the story, which included scathing comments from the San Diego hotel workers' union.

Well, someone apparently cared because the story got picked up by the wires and ran on the front pages in Detroit, so it wasn't surprising that some of these guys had come to San Diego in a particularly irritated state of mind. At least they had read the stuff and reacted—no small point given the general direction of newspaper circulation. Their reaction may have been a bit over the top, but it was based on passion—and it was an earned passion. This isn't abstract stuff to them; it's about their livelihood, their future, their survival, and their collective struggle to take care of their families, and that emotional substance is part of what makes the labor beat worth covering.

Despite what it felt like on the roof and in the street, I learned a few days into the convention that it wasn't personal. Enough reporters had apparently been lit into that union officials felt the need to hold a fence-mending reception one evening. But that session quickly degenerated as they started berating reporters from Chicago, New York, and Detroit, along with St. Louis. A reporter from one city was called a "lunatic," while a top UAW officer warned another newspaper reporter that if he tried to talk to certain union officials, he risked being "knocked on his rear." Even a laid-off autoworker-turned-journalist wasn't spared from the harangues.

If the UAW folks were acting tough, it was because they felt cornered. Their union was reeling from a humiliating confrontation with Caterpillar in Peoria, Illinois, they had been rocked by plant closings and layoffs, and they were facing what loomed as difficult negotiations with the Big Three the following year. Their membership had plummeted to 900,000 by now—summer of 1992—from a high of 1.5 million a dozen years earlier, and the decline showed no signs of abating.

Since these problems couldn't possibly be the fault of union leaders, and since the UAW's massive political efforts were backfiring—speaking to the convention, presumptive Democratic nominee Bill Clinton had reiterated his support for a free-trade pact with Mexico—the press was a handy scapegoat. Even with all the weighty issues facing the UAW, it took the time in San Diego to draft a lengthy resolution blasting the media. The result of all this: not only did the union waste a good deal of time and energy at the expense of attending to serious matters, it needlessly damaged relations with a number of reporters well after everyone had left San Diego.

This particular manner of dealing with the press—media relations through intimidation—may seem a bit unusual, but I would learn subsequently in other settings that it wasn't wholly out of character for the UAW, though in fairness it has abated under the current leadership. Nor, more importantly, have the autoworkers been alone among unions in practicing a strategy that only compounds labor's problems. Unions typically don't execute their press strategy atop rooftops or in front of buses, but they have managed to find a number of ways to shoot themselves in the foot.

More common than outright bullying is the "ostrich approach," the second of four strategies I'll discuss, in which unions duck for cover the instant news breaks, lifting their heads only when the coast is clear. One day in St. Louis a management spokesperson called to inform me that his manufacturing plant would soon lay off a sizable crew of workers. It was bad news for the company, and clearly not something he was eager to share, but evidently the firm had decided it would be advantageous to get ahead of the news and put whatever imprint they could on it. He answered all my questions and provided a couple of ways to get hold of him after hours if need be. Fairly new on the beat, I figured the union local would be only too glad to respond, even grateful for the opportunity. They stood to be the good guys in this, fighting for the workers' jobs, urging the community or public officials to help. Perhaps they could actually save some of the positions, delay the move, or at the very least secure a decent severance package for those being let go.

The first call ended in a quick click. I phoned back and said we'd been cut off and that I was just trying to get a comment about a planned layoff. I was answered this time with a slamming sound in the receiver. "Listen," I said on my third try, "I don't really care whether you say something or not. It'll make my job easier if you don't, but you're going to look pretty callous in the paper tomorrow." Well, beyond an epithet or two, he had nothing to say before hanging up, and yes, the next day his union indeed looked oddly disengaged.

This head-in-the-sand tactic is based on the notion that if union officials just lay low, the story might go away. All that does go away, of course, is a chance to provide their point of view, to indicate what they're going to do about the matter at hand, and to somehow balance the story. Still, this behavior is somewhat understandable. The head of a union at this local level is unlikely to have had much schooling in dealing with the media. He may be just a few months off the line himself, and depending on the union's size, might have little if any support staff. He knows he's up against a polished spokesperson for the company, maybe its attorney or its vice president for communications, both slick and armed with enormous resources. He has also probably had a few unfavorable encounters with the media, perhaps as simple as the local paper's ignoring a release he sent in about a union event of some type, and ever since then he's been convinced the media are indifferent or even hostile.[2] So why on earth should he expect to get a fair deal, especially matched up against high-paid company flacks who do this kind of thing for a living?

This attitude is found less often on the state or international union levels than on the local level, where unions have fewer resources. But that's the place where people live, workers work, and labor-management disputes typically break out. It's also where residents take their news most personally, forming views based on what they read and hear. This isn't a problem that has suddenly popped up as labor faces tougher times and has fewer resources, nor are the ostriches found only at the local level. Here's part of a letter I wrote on May 8, 1991, in St. Louis, to James La Sala, president of the Amalgamated Transit Union (ATU):

> Dear Mr. La Sala:
> I have tried for several days now, with no success, to get a comment from your union on a matter that involves members here as well as the International.

After detailing about a dozen calls to the union, promises from various officials to respond that weren't kept, and buck passing from the general counsel to the president to other officials and back and forth, I concluded:

> So, bottom line is, despite my efforts, I'm left with no comment and no one to reach now.
> A story tomorrow, Thursday, about the ATU—read by our 400,000 readers including tens of thousands of union members—will therefore say that you and other members at the Amalgamated Transit Union wouldn't com-

ment. Readers may wonder why the leaders of a union wouldn't comment on a matter involving itself and its own members, but I can only report what happens.

As someone who covers labor, I know that unions often complain about press coverage, often with reason. But it must also be said that sometimes labor can be its own worst enemy in getting its message out.

The ATU ended up responding that it had no one who dealt with the press, though what was occurring at the time was the Greyhound Strike, which had sparked a great deal of public interest. But that wasn't as bizarre as the actions of the Twelve-Counties Laborers District Council unions in southern Illinois, which shut down $100 million in construction, yet refused to tell the media—or even the thousands of members of other unions honoring the picket lines—what the strike was about. With no understanding of why they were losing paychecks, cement masons, sheet metal workers, and members of other building trades unions grew increasingly frustrated, simply because the laborers' leaders felt communicating wasn't part of their job description. Stranger yet might have been the attitude of the International Association of Machinists (IAM) when it was competing in a hotly contested campaign with several smaller unions to represent TWA's flight attendants. The IAM kept its intentions for the TWA employees shrouded in secrecy—so much so that neither the airline, the attendants, nor the public had any idea of what the IAM was up to. At least the union had an explanation; the IAM official leading the effort said, with admirable clarity: "I don't talk to the press."

Then there's the "good-guy syndrome," in which unions speak only to reporters they personally know and trust or who have been vouched for by other union insiders. The Teamsters have turned this into an art form, an occasionally entertaining one at that. I've lost count of the Teamster gatherings I've covered, or tried to cover, where merely getting into the event to do your job is a roll of the dice wholly unattached to any formal process. One time, the Central Conference of Teamsters, largest of the four geographic Teamster groupings, was holding a key meeting in St. Louis. Having been alerted by officials at conference headquarters in Chicago, I walked the few blocks over to the hotel, I asked where the press was supposed to register, and I was told there was nowhere to register. I tried to enter the auditorium, only to be blocked by a couple of doorway-sized Teamsters. I said I was from the local newspaper and covered labor, but they didn't budge. I showed them my press credentials, but they had no interest. I told them I knew about the event because their guys in Chicago had suggested I attend; by now their gaze was fixed elsewhere. At that point the double doors to the auditorium opened as someone left and a Teamster official I knew spotted me. He quickly sized up the situation, gave the guards the magic words— "He's all right"—and they instantly cleared a path. "Sorry, brother," one of them said, "we didn't know you."

This personalized approach can take more than a few minutes. In 2000, I was sent to Cleveland to write a worker story related to the approaching election, but upon arriving there, I stumbled upon something far more compelling—the Mr. Coffee situation, in which production of the item once endorsed by Joe DiMaggio was slated to be moved to Mexico.

As mentioned earlier, the employees were mostly welfare-to-work single mothers, and their union, Teamsters Local 473, once run by Jackie Presser, had now been led for years by another legendary figure named Carmen Parise, as colorful a labor leader as you'd want to find. He ran a tight ship, and it was clear that the only way I'd get access to workers willing to talk would be through the local. Morning turned into midafternoon as I cooled my heels in the waiting area, the receptionist never giving me a straight answer on whether I could meet with Mr. Parise, when I might find out, or even whether he was in town.

Convinced I was being strung along until I gave up or had to catch a plane, I was startled when a door finally opened and Parise waved me into his office. Gracious as could be, he talked at length about the plant's situation; he picked up the phone and ordered some workers to get over there; we visited others; he showed me union documents about the company and the state of the labor-management showdown; and he patiently answered every question I had. Hours later, I told Parise I greatly appreciated the access and the insights, but I was curious why he had suddenly agreed to see me. What had changed between 9 a.m. and 3 p.m.?

"I reached Bobby Sansone," Parise said. "He vouched for you." Those few words explained everything, just as Ken Mowbray's had in another context. I was accepted by the brotherhood. Bobby Sansone, the longtime head of the Missouri-Kansas Teamsters, had been thrown out of the International Brotherhood of Teamsters—albeit on highly flimsy evidence—in the 1990s as a result of the federal cleanup, and he had faded from the limelight in recent years.

"I think we finally found him in Florida," Parise added. Parise ended up providing enough information that the story prompted Democratic presidential nominee Al Gore, on a visit to Cleveland, to hold a mini-press conference at the airport to address the matter. As mentioned earlier, the Teamsters, helped by an outpouring of community support, initially blocked the move to Mexico, though they were unable to prevent a subsequent shift of production.

Four years later, around Labor Day of 2004, I was once again on hallowed Teamster ground for an election-related story, this time at Local 299 in Detroit, formerly run by none other than the original Jimmy Hoffa. Wiser now in how this worked, or so I thought, I'd arranged the visit ahead of time, and I was whisked right into the office of the local's president, Kevin Moore. Seated at the same desk his idol had used 50 years earlier, Moore couldn't have been more forthcoming. He even acknowledged his struggles to keep the membership up, among other internal problems, and he discussed his strategies for addressing these matters. I told him how different this was from a previous visit to a local in Cleveland, where they'd carefully vetted me before granting access. Moore chuckled. "I did exactly the same thing," he said. "I just did it before you got here. They told me in Washington that you were a good guy, that I might even like you."

This is a highly human approach, sometimes even an endearing one, as long as you're eventually given permission to do your job. You make it into the inner sanctum and they'll tell you pretty much everything you want to know, even weigh you down with union-memento type offerings you'll be professionally bound to refuse or donate to charity. Sometimes I think I'm back reporting in Afghanistan or Kuwait or Albania—once someone assures themselves they can trust you enough to let you into the house, you practically become part of the family and they can't do enough for you. But how efficient is this elaborate process, starting with the private-eye work, for an American labor movement under great duress in 2007? It's not like reporters are beating down the doors to cover labor or to glean the union perspective on every story, so putting an inordinate amount of effort into deciding whom to admit and turning down some opportunities to get out their message seem self-defeating, especially since labor's foes on the corporate side have no such compunctions. They'll speak to anyone, several at a time, known or unknown, on the phone or in person or even via e-mail, in a crisp, professional, and informative manner. Given that, who do you think starts with the edge in terms of spinning the story and influencing public opinion?

And it's not just the Teamsters who want to peer into your soul: I was confronted with an entire city of distrustful labor leaders when I started on the beat in St. Louis in the late 1980s, including the St. Louis Labor Council, the AFL-CIO's umbrella group in the region. It was dominated by construction unions, which tend to be particularly insular and suspicious and are notorious for relying first and foremost on their gut instinct in terms of talking and trusting. For weeks, I was making no headway with Bob Kelley, president of the 200,000-member Labor Council. One early afternoon I called on a story and, as usual, was told he'd gone for the day and wasn't reachable. I suggested to the secretary that there must a way to get hold of him, but she insisted there wasn't. There was, because soon I got a call from an annoyed Bob Kelley, who sternly demanded: "Why are you harassing my girl?" The conversation went downhill from there.

How do you cover a beat when nobody will talk to you because they don't know you well enough to trust you? To break the logjam, Laszlo Domjan, the paper's executive city editor, suggested I take a labor leader out to lunch. I settled on Tommy Harvill, a colorful figure and a major local player as head of the Eastern Missouri Laborers' District Council, which long had been awash in rumors. In the recent past, Laborers' locals, mob feuds, and car bombings had periodically crossed paths in St. Louis, but Harvill was a serious labor leader. He was also a big, gruff guy. I brought him to a nice restaurant at Union Station. To show we were kindred spirits and to make him feel comfortable ordering whatever he wanted, I told the waitress to bring me a bowl of soup, a large steak, and a slice of pie with ice cream. She asked Harvill what she could get for him. "Nothing," he said. The waitress stared at him. This was starting off badly.

"Mr. Harvill," I pleaded, "I really don't want to eat all that food and have you just watching me." He was unimpressed. "I'm on a diet," he barked. The waitress tried to help out. "Can I at least bring you something to drink?" "Yeah, okay," he replied, "a glass of water." She had a better idea—perhaps an iced tea? Finally, he relented and put something on Joe Pulitzer's tab. "Iced tea. Unsweetened." So, as I ate, he talked. I listened, learned a lot about him, and ended up writing a decent story. He was startled, and he began returning my phone calls. The world didn't end, and he had a way to get his views across not just to his members—that, remember, was what the local labor press, the *Labor Tribune*, was for—but to the general public, the politicians, and the business leaders. He began putting the word out—"this guy's okay," to be exact—at the Labor Council's executive board meetings, and from that moment not only was pretty much every labor leader in St. Louis reachable but if the official was out of town, the secretary tracked him or her down.

I had to recalibrate my strategy on deadline. Previously if I needed a comment from labor, I'd call 10 of them and hope to get one timely response; now if I called 10, I'd hear from 15— those I'd phoned and others who had heard about it—and I'd never finish the story. The gates had opened. When Bobby Sansone was fighting his pending ouster from the Teamsters union he had proudly, and ably, represented for 30 years, he brought me to his house—albeit after swearing me to secrecy about its location—to get ahead of the federal allegations he knew would be coming out. Once accessible, the Kelleys and Harvills and Sansones and the others turned out to be forthright, informed, and as sharp as tacks.

But beyond the investment in time and energy this requires on both sides, it often runs into the chicken-and-egg dilemma—labor won't talk to you until they trust you, but they don't trust you until they know you. Jeff Weiss, who for many years was the communications person for the 500,000-member Chicago Federation of Labor, once lamented to me how labor has "such wonderful stories to tell, and unfortunately, our stories are shut out." After the obligatory critique of editors' news judgments and reporting cutbacks and the like, Weiss acknowledged that there was another side to it. He told me about a labor reporter at a major Chicago paper who, enthusiastic about being assigned to the labor beat, promptly placed 100 calls to local union leaders—without getting a *single* return call.[3]

Last, there's the frequent tendency of unions, especially on the international level or at the AFL-CIO, to employ the "put 'em to sleep strategy." That, of course, isn't the goal, but it most definitely is the result of the mass-produced, mind-numbing press releases so many unions churn out on every conceivable subject. These boilerplate products invariably end up in the nearest wastepaper basket. Not only do these generic statements take up union communicators' time that could be used for the type of purposes we'll discuss shortly; they pretty much condition journalists to automatically ignore whatever labor sends across their desks. A recent corollary of this tactic is the AFL-CIO reliance on conference calls, with the usual suspects—federation experts, perhaps a friendly economist, and the mandatory anecdotal worker—on the line with reporters. It's a modest improvement because of the opportunity to ask questions, but it still reflects the same predictable focus on the story of the day, relying on the same, one-size-fits-all approach. This is not to demean the communications folks at the AFL-CIO or its affiliates; there are some dedicated individuals working in this field, more energetic than in the past, but the approach remains tired and not very productive.

Labor's proclivity to act as an intimidator, an ostrich, a sleep aide, or a wary suitor would be amusing if its survival weren't on the line. These types of attitudes and behaviors contribute significantly to the poor press coverage labor gets, which is part and parcel of its failure to find its voice and project a clear message. All the more since finding its voice and making it heard is arguably the overriding challenge facing trade unions—a challenge they won't solve until they first recognize their culpability in the matter. Doing so is a prerequisite to taking steps to remedy the situation, but it's unlikely to happen any time soon—in part because this kind of discussion is something that labor just about never has.

Any labor leaders or union activists who are reading this, even rank-and-file members, are surely shaking their heads. "He must be kidding. He's got it backwards," they're thinking, or yelling. "Doesn't he know that it's the media that ignore *us*, or that treat us unfairly when they bother to pay attention? Is he really that clueless?"

I'm quite aware they feel that way, having spoken to a number of gatherings of union communicators or general union officers, as well as conferences involving both management and labor, and having seen what kinds of points and grievances trade unionists raise in the discussion. I'm familiar not only with their belief that they're getting a raw deal but also with the intensity of that conviction. Nor am I surprised by their stance, which stems both from what they experience themselves and from what I'll call their "enablers" in this respect— the academic experts, labor intellectuals, and leftist media critics who reinforce through research and analysis what labor already suspects.

Groups like Fairness and Accuracy in Reporting (FAIR) have done periodic studies showing the dearth of coverage of labor issues in the American press, so union officials and members know their particular situation reflects a broader reality.[4] That reality is, in short, that news outlets stiff labor. Why they do so is, in turn, explained by the professors and the experts as resulting from the bias, ownership structure, and ideology of the media, in essays or an occasional book, such as *Through Jaundiced Eyes: How the Media View Organized Labor.*[5] The common theme is that the combination of advertiser pressure and the influence of media ownership, increasingly concentrated in the hands of a few large companies, exerts an inexorable pro-business tug on journalists. Snobbery or class bias by individual journalists, too elitist to care about the problems of bricklayers or janitors, fills in the gaps. Even if a given reporter isn't hostile, his or her editor may well be and the generally conservative publisher almost certainly is, and that's before advertisers weigh in, so labor is unlikely to get a fair deal from today's increasingly corporate media.

That's a tidy bit of analysis, and as a theoretical framework, it holds up well in textbooks and journals and classrooms. There's even some truth in it, especially the first part—about the status of labor coverage—which *is* abysmal. It's actually worse than the critics realize. Just look at the language that journalists typically use, starting with the term "labor bosses." Why, exactly, are the only elected people at the workplace or in the labor-management system—folks who therefore can be voted out—pejoratively termed "bosses," while those who truly qualify for that moniker—since they hire, fire, and discipline employees—are respectfully dubbed "executives" or "managers"? Why is a showdown at work so often called a "labor dispute," when in fact it's a labor-management spat? If it's going to be short handed, it could just as easily be labeled a "management dispute." And perhaps most insidious, why in those contractual disputes is the company always said to be offering certain terms, while the union is demanding this or that concession? That terminology juxtaposes, a priori, the picture of a greedy union with a generous company. It could just as easily be written that employees are offering to work for a given contract but that management is demanding they accept something else. For people who make our living using words, we're pretty careless in this regard, at best. At worst, we're making some highly questionable assumptions or value judgments. Either way, there are consequences in terms of readers' or viewers' perceptions.

And the failings in the coverage of unions and workers extend far beyond semantics. The coverage is flawed in three major ways, even when one gets past how paltry it is. First, it is generally sensationalistic, focusing on strikes, corruption charges, picket-line violence, boycotts, and the like. Second, it almost always fails to provide any broader context about what unions do, about their day-to-day role in the workplace and in the industrial relations system, about how they contribute or fail to contribute, as the case may be, to worker safety or training or productivity. Finally, stories are often flat-out unfair, with the perspective of labor or even, amazingly, of the employees, being left out of work-related stories, which often resemble lengthy corporate press releases.

So let's posit that labor coverage is sorely lacking in virtually every way. The salient questions are why is that the case and what can labor do about it? This is where labor is missing the boat, and its enablers—those professors and experts with their simplistic, ideologically driven analyses—are doing it no favor. They encourage unionists to lament a situation about which nothing seemingly can be changed, which has the effect of absolving them of any responsibility or need for action—when labor needs just the opposite approach. What labor should do is stop dwelling on how unfairly it's treated, stop devoting so much energy to cataloguing media neglect, and instead focus on how to improve what *it* does. That's the half of the equation labor has the power to change, and doing so would also affect what journalists do in terms of covering labor because while labor coverage is indeed every bit as bad as labor contends it is, the reasons behind this are not as monolithic or conscious as typically described. The causes are far more pedestrian at their roots than is suggested by the talk of conspiracies or ideological and economic motives. Yes, there's some anti-union bias at various stages of the news chain, but there's bias about a lot of things—social conservatives and their causes come to mind—without that precluding virtually all coverage of, for instance, the religious right. If labor receives dismissive treatment from the media, it's attributable not to some grand capitalist or right-wing plot but largely to practical matters that are amenable to change if labor would pay attention.

Let's consider how the typical newsroom operates: picture a confined space, a group of people, and an overall atmosphere that can be described as hectic, harried, and even hapless. That pretty much goes for all types of media outlets, all sizes, all locations—and getting more so by the day. An increasingly shrinking and wired world generates ever more news to cover, even as cost-cutting mandates from above result in fewer people and resources to do it, all this occurring amid mounting competition from 24-hour news sources. More to do in less time with smaller staffs spells constant pressure on all involved in the news gathering process.

Now let's look at how this translates into day-to-day operations. It's morning and those who make decisions about what news to cover and which events to staff, and those who carry out those decisions, are already being pulled in a hundred directions. They didn't arrive in the office with a grand scheme in mind, bent that day on shortchanging a union campaign for improved safety so that they can boost a company's bottom line. If that were the choice they were consciously pondering, they'd probably make quite different decisions than they do—but none of this even crosses their minds. What they're doing is trying to make sure the important stuff that's swirling all around gets covered so that they don't get called on the carpet for missing something, and that they have some enterprise initiatives—such as features or investigative projects—going on as well. Once the mayhem and the politics and other necessary covers are taken care of—the "spinach" of the daily report—whatever resources and energy they have left will go to produce work—the "dessert"—they hope will captivate, entertain, or startle. What they select will depend on how many readers or viewers a story is likely to grab, as well as the likelihood of actually getting the story in timely fashion. Simply put, they want good stories that are quickly gettable, perhaps exclusive ones with the help of reliable sources.

Given what's been said in previous chapters about labor's waning numbers and about its diminished impact, as well as the perception of an increasingly irrelevant movement, any story about labor has a steep climb just to be put in the mix. Those running newsrooms see the same figures indicating labor's decline, and so they don't instinctively regard union stories as jazzy items when they're deciding, at the afternoon news meeting, the schedule for the evening broadcast or the layout of the next day's paper. "Who's going to care?" will be the typical ranking editor's response if anyone even proposes a union-related story in the first place; unless a subordinate is highly knowledgeable about the labor movement and self-confident to boot, that seems like a good question to avoid engendering in the first place. This attitude percolates down the food chain, as assignment editors schedule news stories and dole them out every morning. Nobody wants to come across as out of touch at those all-important news meetings where the top editors gather.

Even on breaking news, labor is up against it because reporters typically have large Rolodexes replete with home and cell phones of political, community, or business leaders— and precious few for labor leaders. That's all the more problematic because unions tend to be open during hours that mirror the schedules of their members, starting much earlier than do reporters, and going home around 4 p.m.—long before most deadlines. Those stories that look like corporate releases sometimes do so because it was the company or a business group that put out the news in the first place and then provided various contacts for follow-up—all at a time when the union had already closed up shop. Of course, it's about more than availability; many of the political or community activists or leaders are as eager to be on-the-record or off-the-record sources as labor folks are eager to avoid talking to a reporter in the first place.

So news about unions and their issues is generally absent from newsroom discussions and decisions—and from the stories that flow from them. And this affects how newsrooms are organized because business, metro, and national editors take this all into consideration as they periodically assess the beats to be handled by their staffs; the decisions they make generally mean still fewer labor stories. And from the other end, reporters absorb the clear message that labor coverage is hardly the way to get to the top of the newscast tonight or on page 1 tomorrow—let alone to advance one's career.

But labor's invisibility is attributable to more than a series of news judgments reflecting the slipping status of unions; sociological and demographic currents also play a role. Thirty, forty, fifty years ago, not only was union membership much higher and labor's clout clearer, not only was the beat brimming with great stories and outsized personalities like Jimmy Hoffa and John L. Lewis, Walter Reuther and George Meany, but journalists themselves were different. They cussed and drank, often had blue-collar outlooks instead of graduate degrees, and they understood the rough-hewn world of labor instinctively. Editors were all ears for a story about Lewis's brave coal miners or Reuther's bold merging of labor and civil rights, and hungry young reporters out to make a name clamored for the beat. But now, even as the ink-stained character of journalists has evolved into something more privileged or at least more standoffish and even as there are fewer newspaper or television managers who have a working-class background or even basic knowledge of the labor movement, their prime readership also tends to be among white-collar suburban dwellers. And on top of those trends, journalism itself has become increasingly superficial and celebrity conscious, and it is driven more and more by what's topical and popular in today's culture. Compounding this is the move away from a past when hard-boiled editors trusted their gut about what was important and toward a survey-driven desire to dish up news that will appeal to ever-more-elusive news consumers. On these latter counts, unions and their issues are almost the absolute antithesis of what is valued.

These various developments generate several consequences that all work in the same direction—keeping labor out of the news. First, few reporters, whether print or electronic, cover labor these days. Broadcast outlets almost invariably have none. A typical major metropolitan newspaper might have 12 or 15 business reporters, all covering their beats—manufacturing, banking, retail, aerospace, the economy—largely from the corporate and/or consumer point of view. If labor is covered at all, it's usually handled by one of them as a sliver of his or her beat, or divvied up on the basis of whoever happens to be available at a given moment when an editor looks up. Either way, it's generally regarded by the person doing it as insignificant at best, a nuisance at worst. So little knowledge or continuity accumulates, and few contacts get built up. And labor's typical placement on the business side, as opposed to, say, metropolitan or national news, means that the beat is viewed in its most limited form—the struggle for better contracts for union members—and not in its broader social or political context. That affects coverage even at those rare media outlets that do have someone focusing exclusively or primarily on labor, keeping it marginal and separate from the grand sweep of issues out there. And when the political season arrives at most news organizations, the person handling labor's role, if anyone does, is a political reporter who doesn't ordinarily cover labor and is now doing it—and treating it—as a sidebar-type of story to his or her main work. That explains in no small measure why the firefighters slipped so easily under the radar screen in the 2004 presidential primary and, more generally, why labor's overall role was so misconstrued.

This, of course, translates into less news about labor and more superficial handling of those issues that are covered—which, for the most part, means quick hits on fisticuffs or protests or graft. What's lost is sustained, analytical, or investigative coverage of more complex matters, such as the role unions fill at the workplace, the level of shop-floor democracy, labor efforts around job outsourcing, or about the links between a reduced union presence and rising economic inequality or coalminers' deaths.

Labor leaders, staff members, union activists, and rank-and-file workers notice these things and become even more convinced that the media have it in for them and are instead kowtowing to corporate interests, publisher pressure, and advertiser preferences. Having little idea of how the media actually work, they regard the scatter-shot coverage and the unfairness as an intentional slight based on inherent hostility toward unions and their members and, more broadly, toward worker issues. It is not illogical for them to conclude that the media simply won't give them a fair shake and so it's barely worth the effort to try. Why work with a reporter on a story, let alone propose topics for coverage? The already-thin relations between journalists and trade unionists wither further, making stories even harder to get.

And so the notion of editors that labor is not worth paying attention to appears to be justified, which only serves to reinforce the story assigning, news placement, and staffing decisions they have made. Why waste precious resources on an infertile beat? Once again, labor finds itself caught in a vicious cycle—actually a hat trick here—within newsrooms as fewer stories beget less interest; in the labor-media interaction as each side tires of the other; and in the way a declining labor movement and waning coverage exacerbate one another.

Despite all that, there's some good news here for labor. Since much of this hinges on practical, even mundane, factors—as opposed to some nefarious, class-driven plot—there are steps that labor could take to influence the coverage it gets. In fact, the very problems we have outlined as contributing to inadequate media coverage suggest the elements of a media strategy for labor, one that would serve not only the interests of labor and workers but of the media and indeed of an informed public. The obstacles within the world of journalism that block robust labor coverage could become the stepping stones of a productive course of action by labor to boost its presence in the media. As for the more implacable problems of corporate influence or ideological hostility, labor needs to focus on what can be changed and to fruitfully direct its energies.

Much of this revolves around the frenzied journalist syndrome, with our hapless reporter needing contacts, needing stories, and needing ways to sell them to his or her editors.

Let's start with the simplest of these three—the purely practical matters of communications and contacts and the attitudes associated with them. Why were the efforts of the new labor reporter in Chicago to reach out to union leaders rebuffed, something that could only squelch his enthusiasm and thus hurt labor? Why, for that matter, was he the one making the effort in the first place? Shouldn't the unions have been drowning him in phone calls and visits, with lists of cell phone and home phone numbers? Not just of communications people but also union officers, organizers, and various staff members? If need be, labor ought to shift some public affairs people from the international unions in Washington or New York or wherever they're based, to the local levels where the problems are often the worst and the consequences most serious. That's also where reporters would likely be most grateful for ideas. If union folks at that level are overwhelmed, then provide not just more troops but also more training, and deploy rank-and-file members willing to talk to the press. Labor will never match the sophistication of corporate PR efforts, but it can certainly surpass them in terms of speaking from the heart. If the catfish workers in Mississippi could so effectively boost their own cause, despite personal backgrounds that provided little preparation and in that environment, so too can other workers.

Beyond properly allocating resources and providing contact information relevant on deadline, this also requires a change in attitude within the unions. The head-in-the-sand trick needs to be exposed for what it is—a denial of reality that hurts workers' interests while moving unions one step closer to extinction. And the personalized, comfort-level approach that has so long characterized many Teamster and construction unions around the country needs to be sacrificed, colorful as it may be, to the imperatives of efficiency. Labor has little left to lose, and at this point if someone shows interest, that person and that interest need to be welcomed, not evaluated. Even if labor gets burned now and then, it's worth the gamble.

More profoundly, a change in culture is needed. When the UAW gets tough with reporters, when a key International Association of Machinists (IAM) official boasts that he doesn't speak to the press, when a former Teamster president snaps at reporters that the breakdown of a critical executive board vote is "none of your business," there's a potentially harmful subtext here. To a large measure they're playing to the gallery, tapping into a strong us-versus-the-world sentiment within the union, a quasi-jingoistic strain. It's a macho pose, one that resonates among the base and that shows the guy is "strictly for the members, could care less about the PR," as one Teamster put it, but it's also a dangerous pose given the labor movement's tenuous status. Labor leaders need to grasp—and let their members know—that their collective futures rest not on hunkering down but to the contrary, on rising up and shouting out their message.

Putting the stories themselves aside for the moment, labor could do much to help reporters convince skeptical editors that labor news is worth running, even deserving of prominent play, by helping journalists see the bigger picture and understand why labor still matters, whatever its current membership figures are and however weak or vulnerable it may be on a host of fronts. Trade unionists should help reporters comprehend the links between the growing gap separating rich and poor and the assault on the right to organize, or to appreciate how labor's woes tie in with a panoply of issues everyone agrees matter, such as vanishing pensions or the exporting of jobs. Showing that labor is still relevant is not an overly tough case to make in the sense that it doesn't depend on proving that labor's stance is right on any given issue. It simply rests on the premise that the economy and industrial relations systems work best—and the soundest policies emerge—when the various groups and points of view involved are effectively represented.

To accomplish this, trade unionists need to be the ones coming around when there's nothing going on, when they're not trying to peddle a story or talk about a particular issue, but just to discuss labor's multifaceted significance in today's America. If we know that reporters, whose lives revolve around deadlines, tend to appear only when something has *happened* and they need a specific comment or insight, then union officials ought to take the initiative to open a broader discourse. Helping the reporter gain a bank of insight that he or she can use not only to discern good stories and spot linkages but also to make the importance of those events clear to decision-makers in the newsroom is akin to teaching him or her how to fish as opposed to simply giving him or her a fish/story. And there's no reason this couldn't be done as well with the only people on the editorial side of news operations who have the time and luxury of actually batting around ideas, the editorial boards. Virtually every other cause, interest group, or political entity does this. So should labor.

Finally, these two missions accomplished, the matter of stories is the easiest and most straightforward. It involves labor's doing several things it doesn't sufficiently do now: humanize, regionalize, and think big. On the first, rather than bemoan the oft-noted shift in journalism away from investigative, hard-edged journalism toward a softer, more human tendency, labor should take advantage of it. There are few beats with as rich and intriguing a human side as labor possesses, and the union movement could tap into this in several ways. One is by proposing stories featuring workers with noteworthy accomplishments or interesting tales to tell. How many people wouldn't read about the group of aerospace workers who, motivated by their union, discovered how to reconfigure the assembly process for a key U.S. military aircraft, saving American taxpayers large sums of money that could instead go toward making the jet fighter safer and more capable? Might that not affect the image of unions as simply out for themselves, costing everyone else money, and working against the greater good? On a community level, rather than sending out those infernal grainy photos of old-timers receiving their 50-year union pins, photos and captions that rarely get used and change nothing if they do, how about seeing if there's a powerful human interest story there? Perhaps one of the veterans, whose union involvement has been a strong factor throughout his career, helped build the early batch of factory-produced automobiles or kindled a spark in a first-grade student named Colin Powell. Or unions could proffer one of the countless untold stories of racial or gender teamwork or breakthroughs on the job that are waiting to be told.

News about public policies or corporate practices, important as it might be, can be boring for the reporter, difficult to sell to an editor, and impenetrable for the reader. But unions have the wherewithal to help journalists put a human face on such topics. Worker safety programs, for example, are not the stuff of a riveting story, but the local fellow whose life was drastically changed because his plant lacked union-management safety procedures might make a compelling story—one that grips readers, promotes debate, and even sparks changes. Particularly so if the plant down the road has a union and a solid safety program and as a result, experiences fewer injuries.

Adopting a regional strategy might well be the single most effective thing labor could do to get its message out, and it wouldn't involve much additional work—just smarter work. Labor could jettison its confounded press releases and mass-marketing approach (already a net plus right there!) and replace it with a more targeted policy aimed at maximizing coverage by matching story pitches with reporters' strengths and interests, a media outlet's tendencies and audience, local labor situations, and a region's market and economic conditions. The strategy employed by the United Food and Commercial Workers (UFCW) in the case of the catfish workers in Indianola was an example of how such activities can take root—and take off. This would require the initial effort of collecting and analyzing information about news organizations, relevant journalists, and regional economies, but once done, a network of efficient and productive relationships could be built on that foundation. And the preliminary work itself would be invaluable for union communicators.

This type of regional approach offers several advantages. It would allow labor to suggest stories of local relevance to reporters, they might even be exclusive (presently, when you read a generic news release, you know hundreds of others are doing the same), and follow-up by labor would be facilitated because given stories would be tied to specific reporters. Additionally, stories might well take on a continuing life of their own because they would stand a far better chance of resonating among the readers in a newsroom's audience.

Labor also needs to think big, to look for a knockout punch every now and then. It needs to occasionally capture the public's imagination—not just provide information to people but inspire them, showcasing struggles that transcend workers' self-interest. Whether it's because labor spends too much time ducking, vetting, occasionally bullying, or churning out those daily missives, it seems to let the big ones get by. The ones, for instance, like Al Shanker and Eastern Europe. This was something I accidentally stumbled onto, starting in 1989 at the executive council winter meeting of the AFL-CIO, and pursued intermittently, as opportunity allowed. My editors had agreed to send me to Florida for the annual session, a good chance to get to know top labor leaders because, unlike the crush of a labor convention with thousands of delegates, this involved only the couple of dozen council members and some labor reporters. I approached Shanker, president of the American Federation of Teachers (AFT) and an AFL-CIO vice president, as he sat near the hotel pool one morning. I did so with hesitation because I was relatively new on the labor beat and he was a figure of immense stature—and more than a little gruff. But I was interested in foreign developments, he headed the federation's international affairs committee, and I wanted to hear his thoughts on the world.

Within a few minutes I was listening intently as he discussed what he called "incipient independent labor movements" in Eastern Europe. Other than Poland's longstanding Solidarity, they were getting almost no attention, but they were potentially crucial, he said, because they signaled worker dissatisfaction with the status quo. If they grew large enough, they could threaten Communist hegemony over the trade union movement, which served the indispensable role of transmitting production plans and discipline to the very working class upon which these states, in theory, rested. If the upstart free labor unions blossomed, they would rob the regimes of legitimacy in a way that protests by students, intellectuals, or consumers would never be able to. This was February, and the events that would unfold later that year in Eastern Europe were unimaginable.

Hungary's Liga, the strongest of the new union federations, was starting to spread from fledgling groupings of scientists and academics to industrial workers and taxi drivers as it challenged the official Communist-controlled unions. Most important, Shanker told me that the AFL-CIO was quietly working on ways to help such unions without endangering them, and he said he was about to be named head of a new labor panel to forge closer ties with the rebel unions. Three AFL-CIO staffers had just returned from Budapest after lending support—a delicate exercise that could easily have boomeranged, with both political and personal repercussions for the local trade unionists.

This seemed like fascinating material, and I wrote about it, at least the portions that wouldn't compromise anything. My editors in St. Louis held the story as long as they could—wondering, they later let on, why someone supposed to be covering labor-management relations was writing about Hungary—before finally burying the story somewhere in the newspaper. Inexplicably encouraged, I placed a call to the Budapest residence of Pal Forgacs, an acquaintance of Shanker and a labor leader for a half-century who headed the Liga. He spoke at length and with considerable passion about the restiveness bubbling throughout portions of Eastern Europe and about ties quietly developing among autonomous unions in Hungary and Poland and perhaps the Soviet Union. I wrote about him too. My editors, now convinced I was dialing people in Hungary at random, published the story but asked me to kindly refrain from trying to cover Eastern Europe from St. Louis, via Florida.

And so I did, until the fall of that year, when I was sent to Western Europe to write about economic integration. Suddenly, thousands of East Germans "vacationing" in Hungary fled westward to Austria. Maverick unions were playing a key role in the rapid liberalization of Hungary, which hard-line states such as East Germany denounced as a Warsaw Pact traitor. I was dispatched overnight to Budapest. Forgacs was out of town, but Shanker's office put me in touch with another Liga leader, Mihaly Csako. Soon I was in his tiny apartment, full of bookshelves crammed with tomes about working-class sociology and politics, taking notes on what he termed the "imminent dissolution of the Marxist hold on Eastern Europe." Two years later, I would return to report extensively on the changes engulfing the region, including the role these maverick worker organizations played in bringing about the changes and then in facilitating the arduous transition to democracy and free-market economies. In Bulgaria, whose small free trade union movement was known as *Podkrepa*, as well as in visits to Albania's labor camps, eastern Germany's psychiatric clinics, Romania's still-fearful schools, and elsewhere, Shanker's contacts and focus on the role of ordinary people in the tumultuous events proved invaluable. As the curtain was slowly pulled back and people felt somewhat freer to speak out, I gained an appreciation for the role that he and the broader American labor movement had played in providing moral and material sustenance at a critical time.

When Shanker died in 1997, I scoured the obituaries and the news stories. As lengthy and impressive as many were, something important was missing. I wrote a commentary piece that began like this:

> Al Shanker was described in his obituaries as a legendary labor leader, as a teacher's teacher, as the man who made the American Federation of Teachers into a power, as a brash New York City activist who closed down the schools, and as a national leader in educational reform.
>
> He surely was all these things, but he was something else as well: a visionary when it came to workers' struggles in communist countries, a no-excuses human-rights advocate who understood earlier than most how labor's concerns transcended national borders.

I went on to describe Shanker's prescient understanding and little-known role, and thereby that of the AFT and AFL-CIO, in the transformation of Eastern Europe. The *Wall Street Journal* editor who handled the piece said that it covered an angle and contained information he and his colleagues had not seen anywhere and that they wanted to run it "as a part of the historical record."[6] That was good for me, but I wondered then, and still do, why people didn't know—and where labor has been in telling the story of its involvement in one of the key events of our time. And I wondered how the popular perception of labor as a dwindling, hidebound institution would be altered if more were known about the part the American labor movement has played—there and elsewhere—in bringing freedom to millions of oppressed people.

Labor's involvement with democratization isn't limited to exotic locales; it also includes some initiatives much closer to home, developments that the labor movement not only should be talking more about but also needs to expand if labor is to realize its potential. Look no further than the brown-uniformed United Parcel Service delivery driver who may be leaving a package at your door as we speak. Ask about the recent election for Teamsters president and brace yourself as he or she puts down the boxes and expresses some heartfelt views. Given what that driver has probably seen, having an election—and being able to talk about it—are not things that he or she is about to take for granted any time soon.

CHAPTER 6

JOE T! JOE T!

I t was a presidential entrance like no other. The handful of Teamsters carrying their leader, Jackie Presser, into the convention hall in Las Vegas were perspiring profusely under the strain of his 300 pounds. They moved slowly, holding him aloft in a reclining seat as if he were a Roman potentate. Though the rules of the union required a formal vote, this was less an election than a coronation. Those few brave delegates who didn't join in the show of hands for their current and future general president wound up later with broken arms or legs, some just a few yards outside the hotel doors. If that type of brutal enforcement was required only on rare occasions, it reflected the fact that these delegates had been carefully chosen, with loyalty and obedience uppermost. There was, to be sure, an undeniable logic to the whole process. With billions in contracts and pension funds at stake, lucrative kickbacks to be distributed, and casinos to be built in this very city, matters could hardly be left to chance or to the riffraff who hauled freight or loaded warehouses—even if their work and dues funded it all.

This was the early frame of reference for many of today's 1.4 million Teamsters, and it helps explain why the United Parcel Service (UPS) deliverymen who service the Washington, D.C., office building I work in relish the opportunity to speak their mind, tight schedules notwithstanding. So do their fellow truck drivers, brewery workers, or warehouse workers. If they marvel at the array of political choices now available to them within their union's newly boisterous political culture, it's because lockstep events like the 1986 Las Vegas convention were the rule when most of them began their careers and joined the union. They know from personal experience how far the International Brotherhood of Teamsters (IBT) has come, even if it remains a work in progress. The notion of competing candidates—whose merits and liabilities can be openly and honestly discussed, evaluated, and voted on by all members—marks an almost incomprehensible break with history for a union that until relatively recently was shrouded in fear and run by intimidation.

I made a somewhat ironic reference to reporting in East Germany in an earlier chapter, but a comparison between the Soviet Union and the Teamsters' union is not so far-fetched. Both were born early in the twentieth century into a hostile environment of capitalist adversaries or ruthless employers, and they quickly grew suspicious of perceived external threats. Neither entity shied away from using force against those enemies when necessary. Both behemoths ruled in authoritarian fashion, brooking little internal dissent and using muscle to crush the independent souls—be they refuseniks or members of Teamsters for a Democratic Union—who dared challenge the leadership. The rulers answered not to the people but to a higher authority, the writings of Marx or the wishes of the Mob. Soviet industrial might and Teamster muscle earned grudging respect from the outside world. But both began to thaw in 1989, the USSR as a result of Mikhail Gorbachev's acknowledgment of internal contradictions, the IBT because of federal supervision imposed by the Department of Justice. The Soviet Union disappeared in 1991, and so did the old Teamsters, with the first democratic elections the union had seen. Now both Russia and the Teamsters, ironically, have a leader who evokes the past: Vladimir Putin of the former KGB, and Jim Hoffa of, well, the Hoffas.

The difference is that while Russia's democratization path has doubled backward, the Teamsters' has continued and deepened, even if marked by detours and stumbling. It is the type of journey that, writ large, has much to say about how the labor movement will evolve and, indeed, whether it will survive. That's so because the Teamsters have long been the face of the American labor movement, the one union everyone can name—a huge, colorful, and powerful labor organization whose late president remains the most recognizable union leader of the past half-century. If a corrupt, violent, and authoritarian IBT can color the public perception of labor, so too could a visibly clean, progressive, and grassroots-dominated Teamsters' union. And there's a bigger picture here: corruption has been an integral part of the story of a number of unions, including some of the building trades, hospitality unions, the East Coast longshoremen, and, periodically, normally clean labor organizations. Beyond playing into the hands of labor's foes, this weakens unions by squandering their resources, perverting their mission, demoralizing their members, and subverting democracy. In the case of the Teamsters, their journey away from this pattern began in the apt venue of Orlando, Florida, in the summer of 1991.

This was the IBT's first nominating convention, part of the settlement of a federal racketeering suit against the union. From across the country, thousands of newly elected Teamster delegates were gathering to take part in this strange new experiment at self-governance. Their job would be to nominate candidates for general president and various other slots, with the subsequent election slated for December. They labored under extraordinary scrutiny in a Disney World hotel crawling with federal officials. This event, after all, was only five years removed from the charade of Las Vegas and decades of similar events, and the feds were visibly nervous. Having built special rooms and walls of specified size and thickness, and placed voting machines at carefully predetermined locations, federal lawyers were now monitoring every aspect of the proceedings, even scouring and editing union press releases and satellite feeds before approving them. They sat on the podium near international Teamster officers, drawing derision from Teamster delegates—who may have wanted reform but weren't sure they wanted it imported in this fashion—and their guests. Congressman William L. Clay (D) of Missouri, a veteran civil rights and labor activist, drew laughter and cheers when he told the delegates: "This convention reminds me of the ones I used to go to in the early sixties—the NAACP, CORE, SNCC— where you had two FBI agents for every one delegate."

But while the omnipresent government lawyers were annoying and constituted a financial drain on the union, which was bearing the cost for all this, at least they weren't breaking anyone's legs. And so, after years of having no voice, with fear and intimidation finally lifted, the Teamsters had jumped full throttle into democratic mode, acting it out as they defined it—which apparently meant saying and doing whatever they pleased. The 5,000 delegates, officials, and guests lustily jeered President George H. W. Bush when he addressed them on a giant video screen to thank them for their early and vociferous support of the Persian Gulf War. Almost alone in the labor movement, the IBT had endorsed Bush three times in the 1980s—twice for vice president, once for president—but now the members were drowning out his remarks. When Teamster President William McCarthy took the microphone to plead with delegates to "use their manners" and respect the president's right to speak, he too was booed—something that had never happened in the union's 88-year history.

Under government prodding, the Teamsters did their best to adopt the trappings of elections and emulate the appropriate activities. Signs bearing union candidates' names bobbed up and down, and loud chants echoed through corridors jam-packed with large and boisterous men. They sported buttons promoting R.V. Durham, presumed frontrunner from North Carolina; Walter Shea, longtime insider from Washington, D.C.; or Ron Carey, former UPS driver from Long Island, an earnest, nasal-voiced firebrand who aimed to shift the union sharply leftward and away from its coziness with the GOP. There was also some support for a young Jim Hoffa, a lawyer and bearer of a fabled name who was pondering a run, but he had been ruled ineligible by federal officials because he lacked the requisite time in the trade. They remained wary, however, of the potential resonance a populist appeal by Hoffa to get on the ballot could have among convention delegates, many of whom wore buttons that implored: "Let Hoffa Run."

With control of the union up for grabs, and the iron fist retired, the efforts to persuade fellow union members were gaining momentum each day—stopped by one thing and one thing only: the periodic appearance of Joe T. He was all of five-foot-five, at best 130 pounds, and 82 years old, but he was the undisputed chief of the Eastern Conference of Teamsters, which includes such strongholds as New York City, Philadelphia, and New Jersey, and he was also the union's senior international vice president. More important, the word was he was highly connected in the way Teamsters understand it. And so, even in this environment sanitized by the presence of so many federal officials, when Joe Trerotola gingerly made his way through the crowded halls, the seas parted as hulking men suddenly grown silent cleared a path. The cacophony of competing chants for rival candidates would yield to a unified staccato: "Joe T! Joe T!" Government lawyers stared in amazement, but it seemed that old fears die hard, and deference still came surprisingly easy to these rough-and-ready men. Democracy was a laudable goal, to be sure, but Joe T, a legendary power behind the throne, was not a man to be trifled with or diminished in any way. He was to be shown only the greatest respect, and playing politics in his presence, with his union, by yelling out in jarring fashion the names of so many would-be office holders, didn't qualify.

A few brave souls would approach to shake his hand, but nobody dared address Joe T directly because that would be to demand a response. For his part, he glided above it all, barely recognizing the tributes with an almost imperceptible nod.

The press, meanwhile, he didn't recognize at all. Sunlight had never been his ally. He had nothing to gain from reporters—his support hardly flowed from public affirmation—and much to lose, particularly at this moment. The last thing he needed was to draw attention to himself, not with Justice Department officials investigating his background, actions, and alleged ties to determine whether he should be among the dozens of Teamster luminaries or lesser lights tossed from the union. His silence was a shame because there's nothing he didn't know, having helped shape the fate of this union for so many years.

For days I'd been looking to break out a story from the small but knowledgeable group of journalists covering this convention. I owed it to my editors, who had taken a bit of a leap sending me here. The problem was that I was the new guy on the block while everyone else was a grizzled veteran, reflecting the lack of new blood assigned to the beat. My competition had been acquainted with many of these guys for years, and we've seen what personal ties mean to Teamsters.

But I knew of someone they hadn't spoken to. And maybe there was an edge I could exploit. So what the hell:

"Giuseppe, come stai?"

His eyes narrow, and Joe T slowly turns toward where he thinks the familiar greeting has come from.

"Bene, bene. Grazie."

The hallway falls deathly silent. Even the "Joe T" chants cease. All movement stops, including his. He's focused on me, waiting. Now what, wise guy, I'm thinking. And do I identify myself as media or just keep going?

"Joe, are you a kingmaker?"

"Not so," he quickly retorts. "I just voice my opinion."

"But you're said to have a lot of respect and influence within the union."

"I just pick the best man."

As I'm trying to unravel that one, I wonder about something else as well; will this qualify as an exclusive interview, if other reporters are present but nobody understands a word of Italian?

Joe T, meanwhile, is apparently starting to enjoy it for some reason. He's evincing no impatience, showing no need to be on his way. He's just waiting for the next question. Maybe he figures that no one who shouldn't will know what's being said. Maybe he's like a gorgeous actress everyone's too scared to ask out. He uses the opportunity to make it clear that he doesn't approve of all the changes he sees around him in this union he's belonged to for 56 years and helped run for much of that time. Nor does the confusing setting around him this week reflect the best way to govern a union.

"There are a lot of young fellas here. With all due respect to them, they really don't know what the labor movement is. The fact that you drive a truck for UPS or whatever doesn't give you the right to say what should happen here."

In his day, Joe T recounts, he concentrated on winning good contracts for his members, not on changing the world. Some, of course, contend that he also found time for more unsavory activities, such as allowing mobsters to gain footholds in New York Teamster locals or at the very least, that he turned a blind eye to the role of organized crime in union affairs.

He scoffs at the very idea. Then he takes the conversation to a more personal level.

"I never broke bread with these people. They've never been to my house. I've never been to their house. I've never spent a day in jail, never was indicted. I had four depositions, two grand juries. What did they find? Zip, nothing."

So why is the government picking on you, Joe?

"I can't explain this to my wife, who I'm married to 62 years. I say, 'Sweetheart, I don't understand it.'"

On a roll, I'm feeling bolder than I perhaps should. Did this union make a devil's pact with La Cosa Nostra?

"How the hell do I know?" Joe T retorts, flashing the temper that those who know him—better than I know him—try not to provoke. "I know I never associated with those people."

I sense it's time to wind down here, and ending this on a cordial note seems a good idea. Joe, you've been at this a long time. Why not just step aside, with all the chaos surrounding the union these days and the personal grief you're taking?

"Why should I? God's been good to me. I've got my health, and a lovely family. And I wanta clear my name."

But Joe T ended up getting bounced from the union, along with so many others. In a stunning upset, Teamsters nationwide elected the maverick Carey, and the reform of the IBT was on its way. It has proven to be a brawling democratic process that most definitely is not for the faint of heart, and it's been complicated by the vicious Carey-Hoffa hostilities that continue to resurface in various forms. Yet it is light years removed from the way this union once was administered. As the New York–based Association for Union Democracy (AUD) puts it: "The supervised Teamsters elections represent this country's most significant continuing experiment with the direct election of [union] officers."[1]

There are various theories about why corruption has afflicted parts of the labor movement at times. One, postulated by Robert Fitch in his book *Solidarity for Sale*, focuses on the structure of American unions, which he says "still haven't broken out of nineteenth-century models of labor organizations. The classic aim of the American union is still to monopolize a territory; the means—an exclusive bargaining contract; the result—20,000 local unions that inevitably behave more like semiautonomous fiefdoms than like a genuine labor movement pursuing the common good for working people."[2] He contrasts that with the situation of unions elsewhere, saying that "you don't find gangsters running European unions." Others note that the U.S. labor movement is focused largely on money—getting more of it so workers can join the middle class—as opposed to being based on ideology, as are several major European labor movements, including those in France and Italy. And money, combined with the type of power many union leaders have wielded, tends to corrupt. Finally, key European labor federations, such as the (German) Deutscher Gewerkschaftsbund (DGB), tend to be full-fledged partners with employers and government, while American unions often have more of a combative, even isolated, stance.

But these are, at best, partial explanations. Union corruption, violence, and links with the Mob did not arise in a vacuum; intimidation worked both ways. As labor began to take off in the early decades of the last century, U.S. employers frequently responded ruthlessly to keep unions out of their plants and workplaces, sometimes resorting to the use of goons. This often occurred with the tacit, or even active, support of local law enforcement. Multiply the beatings young Jimmy Hoffa absorbed in a single year while trying to organize truck drivers outside Detroit by hundreds of organizers in dozens of cities over a number of years, and it becomes clearer why unions developed their own "muscle" and sometimes even agreed to unholy arrangements. As pointed out in the book *The Teamsters: Perception and Reality*,[3] some Teamster leaders found it "necessary or expedient to have dealings with gangsters [and] formed alliances with underworld figures during the labor struggles of the 1930s, when muscle was needed to counter the violent tactics of employers." The impetus also came from the other side. Racketeers had sought to gain a foothold in the Teamsters' union since its founding, given its stature and size in the labor movement, its strategic position as the transportation force for a variety of industries, and its multi-billion-dollar pension or health and welfare funds. On the latter count, the union's huge Central States Pension Fund was so abused it was dubbed the "Mob's bank."

Whatever the genesis of the violence and corruption that have plagued a number of unions—the Teamster-Mob nexus being merely the most celebrated example—efforts to reverse such developments have produced some of the most compelling episodes in labor history.

While the country was focused on the war in Vietnam in the early 1970s, coal miners were fighting their own internal war, with grassroots elements locked in a bitter struggle to take back their union from Tony Boyle, the corrupt president of the United Mine Workers of America (UMWA). Arnold Miller's Miners for Democracy ended up winning a government-supervised rerun of the previous election, called because Boyle's challenger, Jock Yablonski, had been murdered along with his wife and daughter. As it turned out, Boyle had ordered the killings. This was a union that, in response to a past replete with company towns, corporate thugs, and machine gun–toting law-enforcement officers, had long been run in autocratic fashion, but now it had gone over the pale. With the help of some very courageous people, the UMWA emerged from the period of change with a highly democratic constitution. Among those instrumental in Miller's gutsy reform movement was a young coal miner-turned-attorney named Richard Trumka, who was later elected the youngest president of any union in the country at age 33. In the mid-1990s he became vice president of the AFL-CIO on John Sweeney's ticket. In a labor movement largely bereft of charismatic leaders, Trumka speaks with quiet passion of what black lung disease did to his father and grandfather. Listening to him not only brings home the continuing need for strong trade unions, it also suggests that he is the type of person the labor movement needs to use more to communicate its message.

Even in the case of the Teamsters, where the government played a major role by using the federal Racketeer Influenced and Corrupt Organizations (RICO) Act to secure a consent decree from union leaders intent on avoiding prison terms, the original push for the cleanup came from inside the union. In 1976 a group of dissident Teamsters banded together to reform the nation's most powerful union. It was a daring—and dangerous—enterprise for the fledgling Teamsters for a Democratic Union (TDU). The group was, and remains, reviled by the Teamster establishment and by many members. At that year's Teamster convention a sturdy, bearded 29-year-old named Pete Camarata was the lone TDU member among the delegates. On the last day of the convention, Camarata rose and told Teamster President Frank Fitzsimmons, who was Presser's predecessor: "Mr. Fitzsimmons, yesterday your election was declared unanimous. I couldn't rest if I didn't declare my opposition."

"You could have heard a pin drop," Steve Kindred, a colleague of Camarata's, told me.[4] That night, Camarata and Kindred attended a union reception. Surrounded by unfriendly Teamster leaders whose hostility was rising by the minute, the two decided they would be better off elsewhere. Several beefy sergeants at arms offered to escort the two men outside. But once there, they pounced on Camarata—knocking him down, kicking him repeatedly in the head, and leaving him unconscious on the ground. When Kindred came to Camarata's aid, he too was attacked, and both his shoulders were dislocated. But Camarata's action had, symbolically at least, put the issue of the right to vote on the convention floor.[5] By the 1981 convention, some 20 dissidents had joined Camarata as delegates, and TDU eventually swelled to over 10,000 members. Though that was less than 1 percent of Teamsters, the group constituted, by the clarity of its message and courage of its members, a powerful force for change. After Carey was nominated at the June 1991 convention, TDU was pivotal in his upset win. Along with shining the light on Mob ties, TDU focused attention on the multiple—and hefty—salaries pulled down by union officials holding simultaneous positions on international, regional, state, and local levels, while also pointing out lingering anti-democratic practices within the union.

The Teamsters are not the only union to have recently shed an authoritarian past and moved to clean itself up. Because of the direct control they exert over hiring for construction jobs, unions in the building trades have often been run in an authoritarian manner, demanding obedience from members. In addition to nepotism, these unions have sometimes been susceptible to corruption running in various directions among the unions, the employers, and outside criminal elements. And if the old IBT resembled the Soviet Union, the Laborers' International Union of North America (LIUNA) bore a closer similarity to Stalinist Albania. At the international level, this was a hermetically sealed union about whose inner workings one could only guess. The old Teamsters at least had a spokesman, even if he rarely practiced his trade. ("Duke Zeller had the very best job in the world," an envious flack at another union told me, with poetic license. "He would never ever talk to a reporter, he'd show up at work, have a Teamster lunch, and then go home.") The Laborers didn't even bother going through that pretense.

Finally, in the mid-1990s, under the weight of accusations it was mobbed up, LIUNA reached an accommodation with the Clinton White House to tackle corruption and adopt democratic reforms. Some who had dismissed the Teamsters' evolution as nothing more than government-mandated change criticized the Laborers for allegedly securing a sweetheart deal from the administration that allowed the union to clean itself up on its own. That would appear to be an example of labor's foes having it both ways: showing disdain for a union forced by the government to cleanse itself, then showing equal disdain for a union allowed to do the same on its own. In any case the latter deal sparked Republican fury on Capitol Hill that led to one of the most entertaining congressional hearings I've seen on any subject.

The GOP-led House Judiciary Committee's crime subcommittee scheduled a hearing into why the federal government was letting LIUNA officials stay in power as the union sought to rid itself of Mob influence, and whether the friendship between President Bill Clinton and union President Arthur Coia had led to special treatment. It seemed a good opportunity to embarrass both the union and the administration in one fell swoop, and the committee announced the session in rather breathless fashion. To lend further mystery and drama to the proceedings, the Republicans let it be known days in advance that the hearing would feature a secret witness whom Chairman Bill McCollum of Florida identified only as a "confidential organized crime informant." He was an insider capable, it was promised, of definitively linking organized crime and LIUNA through personal knowledge.

The first crimp in the plan surfaced when labor found out beforehand who the witness was going to be and publicized his identify in half-page newspaper advertisements in Washington. But that didn't deter the Republicans, who continued to act as if they were handling high state secrets. They fully expected this to take its rightful place with memorable congressional hearings of the past, whether Bobby Kennedy's confrontation with Jimmy Hoffa and the Teamsters, or various organized crime investigations. And so, on July 24, 1996, a black-hooded man entered Room 2141 of the Rayburn House Building and made his way to the witness table or, more accurately, to a three-sided cardboard partition erected minutes earlier. It was designed so that only congressional committee members could see him and, most of all, to prevent photographers from taking his picture. One had to listen carefully to hear the few soft snickers as he sat down.

"You're now in the clear, as they say," McCollum assured the witness, advising him he could remove his mask. The chairman sternly advised photographers not to peer around the cardboard contraption and take a picture, but that hardly mattered because a union consultant seated in the audience was cheerfully handing out a stack of large color photos of the witness to anyone who wanted one.

In moving and solemn words, Republican committee members praised the man's courage and service to his country. Democrats were less reverential. Pointing to the partition, North Carolina's Melvin Watt asked facetiously, "Is that bullet-proof? I just want to know if I'm in danger if somebody opens fire."

McCollum insisted that nothing had been staged for theatrical purposes: "It is being done strictly at his request, to protect him from personal harm." The witness, Ronald M. Fino, who had previously run a Laborers' local and who now was a government-protected witness, testified about the criminal control of LIUNA and jobs, how Mob bosses spoke with hand gestures to avoid uttering words that could convict them, and the murderous code of silence. He said his father, though a member of La Cosa Nostra, had "instilled in me values that led to my eventual cooperation with the FBI." Democrats said his testimony shed no light on the union's past or its transformation and that the hearing was rank politics. Meanwhile, a supermarket tabloid containing a story purportedly written by the witness claiming that O.J. Simpson had been framed by the Mob, was making its way around the room in an effort to ridicule him. AFL-CIO officers outside the hearing room said the whole thing was retaliation for labor's criticism of the newly elected Republican Congress for its votes on minimum wage, Social Security, and other matters.

Whoever was right, the Laborers' union continued its evolution, and today it stands as a progressive union that is active in politics and is led by President Terence O'Sullivan, who has brought the union squarely into labor's mainstream. At LIUNA's convention in September 2006, the federal oversight that had been part of the original deal was lifted, and when the Change to Win federation was formed with the stated goal of organizing new members, not only were the Teamsters and Laborers among the driving forces, they provided a good third of the group's membership.

These changes in the Teamsters and the Laborers are the most visible part of a broader set of developments that cover how unions are run and how they relate to their members. In addition to robust elections and cleaning up vestiges of corruption, the internal reforms have included efforts aimed at boosting rank and file involvement in union decision making and actions, strengthening the diversity of the membership and the officers, and achieving greater transparency in union affairs. Addressing matters of pluralism, membership participation and similar goals are key for two reasons. The shortcomings in these areas are far more endemic than are instances of actual corruption or Mob influence in the labor movement, and every bit as hard to resolve. And truly harnessing the energy of members depends on much more than the lack of criminality in a union—much as creating genuine peace requires more than the absence of war. Just because members aren't being beaten or their money stolen doesn't mean their voices are being heard or their energy effectively mobilized on behalf of their interests and their unions' activities.

Notions of union democracy and grassroots participation as a means of revitalizing unions were downplayed during labor's period of self-examination preceding the split. The issues considered important were whether labor should focus on organizing or on politics, or perhaps on better servicing of existing members through more aggressive collective bargaining. Internal reform was relegated to a second-tier level—a possible avenue to pursue rather than the indispensable part of a rejuvenated labor movement it actually is. At times it was even deemed an impediment to what labor really had to do to turn things around, such as consolidating into a few larger unions able to better confront their corporate adversaries in a given multinational company or even an industry. And so, for example, Gregory Junemann, president of the International Federation of Professional and Technical Engineers, found himself debating leaders of more-powerful unions at New York's Labor at the Crossroads conference over the idea of forced mergers. Not only was the very concept of forcing unions to be subsumed into other bigger ones undemocratic, he maintained, but the consequences would be as well, by further distancing the rank and file from the leadership while simultaneously reducing the autonomy enjoyed by local unions.

Getting members more engaged in their unions is neither an inconvenience nor merely one possible strategy among others: it is a prerequisite to a revamped movement, a building block for whatever else labor attempts or hopes to do. The learning process and personal engagement that workers experience when they become involved in shop-floor activities, organizing campaigns, collective bargaining, political efforts, and in union functions in general have a number of positive consequences. As, from the other end, do the trust and confidence union leaders show in members by seeking their participation and opening up union processes to facilitate it. Together, both unleash the potential of the tens of thousands, hundreds of thousands, or even the million-plus members each union has, and that broad-based enthusiasm and knowledge is the key edge unions have over their adversaries. They can't match business in terms of deep pockets, nor can they equal the one-issue zealotry of those they should be squaring off against in the debate over values. What they do bring to the table are organizational ability and numbers—but those are empty without the full-throated participation of their members.

Encouraging workers to be actively engaged in their union, finding mechanisms to make that happen, and removing impediments to their participation—whether bureaucracy, undemocratic bylaws, inertia, or corruption—gives union actions in every arena a greater likelihood of success. The decisions about what to do and how to do it benefit from a greater level of input, and so does the execution. Not only will members more solidly support campaigns they helped craft but their participation will also improve the prospects that the efforts will work. Members lend their practical insight and infuse the union with energy. As a labor scholar concluded after closely studying a specific local before and after it opened itself up to worker participation, "When unions institute democratic reforms, they are better able to represent member interests."[6] At a time when unions are so imperiled by outside forces, they need to shore themselves up on the inside and face these threats in as robust and unified a shape as possible. Having smart leaders at the helm, no matter how brilliant they are or how sophisticated their strategies may be, will not by itself suffice.

The unexpected successes of the firefighters and the catfish workers rested on the central role local rank-and-file workers played, on the characteristics and commitment they brought to the fight as opposed to simply carrying out instructions. It was the personal history and courage of the striking women that placed the Delta Pride strike in a broader context of human dignity and civil rights, provided an emotional and moral component, and made it a cause the public could embrace. In the case of the Iowa firefighters, their knowledge of the community and its residents, the professional respect they enjoyed from the public, their ability to work in coordinated fashion, and their never-say-die attitude helped overcome odds equal to those faced in Indianola.

Those two instances belie the notion that there is any tension between a vibrant rank-and-file voice and decisive union leadership. It's a false dichotomy that is, unfortunately, often an unspoken fear when the subject of expanding union democracy is discussed. In Mississippi, the women were put front

and center, part of a strategic plan formulated by union officials who realized that the strike could succeed only if they
trusted the women to do something they never had done—
serve as the public face and spokespersons for their own cause.
There is no more hierarchical, disciplined union in the country than the International Association of Fire Fighters, and
arguably no stronger leader than its president, Harold
Schaitberger. But the IAFF's leadership knew that its only
hope, as it went up against far bigger and more experienced
unions in the arena of national politics, was to put the caucus
effort's fate in the hands of local firefighters. In both cases it
was the complementary nature of bold leadership and grassroots passion that prevailed.

Rather than posing a threat to the leaders of a given union,
internal reforms may be a critical factor in the ability of the
leadership to succeed and thus retain control—and in the long
term, for there to be a union to run in the first place. Beyond
engaged members and effective programs, unions that become
more responsive and democratic gain something else as well—
a greater appeal to prospective members. And unions that
grow become yet stronger and more effective, and thus still
more attractive to unorganized workers. This may sound like
a trend that has been sorely lacking in this book: an upward
spiral, a positive cycle for labor. Yet it has the potential to produce just that. To survive today's overwhelming challenges,
unions need to stand on the foundation of a spirited and
engaged membership.[7]

The progress made by the Teamsters and Laborers, among
others, in the area of internal reform, is potentially significant
in another way as well. It counters the negative depiction of

labor by its foes as an occasionally corrupt and violent institution, or as being dominated by out-of-touch "union bosses"
who call the shots to the detriment of average workers. Or it
would, if only unions called attention to the positive trends
they have undergone, and continue to undergo, in this area.
So far it's merely another failed opportunity for labor to communicate a positive message, in this case one about its inner
workings.

The time is ripe for labor to seize this chance to improve its
image. As Congress finally tackles some of labor's most-
favored legislation, such as the Employee Free Choice Act,
labor's business and political adversaries—and some editorial
pages—have gone on the offensive. One of their key targets is
a provision in the bill that downplays the role of secret-ballot
union elections; they claim this would open the door for labor
"thugs" or "bullies" or "goons" to intimidate workers into
approving the union. Labor has largely missed the boat by
responding in a strictly literal way about the legislative details
and not addressing the broader and highly damaging insinua-
tions about itself, though the story is there waiting to be told.
Labor could show, via the Teamsters and Laborers, that its
foes in the corporate suites and their allies on Capitol Hill are
reviving an outdated and offensive stereotype.

And beyond playing defense, labor should seize the initiative and turn those charges and the images that lie behind
them back on its foes, given the corporate world's many well-
publicized ethical lapses. "Yes, we have had challenges to overcome. And we have come a long way and worked hard in
doing so. Now our freight haulers and flight attendants, our
ditch diggers and hazardous material handlers, and all our

members are active participants in a robust democratic process. We're still learning, but look at the progress we've made. And by the way, thank you for raising the subject of internal governance. Since you brought it up, let's look at what's been occurring these past few years in the corporate suites. How has management been watching out for the welfare and interests of employees, and can you see why a stronger union say on the job is so pressing a matter right now?" The spate of corporate malfeasance, lack of ethics, and outright sticking it to workers over recent years have provided an opening for labor to draw a favorable contrast with its own internal reforms. Here's an opportunity to close the loop with a public that has grown weary of corporate scandals, soaring business profits, startling CEO compensation and golden parachutes, and the yawning gap between wealthy Americans and the rest of America. People are busy; labor could do the work for them of comparing corporate and labor track records and recent trends of the two as regards internal governance. The stark contrast can only help labor's cause.

Addressing this would be particularly important because, while much of the criticism of labor is self-serving, often misleading, and sometimes hypocritical, it is not entirely off the mark. Though the extent of union corruption has often been overstated to make a point,[8] the more general issues of governance, including top-down rule and homogeneity of leadership, have indeed been problematical for a labor movement that has been too white, too male, and too old, for too long. Trumpeting the progress in making leadership more responsive and members more engaged, while acknowledging past and present shortcomings and demonstrating a desire to make further changes, could only serve to improve labor's standing. But that would require labor's leaders and communicators to think bigger than circulating a hackneyed reaction to the most recent unemployment report.

If the significance of the changes in the Teamsters and Laborers is not fully understood, the developments themselves are at least visible, far more so than other events that recently have occurred or that are underway. On the next-to-last morning of the AFSCME's five-day national convention in Chicago in August 2006, the nearly 5,000 delegates were greeted by a strange configuration. Instead of the long tables that had filled the cavernous room the previous three days, they now saw some 500 small round tables. Atop each were a laptop computer and 10 small voting machines, one for every delegate. These were the props for an unprecedented effort to take the pulse of the union's members and set priorities accordingly. To do this, AFSCME had hired a firm that had done post–September 11 polling about redevelopment of the World Trade Center site and also led a national discussion on Social Security. For AFSCME president Gerald McEntee, business as usual clearly no longer sufficed.

In the same windy city, as this chapter was being written in April 2007, Local 150 of the International Union of Operating Engineers (IUOE) was holding its first truly contested election in decades. This is a sprawling local, representing 22,000 workers at construction sites in Chicago, northern Illinois, northern

Indiana, and part of eastern Iowa. The election reflects the union's checkered past and tumultuous nature, with candidates throwing mud at each other, and lawsuits and countersuits already part of the mix. But it's an election nevertheless. "It's turned real personal, very nasty," an official with the International told me, "but the membership's getting involved, for the first time in a long time." And "long time" fits the situation; this campaign was scheduled to run from July 2006 to July 2007, assuming anyone is left standing.

These two entities could scarcely differ more. AFSCME is a huge and powerful white-collar union with 1.4 million public employee members, a progressive and politicized union highly active in AFL-CIO affairs, led by one of labor's most recognizable faces. Local 150, with a somewhat colorful past, is a single local in an international union representing construction workers, historically far more concerned with worksite disputes than politics or any other cause larger than itself, and run by a new leader few know. Yet each in its own way is seeking to connect more with its members, to stir the pot and see what happens.

These are among a potpourri of indications, in locals and in internationals, throughout various parts of the country, both among unions that stayed in the AFL-CIO and those that broke away to form the Change to Win federation, that changes are afoot in the world of labor. They are impossible to quantify, but they run the gamut of internal reform, involving greater grassroots participation or increasingly competitive elections, leaders more willing to engage members, or organizing directed at diverse groups of workers. Here's a snapshot of a few more:

A force known as "Stewards' Army" is shifting to local union members within the Communications Workers of America a number of functions that previously were filled by paid union staffers. Increasingly, they are handling workers' grievances or mapping out the contract issues to be focused on and the negotiating strategies to be deployed. The union aimed to have 50,000 members in its "army" by the summer of 2007. CWA president Larry Cohen is a strong advocate of energizing the rank and file, and he's brought the idea to the AFL-CIO as a whole with a threefold goal—to wage campaigns that will be more effective because they engage members and accurately reflect their views; to reenergize the union; and to "make sure the face of working people is out there in the public."[9] Several Change to Win unions, including SEIU and UNITE HERE, are also involving members far more deeply in workplace representation tasks. So there is much happening to engage rank-and-file membership in unions right now.

UNITE HERE's "hotel workers rising" program has helped get new contracts in hotels around the country by unleashing members to bargain, walk picket lines, and put together rallies. In so doing, the union has spotlighted those very workers it needs to attract and organize because they are the growth sector of the hospitality workforce: particularly women, African-Americans, and Hispanics and, in cities like Chicago, Polish immigrants. It was launched in February 2006 because with 60,000 hotel workers' contracts up over the course of the year—particularly in Boston, Los Angeles, Chicago, and Washington—it seemed advantageous to combine negotiating with the raising of public awareness about hospitality workers' role in the economy. An additional goal, a UNITE HERE official says, was to make people realize that "unions are workers, not bureaucracies."

Most successful union organizing campaigns are now taking place in sectors composed largely of women, minorities, or immigrant workers. Education unions are organizing teachers' aides; Teamsters are scoring gains among food processing workers as well as logistics employees at transport distribution centers; and the UAW is making inroads with auto-parts workers after shifting resources from its strike fund into organizing. SEIU grows by dint of impressive efforts with health-care workers, security guards, and janitors; UNITE HERE is organizing heavily among commercial laundry workers struggling with some of the most perilous safety conditions in any industry. CWA scored a coup with wireless workers. The Laborers have hired a Hispanic woman to lead a national unionization drive in immigrant communities. (You might be asking, "Organizing? I thought unions were losing members because they can't organize, given all the obstacles." What is happening is that the labor movement hasn't been able to add enough new workers to increase or even keep up its percentage of an expanding workforce. And in some years, it can't even replace those workers whose jobs are sent overseas or are moved to right-to-work states in this country, meaning that its absolute numbers drop as well.)

Several building trades unions in the Midwest, including the Chicago Regional Conference of Carpenters and Local 134 of the International Brotherhood of Electrical Workers (IBEW), have set up pre-apprenticeship programs to increase the number of minorities employed in what have traditionally been nearly all-white and male occupations. They have part-nered with the Chicago Interfaith Committee on Worker Issues, which established a 14-week classroom program called "Building Bridges" to train African-Americans and women to enter a union apprenticeship program. The unions provide money, facilities, speakers, tours of the union's apprenticeship schools—and they accept the program's graduates. Chicago's Interfaith-Labor model has been adopted in Kansas City and Albany, New York. In addition, Local 134 has a new program called "Jump Start" that provides disadvantaged youths with free tutoring on subjects required for the trade. In the first year 70 people made it to the apprenticeship stage. Maurice King, whose full-time job is to lead these efforts for Local 134, heads to schools, churches, and community groups to find recruits, rather than sending fliers, because "going out and talking to people, we get a better return on that."[10]

IBEW Local 11, with 8,000 members in Los Angeles County, has been highly successful the past few years with its "minority caucus," which mentors inner-city youngsters and trains them in the algebra and people skills required for the trade. That in turn has helped Local 11 secure multi-billion-dollar contracts from public officials over the next three years for work on airports, water treatment facilities, and schools—opening up further opportunities to bring in members, and thus expand the union.

AFSCME's event in Chicago, which it billed as a "town meeting," represented the largest effort yet by a union to measure the views of its members and the intensity of those ideas while allowing real-time interaction among members and between members and leaders on what the priorities should be. As one union official put it, "We were able to take the pulse of that room on issue after issue." McEntee acknowledges that the "future of AFSCME was hanging in the balance," and the event appears to have gone beyond the rhetorical. One message that came across unambiguously was the desire of members for leadership programs that would train rank-and-file activists to take lead roles in union campaigns. The next edition of the AFSCME magazine carried an item announcing that the union's Leadership Institute was being established. A few months later, the magazine announced the opening of the Leadership Institute in mid-April of 2007, with initial training in four areas: advocating for health-care reform, local union treasurers' training, effective communications (!), and study of AFSCME's strategies to organize and to increase its bargaining and political power.

This, union officials say, was part of a larger process aimed at increasing members' "ownership" of AFSCME so that they will take a greater role in union campaigns of various types, similar to the CWA initiative. The goal is to get 10 to 15 percent of the membership involved in communicating with and mobilizing coworkers for efforts such as "contract action teams" during negotiations. Looking toward the 2008 elections, the union hopes to build a force of 40,000 members to engage in get-out-the-vote activities. The union also plans to "drill deeper" into membership preferences before endorsing a candidate—no doubt a reaction to the political embarrassment of 2004 discussed in the first chapter.

Meanwhile, Operating Engineers Local 150 is evolving in ways that go beyond its competitive election. Talk of social justice, once a foreign concept, is heard among activists, and an aggressive organizing approach that reversed a trend and turned National Labor Relations Board delays against employers, combined with an outreach to minorities through city colleges, has led to a rise in membership.[11] The local recently joined the interfaith program as well. Some of the impetus comes from the international union's president, Vincent Giblin, who over his two years in office has instituted several initiatives to spark members' involvement, programs that have, as one union insider puts it, "dramatically changed the face of this organization, though it's still a work in progress."

Why are these myriad shifts occurring across a range of industries, locations, and types of unions, and what do they signify? A key point about the changes—whose common feature is that they aim to pump up members' participation—is that they do not result from any grand scheme or strategic decision by labor as a whole. Rather, each is the product of a practical imperative, as a local here or an international there, seeking to survive the mounting challenges discussed throughout this book, takes whatever steps to strengthen the union it deems promising. Something that works is then adopted more widely within the union or even emulated elsewhere within the labor movement. In a sense, the actions have been forced on unions by a hostile environment and by the institutional weaknesses that are combining to push labor down. But once the process is started, these initiatives are likely to take on a dynamic of their own that stands to change labor in ways as yet unforeseen.[12]

I raised these issues with three highly respected labor scholars, based in different parts of the country yet all possessing broad overviews: Kate Bronfenbrenner of Cornell University, Robert Bruno of the University of Illinois, and Harley Shaiken of the University of California at Berkeley. Their analyses as to the impetus for the shifts were strikingly compatible with each other, though what the changes will mean for the future of the labor movement appears to be more open to question.

With unions facing difficulties on so many fronts, Bronfenbrenner says, they increasingly have no alternative but to try something new, even if it means shaking up union structures and approaches long in place. Employers have become so aggressive that it takes exceptional labor campaigns to organize or secure good contracts, and that is nearly impossible to achieve without enthusiastic rank-and-file involvement. What many union leaders have yet to grasp, she says, is the potential this grassroots involvement has to eventually change the union as a whole because it sets in motion expectations that will continue beyond the life of a specific campaign. Newly engaged members will not quietly shrink back into passivity once a program is completed or goal achieved.

"So the unions that are growing and winning are doing this, are making their members into activists, into leaders," she says. "If they empower their members as part of an organizing or bargaining campaign, you can't just turn that off when it comes to making decisions about political action, or who's going to be an officer—the major decisions about the local."

Pushing in the same direction is the nature of the new workers being organized, many of them women, minorities, or young workers, as a result of the targeting of campaigns toward service industries and vulnerable workforces most in need of improved safety and pay and of labor's overall protection.

"They're coming in as activists, people used to a seat at the table, so they're planning to change the union," Bronfenbrenner says. "They're not going to sit back and let an older leadership keep them in their place. These new workers are going to change the unions. I don't think the unions recognize it yet. Women of color are being organized more than any other group, and they're coming in fighting. They're not up in the leadership ranks yet, and they're going to be fighting for a say. They're more likely to file grievances, more likely to go out on strike, more likely to speak out."

Because the reforms result more from a patchwork of decisions made in response to concrete needs and situations than from policy decisions issued from above or demands from members, they are starting to take on a life of their own that is beyond anyone's control, Bruno says, and he continues:

It's almost getting at union democracy from the side. It's not being demanded from the bottom up, or imposed from the top by reform leaders. There are more locals with minority leaders, more organizing campaigns made up of rank-and-file workers, more coalitions being built with community organizations. This is creating a push to open up the leadership to new voices, new faces, to have a much more interactive process between the rank-and-file and the leadership. If you're going to reach out to all these non-traditional members and community partners, you can't bring them in and not share power with them. It's not so much agitation from the rank-and-file expressing dissatisfaction, not so much the government threatening lawsuits, or from enlightened leaders, as an outside movement coming into the union—and that's because the labor movement is in dire straits and has to reach out. Labor is finding itself working with groups that are different from it—different color, different gender, different nationalities—and these groups are going to compel the unions to share power with them, to be more transparent.

Though the issues of corruption and Mob influence have been favored topics in the media, especially among conservative outlets hostile to labor,[13] cleansing unions of organized crime or crooked officials is actually a minor part of the process of internal reform. According to Bruno,

It's about giving members ownership in the union, not about getting away from the Mob. It's about members speaking and fighting for themselves. It's trust in the members that they know how to fix their workplaces, that they know what legislation they need, that they know what candidates they should be endorsing. It's trusting in and expecting your members to solve the problems of the workplace, to speak for themselves, to contribute to the direction and the policy-making of the union.

The United Steel Workers of America (USWA), no longer his father's union, is a dramatic example of a process of change that took on its own momentum, Bruno says. Historically it has been a clean and well-run union, albeit one with a highly centralized structure and a top-down leadership style. That model worked well as long as the steel industry was flourishing; the union was large and powerful; and labor, management, and government worked together. But once the industry found itself buffeted by trade and the import of cheap steel, plants shuttered, and the union shrinking, a more aggressive approach was needed. The union reexamined its relations with members and how contracts were negotiated, and it soon began educating steelworkers on such issues as trade, the price of steel, and the manner in which the companies were managed. Various action groups were set up, including Women of Steel, Rapid Response, and one involving Hispanics. According to Bruno,

It's a union that transformed itself. They actually turned their rank-and-file into people who could speak to the policy of the union, who could speak for the union, who could go to Washington and speak at rallies, write letters to the editor, hold organizing campaigns. It really mobilized rank-and-file members in ways that were impressive. They set up tent cities wherever steel companies were. They wrote 200,000 letters opposing dumping of imported steel and got President Bush to temporarily place a tariff on certain kinds of imported steel. He did that for a union that had campaigned against him; it was about the only thing he did for labor.

That heightened participation came full cycle in steelworker elections in the summer of 2006, when energized members, concerned about the conditions in the industry and about recent contracts, turned their enhanced knowledge and activism inward as they swept about one-third of their own leaders from office in balloting at their locals.[14]

If there is agreement on the genesis of the changes and their impact thus far, there is more uncertainty about how this will play out and what it ultimately augurs for labor's future. That stems in part from the fact that while rank-and-file involvement and the organizing of workers with an activist bent spark more democracy, two countervailing forces are tugging in the opposite direction. One is that some locals are getting much bigger and covering larger geographic areas because of mergers or consolidations within unions or even across industries, especially as falling numbers and diminished resources demand efficiencies. That saves strapped unions money by avoiding duplication, helps centralize operations, and allows for more efficient coordination, but it also distances rank-and-file members from the leadership, making it harder for them to have a voice in the local. The carpenters union, for instance, has achieved gains in organizing and contracts in part by restructuring and centralizing its efforts in regional groupings, which appears to involve a trade-off in terms of local autonomy. In a few instances, such as with SEIU, organizing success is having the same effect of creating much larger local units.

The other trend is that the crisis faced by labor leaves some in the union movement wondering whether they can afford to worry about concepts like internal democracy or grassroots participation right now. "Unions feel like they're in a state of war with employers shooting at them, and they say, 'We don't really have time for democracy; we're under attack.' The question is whether there's time for the niceties of democracy when you're under attack," Bronfenbrenner says. "I would argue that there is no better time, because you need members who are engaged."

It would seem that how far union reforms go ultimately depends in large measure on which set of factors prevails. If the forces of openness and rank-and-file involvement continue apace and expand to other unions, they have the potential to transform the labor movement.

But democratic changes and internal reform shouldn't be seen as a silver bullet with the power to save labor by themselves, Shaiken cautions, and he continues:

> I think it matters, but I don't think it's defining. The forces that have so undermined labor have largely been from without, whether it's globalization, aggressive domestic employers, a hostile government, and unfriendly labor laws. That said, some of the problems have been self-inflicted—being tardy to emphasize organizing, a failure to inspire members—but they have not been the defining factors in labor's decline. I think we are seeing a more democratic and responsive labor movement, but the outside factors are ferocious.
>
> I do not say all unions get it equally, but in a broad sense there is an understanding that this is a critical moment, and that some bold, visionary approaches need to be tried. What's fascinating here is I think we can see much of the future of labor here today. The question is can you replicate it, can you expand it?

Bruno looks at the various developments in the way that unions are being run and are conducting their business and sees a picture only slowly coming into focus:

Unions are redesigning and redefining what it is to be a labor union in the 21st century. It's still in its infancy stage. It varies from one union to the next. The message is getting out that conditions are very severe; you can't keep your head in the sand. I think labor is seeing a new moment in time, and there is a lot of activity around, 'Whom do we represent, how do we represent them, how do we structure our organizations? Whose job is it to do what, to handle grievances, organizing, run strategic campaigns? What should our executive boards look like?' There are lots of new things happening. It's measurable, it's significant, but I wouldn't say it has reached critical mass yet.

It hasn't, and that is among the factors that imbue labor's future with much uncertainty and some promise. And while it's true that the forces confronting labor are powerful and unrelenting—whether they are employers or global economic trends—the power of those forces is precisely why it's critical that unions be run effectively and that they mobilize their members in every way possible. It's equally true that these various reform efforts are uneven and their fate uncertain, but that's why unions should seize the initiative to push for internal changes that promote transparency and member participation. What they should not do is use the excuse of being "embattled" to push aside some of the very changes necessary to succeed in that battle, nor should they sacrifice democracy for what on paper looks like more efficient management via centralization—not when we've seen what grassroots participation can do to produce truly effective union activities. The labor movement won't be turned around solely by more democratic and dynamic unions, but if developments on this front could mesh with advances in the areas of communications, politics, and values, then labor may indeed have a fighting chance.

CHAPTER 7

WHAT IT MEANS
FOR THE FUTURE

The struggles of the catfish workers, the coal miners, and the nurses are our struggles as well because they touch our lives in ways both direct and subtle. The gutsy women of Delta Pride and the hardened men of Appalachia evoke moral questions about who we are as a people. Will all workers, whichever occupation they practice and in whatever setting, be afforded a measure of dignity on the job? And if their dilemmas are more intractable because they're linked to past discrimination or current attitudes, will we allow that to stand? Do we care about the safety of people who climb underground every day to meet the nation's energy needs, and will we insist that hard-won statutes enacted to protect workers be enforced?

Campaigns being waged by nurses bear upon us in more practical ways, with these workers willing to confront an increasingly profit-driven medical industry so that they can provide better care for their patients. Every American is potentially affected by the efforts of nurses in New Jersey and Nevada, in California and Chicago, and elsewhere, even though few seem to notice. They're fighting on three fronts: battling collectively to restore hospital staffing levels; advocating individually for the specific needs of their patients; and going against the grain by organizing in ever-greater numbers because they need the safety of a union as they challenge their employers.

A union: that's the common thread here. In untold actions undertaken by or against workers every year across the country, the strength or weakness of the union, indeed the presence or absence of a union, is a critical factor. The nurses know they can't protect their patients, let alone protect their own jobs, without the cohesion and the clout that comes from being unionized, something the government has now made even harder to achieve. Rarely are their drives motivated by a quest for more money or better benefits. Instead, they're spurred by a desire to provide more resources for their patients, made necessary in large measure by the failure of our government to provide a national health plan that reduces the profit motive. The catfish workers prevailed against overwhelming odds first because they found the collective courage to challenge wealthy men who held all the economic, political, social, and legal cards and then because their union marshaled the unique attributes they did possess. The coal miners perished, and continue to risk their lives in part because one mine after another has slipped from their union's control, because they have lacked the strength to demand rigorous federal oversight, and because they have been unable to raise a fraction of the public outrage a shock jock's utterances can instantly produce.

The fate of America's labor movement is a matter larger than workplace struggles and more profound than the outcome of any particular issue such as pensions or health care, as important as those are. It is one that goes to political matters of voice, representation, and control, and to socioeconomic questions about what type of society we will become in terms of mobility, equality, and the sharing of power. The widening gap between the very wealthy and that growing segment of the population that essentially lives from paycheck to paycheck, one catastrophe away from losing everything, amid a spike in bankruptcies and foreclosures, has broader implications that spill over into politics. In a society like ours, where influence is tightly linked to money, concentration of wealth translates into a skewing of the political arena, and it does so in a self-perpetuating way. Those adversely affected by economic changes lose their ability to influence the very policies that promote the trends.

What's happening to unions says much about what's happening to the middle class. For decades after World War II, when unions were robust partners with management and government, wages and productivity rose in tandem, leading to an expanding middle class. Unions weren't uniquely responsible for the gains that workers made, but they played an indispensable role. Collective bargaining gains set standards that reverberated well beyond union ranks. As labor declined during the past quarter century, the normal push and tug of the industrial relations system slowly ground to a halt, and much has changed as a result. Productivity is now rising much faster than wages, which helps explain why profits constitute a near-record share of national income, with salaries at their lowest point.[1] A powerful labor movement that once moved workers into the middle class is now powerless to prevent people from falling out of it.

Emboldened corporate interests have turned their attention to the remaining sectors of employment—white collar, technical, services—and a beleaguered middle class is surprised it's getting squeezed. Information technology jobs are being sent abroad, engineers are training their own replacements, and it's all made so much easier by the emasculation of those once-troublesome labor unions. Because no one stood up when they came for the unions and union jobs and much of the manufacturing sector, the middle class finds itself more vulnerable as its jobs and economic well-being are becoming the next logical targets.

Make no mistake; these trends will only intensify if unions continue to decline. Nearly two centuries ago, de Tocqueville described the civic groups that serve as intermediaries between citizens and leaders as the special genius of the young American nation because they promote involvement of average people in public life.[2] Abolishing such groups is the first goal of totalitarian rulers who seek the "atomizing" of society, meaning that nothing stands between the ruling elite and the isolated individual.[3] That abets control and direction from above, encourages passivity and obedience below, and reduces the prospect of rebellion. We are heading in that direction in the sphere of jobs and the economy, albeit without the nefarious intent. Capital is becoming more mobile across national borders, and employers gain, via trade pacts and technological advances, greater ease in moving production and some service jobs wherever is most convenient. And as their collective voice disintegrates, American workers find themselves less able to stand up for themselves. Indeed, an unstated aspect of the "ownership society" and the privatization that underlies it is the transformation of the workforce into so many individual contractors, each fending for himself or herself. The resulting loss of influence over one's own situation is as central as falling real wages or jeopardized pensions in explaining why so many people express mounting frustration with the present and pessimism about the future.

Think about it for a moment, setting aside ideological orientation, just from a practical perspective: absent a revitalized labor movement, who will speak up for hourly workers or salaried employees? Who will meld their voices into a collective entity able to deal with their employers? Where will they turn, and if they have nowhere to turn, will that make our society more or less just, more or less democratic? The economic forces arrayed against average people are growing more powerful and less accountable, more distant and more impersonal, meaning imbalances in terms of affluence and influence will grow. Everyone who works for a living—whether they belong to a union or not—will feel the ramifications if labor can't make a comeback.

Can it? The struggle is uphill, but there are hopeful signs. First, there are some propitious developments amid the gloom. Though the congressional campaign of 2006 represented a missed opportunity for labor to alter the national discussion, the election results reflected underlying shifts in attitudes that could prove significant. There was a sense among voters that the pendulum has swung too far from the average person,[4] accompanied by a rise in the share of workers wanting to join a union.[5] Even as unionization rates tumbled over the past decade, insecurity has spurred more than one-half of workers to now say they'd like a union, up from one-third 10 years ago. But labor's window to take advantage of those attitudes may be limited, assuming unions endure, because at some point not too far off, it may be too weak to mount a recovery.

Second, unions are engaging in several activities that could help turn the tide. Among them is Working America, an AFL-CIO creation that in three years has enlisted 1.6 million members who have no workplace union to join but want to fight for good jobs and a just economy. They're recruited by door-to-door campaigns conducted strategically enough that two of every three people approached end up joining.[6] Intriguingly, the states they are concentrated in—Ohio, Pennsylvania, Minnesota, Missouri, Oregon, and Florida—are swing states that have seen value-oriented campaigns waged to labor's detriment. That suggests the potential of this group. Speaking of Ohio, it was something of an exception to labor's failure to make its issues part of the last campaign's discussion. Trade, wages, and economic justice were front and center in several key races there in 2006, a promising development for labor because of the state's political importance and because Ohio could serve as a model for other swing states full of blue-collar conservatives. Cleveland AFL-CIO President John Ryan, who ran Sherrod Brown's successful Senate campaign, says a confluence of factors contributed. He cites the presence in four races of unabashedly pro-labor candidates who raised those issues, a receptive electorate in light of job loss, GOP scandals that have rocked Ohio, and the wage-hike ballot item. Consultants helped the campaigns reach out to religious voters on such issues as minimum wage and health care, Ryan says. Asked whether that might be the start of a labor offensive on values, as opposed to merely seeking to avoid getting hammered over cultural values, Ryan was enthusiastic. "It's really hard to score when you're only playing defense," he said, as a former basketball coach. "You need to play defense at times, but you also need to grab that ball and put points up on the scoreboard."[7]

Meanwhile, the AFL-CIO received a boost on March 9, 2007, when it reached an accord about joining forces with the independent California Nurses Association (CNA), one of labor's success stories after organizing 75,000 nurses around the country. That boosts to 325,000 the number of nurses in AFL-CIO affiliates. CNA agreed just two days after the AFL-CIO endorsed a single-payer health-care plan, which positions the federation to highlight the need for a national health-care policy, critical since most contract disputes now revolve around medical coverage and workers' payments. It's also an issue with enormous capacity to resonate with the general public. If labor can effectively raise the subject and bring nurses into the equation, this could prove a powerful set of issues.[8] Even in the area of communications, there are early signs of more nimbleness and creativity among AFL-CIO unions, perhaps in response to the challenge posed by Change to Win. And the still simmering if less visible debates over labor's direction have, in some cases, translated into action. The room that SEIU and UNITE HERE have had to focus on organizing, for instance, has led to creative approaches. These unions argue that as manufacturing vanishes, jobs in the growing service sector could provide fertile territory for labor, which could transform them into good-paying jobs that would sustain unions, just as was done with manufacturing jobs a half-century ago. If the fruits of such efforts are shared, then for all its problems, the split may bring some benefits to labor's long-term prospects.

If the labor movement does revitalize itself, it won't be because its leaders have discovered a magic formula or because the officials in Change to Win prove themselves smarter than those in the AFL-CIO, or vice versa. It will be because unions, having strengthened themselves internally and having honed their skills, are able to take advantage of promising trends and developments. It will be because labor is out telling its story in a way that captures imagination, evokes a sense of mission and achievement, and makes clear why a robust union movement is not only relevant but in the public interest. It will be because unions, having decided that democratization is not a luxury but a matter of survival, have reformed themselves in ways that unleash the energy of their members. It will be because political strategies have been crafted to fit the situation at hand, including the traits of the rank-and-file members, not lifted from a dusty shelf. It will be because labor's values—powerful and mainstream as they are—and the public policies that support those values, have been made to resonate throughout the country by local workers every day and twice daily during elections. And most of all, it will be because the needs that gave rise to the labor movement a century ago still exist, as does the idealism that brought it to life—and labor is tapping into that reservoir.

If more young people like Rachel Yanda, the former Sarah Lawrence student now with SEIU in New York, are able to make their careers in a thriving labor movement in the years ahead, the country stands to benefit. For all labor's woes, I have seen what it can do to bring decent wages and a voice to workers who otherwise would have neither. Three years on, I've heard Iowa firefighters, still incredulous that novices like themselves were able to influence national politics, talk eagerly of waiting for the next round to begin. I've seen the women of Delta Pride try to win respect on the job and end up altering the social fabric of their region, gains that have stood the test of time. In the end, unions aren't their leaders, the proclamations they issue, or their imposing headquarters; they're the nurses in Utah, the bakery workers in Ohio, the metalworkers in Mississippi seeking to improve the places where they spend most of their days. On the flip side, I've seen society's increasing polarization in terms of wealth and influence as labor has faltered. And I've seen the wins of the past, struggles over safety, overtime pay, and other matters result in statutes that are now, ironically, used by many to say that labor's time has come and gone. At the same time, these statutes are increasingly ignored as companies cut costs and enforcement agencies look away. This will continue unless some balance is restored. It is equally clear that the factors that imperil labor are precisely what make its resurgence so necessary.

Now I see a presidential election approaching that will dwarf all others in terms of cost, meaning that big money will play a dominant role. I see the issue of immigration looming as a defining issue in this election and as one that will be grappled with for years to come. Virtually all those who have entered this debate have done so on behalf of a particular interest, fueling the intense discord. Conservatives seek to enforce the laws, business groups want an inexpensive and malleable supply of workers, politicians aim for ethnic votes, and national security groups clamor for beefed-up border security. The labor movement occupies a rather lonely perch, by having a broad perspective on the matter and working for policies that take all factors into account. This is due less to any innate goodness on its part than to the fact that its self-interest involves representing American workers and their jobs and wages, while also protecting immigrant workers from exploitation. This symbolizes one of the key functions unions have filled over the last century: uniting people in common struggles across racial and ethnic divides, enabling them to pursue the American Dream, and helping them enter the middle class.

Labor has absolutely no monopoly on truth or virtue on these or any issues, but it represents a constituency that, as much as ever, needs its voice to be heard, whether on the job or in national debates over politics and values. In a time of increasing disenfranchisement of average people, of growing gulfs between the haves and have-nots, labor's most important role may be to serve as a vehicle for the voices of people who are being drowned out. I hope that unions manage to refashion themselves in ways equal to the tasks before them so the American labor movement can survive and continue its work, only more effectively. I do so fully aware of the personal consequences—that Jim Hoffa's vigilant and protective sister will stay on my case, watching everything I miss.

NOTES

Introduction

1. Labor's share of the workforce has fallen from its high of one-third between 1947 and 1953 to its present level of 12.5 percent. The private sector drop is even sharper, from 35 percent in 1953 to less than 8 percent today. Sources: Bureau of Labor Statistics; Richard Hurd, professor and former director of labor studies at Cornell University's School of Industrial and Labor Relations; and the American Federation of Labor and Congress of Industrial Organizations (AFL-CIO) research department.

2. Ezio Tarentelli, *Economia Politica Del Lavoro*, UTET, 1986. By the same author, *Salario, Inflazione E Relazioni Industriali in Europea*, Marsilio editori, 1984. Former professor of comparative industrial relations at MIT's Sloan School of Management.

3. Workplace fatalities rose in 2004 for the first time since 1994, according to the federal Bureau of Labor Statistics (BLS). There is a significant lag in compiling these voluminous figures. In April 2007 the BLS released final results for 2005, showing a slight drop in fatalities from the previous year, back to the level of 2003. Worrisome, however, were the rises for 2005 in fatalities among several worker groups that are increasing in size, including Hispanic workers, foreign born, and young workers. The 5,734 worker fatalities in 2005 do not include deaths from occupational diseases, which may be as high as 60,000 annually, according to the AFL-CIO Safety and Health Department. Given current staffing levels at the Occupational Safety and Health Administration (OSHA), it would take the federal agency more than 100 years to inspect all U.S. workplaces. Fatalities have declined substantially since OSHA was created in 1970, most dramatically in the early- to mid-1990s, but critics complain that funding cuts and weaker regulatory and enforcement activity have curtailed the trend toward safer workplaces during this decade.

4. In 1999 OSHA proposed a rule that employers pay for "personal protective equipment" such as face shields, gloves, or lifelines for 20 million workers, but it failed to implement it. After the suit, the administration agreed on March 16, 2007, to issue a "final rule" by November. The United Food and Commercial Workers (UFCW) President Joe Hansen said that by "OSHA's own estimates, 400,000 workers have been injured and 50 have died while the rule has been in limbo," referring to workers in affected industries.

5. The share of the national income that went to wages and salaries in 2006 was 51.6 percent in 2006, lowest on record, with profits of 13.8 percent the highest recorded; figures from the Center on Budget and Policy Priorities, citing Commerce Department data. Also, see Economic Policy Institute (www.epi.org). These figures tend to fluctuate, making comparisons over time difficult, but the trends are steady.

6. Within a few months of its founding, United Professionals had 7,000 members or affiliate members. Interview in April 2007 with its board chairman, R. William Holland, author of the book *Are There Any Good Jobs Left? Career Management in the Age of the Disposable Worker* (Westport, Conn.: Praeger/Greenwood Publishing Group, 2006).

7. The income of the richest 1 percent of Americans is now 22 percent of the entire national income, the highest since 1929. Interview in April 2007 with Jared Bernstein, director of the Living Standards program at the Economic Policy Institute (EPI), an author of *The State of Working America* published by EPI, and a former deputy chief economist for the Department of Labor.

8. Interview in April 2007 with Theodore St. Antoine, who is also a past president of the National Academy of Arbitrators.

9. National Labor Relations Board (NLRB) decisions awarding back pay to workers wrongly fired or disciplined by their employers, usually for seeking to form a union, stood at a few hundred employees annually in the 1950s. That figure rose to 6,000 a year in the late 1960s, soared to about 20,000 annually starting in the early 1990s, and now stands at more than 30,000 a year.

10. Figures from the Bureau of Labor Statistics, which is part of the Labor Department, show a decline of 3.4 million manufacturing jobs over that period.

Chapter One

1. I interviewed Harold Schaitberger numerous times over the course of 2004 and thereafter, and I spoke to dozens of rank-and-file firefighters, IAFF officials, and retired officers throughout the 2004 election season. I interviewed Rick Kleinman, John TeKippe, and Bill Post several times in January, February, and March 2004 and again in April 2007.

2. Interview in September 2006 with Tom Vilsack.
3. Interview in February 2004 with Senator John Kerry.
4. Interview in February 2004 with Gerald McEntee.
5. Interview in January 2004 with Jim Spellane.

Chapter Two

1. I interviewed dozens of workers, farmers, ministers, town officials, and union leaders involved in the dispute several times each throughout the fall and winter of 1990, and I spoke again to several in the early months of 2007.
2. Jeff Fiedler told me in June 2007 that the key here was not whether bankers or other business leaders actually signed the pledge, but rather the fact of putting them on notice that their actions were being observed, which "got a lot of people to back off" of engaging in reprisals against the workers.
3. Interviews with the various supermarket executives in St. Louis in the fall of 1990.
4. Unbeknownst to the firm, the union was also quietly negotiating with B.B. King to return to Indianola for a major concert and rally on behalf of the strikers if need be, Neel Lattimore told me in an interview in April 2007.
5. Interview with Sarah White in February 2007.
6. A report in May 2007 by MSHA, which pointed to lightning as the likely cause of the Sago incident, has done little to quell the debate over issues of safety and risk. The miners' union and the miners' families reject the theory that lightning was to blame, and add that even if it was, questions of federal oversight as well as safety practices, training, and equipment, both before the explosion and during the rescue operation remain unsettled.
7. Interview in February 2007 with UMWA spokesman Phil Smith.
8. Records of the United Mine Workers of America.
9. The convoluted nomination process for Richard Stickler notwithstanding, he has surprised some industry observers by overseeing more enforcement than they expected, with individual inspectors seemingly intent on averting another tragedy on their watch.

Chapter Three

1. Interview in October 2004 with Harry McCree.
2. Thomas Frank, *What's the Matter with Kansas: How Conservatives Won the Heart of America* (New York: Metropolitan Books, 2004).
3. David Sirota, *Hostile Takeover: How Big Money and Corruption Conquered Our Government—and How We Can Take It Back* (New York: Crown Publishers, 2006).
4. Poll by Peter D. Hart and Associates, November 2006.
5. Senator Chuck Schumer, *Positively American: Winning Back the Middle-Class Majority One Family at a Time* (New York: St. Martin's Press, 2007).

6. Figures from Economic Policy Institute.
7. Tyndall Report Web site (tyndallreport.com); interview in January 2007 with Andrew Tyndall.
8. Interviews with economists and statisticians from pro- and anti-labor groups, as well as with the NLRB, in June 2007.
9. Interview with Robert Shaffer in January 2007.
10. Human Rights Watch (HRW) also found a "systematic abuse of workers' right to organize and bargain collectively in the United States." Study in August 2000: *Unfair Advantage: Workers' Freedom of Association in the United States under International Human Rights Standards.* The group's January 2005 report *Blood, Sweat and Fear: Workers' Rights in U.S. Meat and Poultry Plants* focused largely on workers' rights in the meat and poultry industry and found that little had changed.
11. Again, anti-union groups question polls that produce such findings, saying they are done in ways that encourage a positive response by those questioned. They cite surveys showing a lower level of interest in joining a union among workers. Even their smaller percentage of 12 percent, however, would mean that about 18 million workers would "definitely" join a union if given an opportunity and millions of others would consider doing so.

Chapter Four

1. Labor at the Crossroads, at the City University of New York, was sponsored by the Queens College Labor Resource Center and the *New Labor Forum*, a periodical.
2. International Labor Communications Association (ILCA) Conference, Washington, D.C., November 12, 2004.
3. Separate interviews in March 2007 with Mark Dudzic and Rachel Yanda.
4. Gerald McEntee, president, American Federation of State, County and Municipal Employees (AFSCME), "Labor's Main Challenge: Increasing Political Power for Working Families" (Washington, D.C.: Position paper, AFSCME, 2005).
5. Author A. Sloane, Hoffa. (Cambridge, Mass.: MIT Press, 1992).
6. The year was 2003 and union membership had fallen from 15,978,000 to 15,776,000, according to the AFL-CIO Organizing Department.
7. Interview in August 2006 with Gerald McEntee.

Chapter Five

1. Interviews in 1992 with Joe Rauh, who served as the UAW's general counsel from the 1940s to the 1980s and who worked closely with UAW founders Walter Reuther and his brothers and coworkers Victor and Roy Reuther, to help shape the union. (Rauh also was the attorney for the Mississippi Freedom Democratic Party at the Democratic convention in 1964, co-chaired by Aaron Henry, a key supporter of the Mississippi cat-

fish workers discussed in Chapter 2.) Also based on multiple interviews over 15 years with Victor Reuther.

2. I've addressed conferences or sessions of labor communicators in Illinois, Missouri, Washington, D.C., and elsewhere, and I've asked them about their problems with the media. The responses invariably follow the same pattern. An announcement about a union event didn't get on the local radio station, a union colleague had a similar problem with the newspaper, the international union ran a story in its monthly publication about media bias and voilà—it made no sense to waste any more time on such efforts.

3. Interview in 1999 with Jeff Weiss.

4. Since its study *Lost in the Margins: Labor and the Media* in 1990, the New York–based group Fairness and Accuracy in Reporting (FAIR) has regularly issued reports aimed at chronicling the extent to which unions and their activities are ignored, downplayed, or inaccurately reported by the media.

5. William J. Puette, *Through Jaundiced Eyes: How the Media View Organized Labor* (Ithaca, N.Y.: ILR Press, Cornell University, 1992). See also Christopher R. Martin, *Framed!: Labor and the Corporate Media* (Ithaca, N.Y.: Cornell University Press, 2004).

6. Philip Dine, "A Unionist Cold Warriors Should Mourn," *Wall Street Journal*, March 13, 1997, p. A14.

Chapter Six

1. Barbara Harvey, "Teamster Elections: Inspiration from the Ground Up," *Union Democracy Review*, published by the Association for Union Democracy (issue no. 165), November/December 2006, p. 1.

2. Robert Fitch, *Solidarity for Sale: How Corruption Destroyed the Labor Movement and Undermined America's Promise* (New York: PublicAffairs/Perseus Book Group, 2006).

3. Stier, Anderson & Mallone, L.L.C., *The Teamsters: Perception and Reality; An Investigative Study of Organized Crime Influence in the Union* (Washington, D.C., 2002).

4. Interview in June 1991 with Steve Kindred.

5. In a June 1991 interview, Susan Jennick, then director of the AUD, told me: "I think Camarata's presence at the 1976 convention was the beginning of the rank-and-file movement" in the IBT.

6. Robert Bruno, *Reforming the Chicago Teamsters: The Story of Local 705* (DeKalb: Northern Illinois University Press, 2003).

7. Some of the best discussions on democracy in unions take place in the publications and on the Web site of the Association for Union Democracy.

8. Most unions have sterling records of clean governance without corruption, including manufacturing unions such as the UAW and the various public employees' and teachers' unions.

9. Interview in April 2007 with CWA spokeswoman Candice Johnson.

10. Interview in March 2007 with Maurice King, community relations coordinator for IBEW Local 134.
11. Interview in March 2007 with James Sweeney of the International Union of Operating Engineers Local 150.
12. Interviews in March 2007 with academic labor experts Robert Bruno, Kate Bronfenbrenner, and Harley Shaiken.
13. Few media outlets do this with more creativity and fervor than the *Washington Times*.
14. USWA officials, interviewed in June 2007, said that electoral turnover is not unusual in their union, given their membership's level of activity and demographics, including many veteran workers with considerable time invested in the union.

Chapter Seven

1. As noted earlier, comparisons over time on the national income share of profits versus wages are innately difficult, but figures are near or at record highs. And, according to the Economic Policy Institute, productivity has been rising at least four times as fast as wages. Harley Shaiken of the University of California makes this observation: "The genius of the American system was linking rising wages to rising productivity. The link was the labor movement."
2. Alexis de Tocqueville's seminal work, *Democracy in America*, was published in two volumes, in 1835 and 1840. It was republished by the University of Chicago Press in 2000 and 2002 and by the Library of America in 2004.
3. Hannah Arendt, *The Origins of Totalitarianism* (New York: Harcourt, 1951).
4. Economic Policy Institute (EPI) forum, February 22, 2007, in Washington, D.C. Paper delivered by Thomas Kochan, professor of management at the Massachusetts Institute of Technology and codirector of MIT's Institute for Work and Employment Research, and Beth Shulman, author. "Now," they wrote, "as rising income inequality and the failure of wages to move with productivity are being noticed, America is beginning to recognize the economic and social costs of a severely weakened labor movement."
5. Richard B. Freeman, Harvard University economics professor and director of the Labor Studies program at the national Bureau of Economic Research, Washington, D.C. Paper, "Do Workers Still Want Unions? More Than Ever," February 2007.
6. Interview in April 2007 with Working America's executive director, Karen Nussbaum.
7. Interview in April 2007 with John Ryan. In the summer of 2007, Ryan was selected as state director for Senator Sherrod Brown, Democrat of Ohio.
8. The affiliation of the California Nurses Association with the AFL-CIO was completed on May 21, 2007.

BIBLIOGRAPHY

AFL-CIO. Executive Council meeting, Bal Harbour, Fla., February 1989; National Convention,Washington, D.C., November 1989.

American Federation of Labor and Congress of Industrial Organizations (AFL-CIO). Report, *Death on the Job: The Toll of Neglect—The State of Workers' Safety and Health*, 2006.

Association for Union Democracy. *Union Democracy Review*. New York, bimonthly publication.

Bernstein, Aaron. *Grounded: Frank Lorenzo and the Destruction of Eastern Airlines*. New York: Simon and Schuster, 1990.

Bernstein, Jared. *The State of Working America*. Washington, D.C.: Economic Policy Institute (EPI), annual publication.

Bronfenbrenner, Kate (editor), Sheldon Friedman (editor), Richard W. Hurd (editor), Rudolph A. Oswald (editor), and Ronald L. Seeber (editor). *Organizing to Win: New Research on Union Strategies*. Ithaca, N.Y.: ILR Press/Cornell University Press, 1998.

Bruno, Robert. "Presidential Labor Regimes: Democrats from Roosevelt to Clinton." Paper presented at the Industrial Relations Research Association, Chicago,1998.

———. *Steelworker Alley: How Class Works in Youngstown*. Ithaca, N.Y.: Cornell University Press, 1999.

———. *Reforming the Chicago Teamsters: The Story of Local 705*. DeKalb: Northern Illinois University Press, 2003.

———. "USWA-Bargained and State-Oriented Responses to the Recurrent Steel Crisis." *Labor Studies Journal*, vol. 30 (no. 1), 2004, pp. 67–91.

Change to Win. The American Dream for America's Worker, a federation of unions, founding convention. St. Louis, Mo., September 2005.

Change to Win. *The American Dream for America's Workers*. Report. Washington D.C., April 2007.

Clay, William L. *Just Permanent Interests: Black Americans in Congress*, 1870–1991. New York: Amistad Press, 1992.

Deutsche Gewerkshaftsbund, Confédération Générale du Travail, Force Ouvrière, Confédération Française Démocratique du Travail, Confederation Française des Travailleurs Chretiens. Dissertation research in Germany and France on comparative labor movements, 1976–1978.

Dickmeyer, Elisabeth Reuther. *Reuther: A Daughter Strikes*. Southfield, Mich.: Spelman Publisher's Division, 1989.

Dunlop, John T. *Industrial Relations Systems*. Holt, 1958.

———. *Dispute Resolution: Negotiation and Consensus Building*. Auburn House, 1984.

Dunlop, John T., and Galenson, Walter. *Labor in the Twentieth Century*. New York: Academic Press, 1978.

Fairness and Accuracy in Reporting (FAIR). *Lost in the Margins: Labor and the Media*. Report. New York: FAIR, 1990. See also subsequent media studies by FAIR.

Feldman, Richard, and Michael Betzold. *End of the Line: Autoworkers and the American Dream*. New York: Weidenfeld & Nicolson, 1988.

Fitch, Robert. *Solidarity for Sale: How Corruption Destroyed the Labor Movement and Undermined America's Promise*. New York: PublicAffairs/Perseus Book Group, 2006.

Franco, Joseph. *Hoffa's Man: The Rise and Fall of Jimmy Hoffa as Witnessed by His Strongest Arm*. New York: Prentice Hall, 1987.

Frank, Thomas. *What's the Matter with Kansas? How Conservatives Won the Heart of America*. New York: Metropolitan Books, 2004.

Fraser, Steven. *Labor Will Rule: Sidney Hillman and the Rise of American Labor*. New York: Free Press, 1991.

Friedman, Allen, and Ted Schwarz. *Power and Greed: Inside the Teamsters Empire of Corruption*. New York: Franklin Watts, 1989.

Galenson, Walter. *The World's Strongest Trade Unions: The Scandinavian Labor Movement*. Westport, Conn.: Quorum Books/Greenwood Publishing Group, 1998.

Getman, Julius. *The Betrayal of Local 14: Paper Workers, Politics & Permanent Replacements*. Ithaca, N.Y.: ILR Press/Cornell University Press, 1998.

Geoghegan, Thomas. *Which Side Are You On? Trying to Be for Labor When It's Flat on Its Back*. New York: New Press, 2004.

Gould, William B., IV. *Labored Relations: Law, Politics, and the NLRB, a Memoir by William B. Gould IV*. Cambridge, Mass.: MIT Press, 2000.

Hamper, Ben. *Rivethead: Tales from the Assembly Line*. New York: Warner Books, 1986.

Holland, William. *Are There Any Good Jobs Left? Career Management in the Age of the Disposable Worker*. Westport, Conn.: Praeger/ Greenwood Publishing Group, 2006.

Hoyman, Michelle M. *Power Steering: Global Automakers & the Transformation of Rural Communities*. Lawrence: University Press of Kansas, 1997.

Human Rights Watch (HRW). *Unfair Advantage: Workers' Freedom of Association in the United States under International Human Rights Standards*. Study published August 2000 (www.hrw.org).

———. *Blood, Sweat, and Fear: Workers' Rights in U.S. Meat and Poultry Plants*. Study published 2004 (www.hrw.org).

Hurd, Richard W., Rudolph A. Oswald, Ronald L. Seeber, and Sheldon Friedman. *Restoring the Promise of America Labor Law*. Ithaca, N.Y.: ILR Press/Cornell University Press, 1994.

International Association of Fire Fighters (IAFF). National legislative conference, Washington, D.C., March 2004.

International Brotherhood of Electrical Workers (IBEW). National convention, St. Louis, 1991.

International Brotherhood of Teamsters. Nominating convention, Orlando, Fla., June 1991.

———. National election, Washington, D.C., fall 1996.

International Labor Communications Association (ILCA). Media workshops, Washington, D.C., November 12, 2004.

Kindleberger, Charles P. *Europe's Postwar Growth: The Role of Labor Supply*. Cambridge, Mass.: Harvard University Press, 1967.

Kochan, Thomas A. *Restoring the American Dream: A Working Families' Agenda for America*. Cambridge, Mass.: MIT Press, 2006.

———. *Challenges and Choices Facing American Labor*. Cambridge, Mass.: MIT Press, 1984.

Kochan, Thomas A., Harry C. Katz, and Robert B. McKersie. *The Transformation of American Industrial Relations*. Ithaca, N.Y.: ILR Press/Cornell University Press, 1994.

Martin, Christopher R. *Framed! Labor and the Corporate Media*. Ithaca, N.Y.: Cornell University Press, 2004.

McEntee, Gerald, president, American Federation of State, County and Municipal Employees (AFSCME). "Labor's Main Challenge: Increasing Political Power for Working Families." Position paper, Washington, D.C.: AFSCME, 2005.

McGaughey, William. *A U.S.-Mexico Free-Trade Agreement*. Minneapolis: Thistlerose Publications, 1992.

Mehta, Chirag, and Nik Theodore. *Undermining the Right to Organize: Employer Behavior During Union Representation Campaigns*. Study published by the Center for Urban Economic Development, University of Illinois, December 2005.

The Nation. "Let's Get Organized." *The Nation*, Special Labor Day Issue, September 2001.

O'Connor, Richard. *Heywood Broun: The Life and Career of the Most Famous and Controversial Journalist of His Time*. New York: Putnam, 1975.

Parker, Mike, and Martha Gruelle. *Democracy Is Power: Rebuilding Unions from the Bottom Up*. Detroit, Mich.: Labor Notes Book, 1999.

Puette, William J. *Through Jaundiced Eyes: How the Media View Organized Labor*. Ithaca, N.Y.: ILR Press/Cornell University Press, 1992.

Puddington, Arch, and Lane Kirkland. *Champion of American Labor*. New York: Wiley, 2005.

Queens College Labor Resource Center and the *New Labor Forum*. Labor at the Crossroads conference, New York, December 2004.

Ragano, Frank, and Selwyn Raab. *Mob Lawyer: Including the Inside Account of Who Killed Jimmy Hoffa and JFK*. New York: Scribner's, 1994.

Reuther, Victor G. *The Brothers Reuther and the Story of the UAW: A Memoir*. Boston: Houghton Mifflin, 1976.

Reynaud, Jean-Daniel. *Les Syndicats en France*. Paris: Editions du Seuil, 1975.

Schmitt, John, and Ben Zipperer. *Dropping the Ax: Illegal Firings During Union Election Campaigns*. Washington, D.C.: Center for Economic and Policy Research (CEPR), January 2007.

Schumer, Senator Chuck. *Positively American: Winning Back the Middle-Class Majority One Family at a Time*. New York: St. Martin's Press, 2007.

Sirota, David. *Hostile Takeover: How Big Money and Corruption Conquered Our Government—and How We Can Take It Back*. New York: Crown Publishers, 2006.

Sloane, Arthur A. *Hoffa*. Cambridge, Mass.: MIT Press, 1992.

Stier, Anderson & Malone, L.L.C. *The Teamsters: Perception and Reality; An Investigative Study of Organized Crime Influence in the Union*. Washington, D.C., 2002.

Stern, Andrew, president, Service Employees International Union (SEIU). "Unite to Win." Position paper, Washington, D.C.: SEIU, 2004.

Tarentelli, Ezio. *Economia Politica Del Lavoro*, UTET, 1986.

———. *Salario, Inflazione E Relazione Industriali in Europea*, Marsilio editori, 1984.

Teamsters for a Democratic Union. National convention, St. Louis, October 1992.

———. National convention, Pittsburgh, 1989.

Tyndall Report Web site (tyndallreport.com).

United Auto Workers (UAW). National convention, Anaheim, 1989.

———. Midwest region election, Oklahoma City, 1989. Economic convention, Kansas City, 1990.

———. National convention, San Diego, June 1992.

———. New Directions Movement convention, St. Louis, November 1992.

U.S. Chamber of Commerce. *Symposium: OSHA at 35—Midlife Crisis or Just Hitting Its Stride; Examining OSHA's Impact on and Role in Workplace Safety*. Washington, D.C., May 15, 2006.

U.S. House Judiciary Committee. Subcommittee on Crime, hearing July 24, 1996.

INDEX

Afghanistan, 112, 186
AFL-CIO, xxxv, 21, 32, 33, 48, 113, 117,
    139, 148–150, 186, 222, 226–227
  and AFSCME, 235
  breakup of, 151–160, 235
  and California Nurses Association, 255
  and Delta Pride, 68, 70
  early presidential endorsements by, 172
  and Eastern European trade unions,
    xxxiii, 205–206, 208
  and Kerry campaign, 7, 26, 37–43
  and NLRB, 99, 100
  "put 'em to sleep strategy" used by, 189
  and 2006 congressional elections,
    50–53, 118
  and Working America, 256–257
African Americans, 59, 60, 63, 129, 236
AFSCME (see American Federation of
    State, County and Municipal
    Employees)
AFT (see American Federation of
    Teachers)
Ainsworth, Bill, 68–69
Albania, 186, 208, 224
Amalgamated Transit Union, 181–182
American Federation of Government
    Employees, 42, 100
American Federation of Labor, 159
American Federation of State, County
    and Municipal Employees
    (AFSCME), 100, 155
  Dean, Howard, and, 32, 33, 38
  Leadership Institute, 239
  town hall meeting of, 165–166,
    238–240
  and 2006 congressional elections, 118
  2006 national convention of, 234–235

American Federation of Teachers (AFT),
    xxxiv, 100, 205, 208
American labor movement:
  avoidance of media by, 179–182
  and 2006 congressional elections,
    118–119
  corruption in, 213–214
  decline of, xix–xxi, xxvi–xxviii, 142,
    160–164
  and Democratic Party, 128, 158
  division within, 151–152
  foreign labor unions compared with,
    xiv
  intimidation of media by, 175–179
  leadership of, xxix
  and media access, 183–189
  political influence of, 161–162
  union membership, 161
  (See also specific headings)
Anti-union consultants, 137–138
Apprenticeship programs, 238
Aracoma Alma Mine fire, 96
Arant, Turner, 58–59, 71–72
Association for Union Democracy
    (AUD), 219
Atlanta, Georgia, 71, 80
AUD (Association for Union
    Democracy), 219

Bakery, Confectionery, Tobacco Workers
    and Grain Millers International
    Union (BCTGM), 134
Battista, Robert J., 99
BCTGM (Bakery, Confectionery,
    Tobacco Workers and Grain
    Millers International Union), 134
Biased language, use of, 191–192

Big Three automakers, 176, 178
Black lung disease, 222
Boeing Company, 148
Boston, Massachusetts, 125, 236
Boycott, Delta Pride, 73–78, 81
Boyle, Tony, 221–222
Bronfenbrenner, Kate, 137, 146, 241, 244, 246
Brotherton, Paul, 28
Broun, Heywood, 83
Brown, Sherrod, 254
Bryant, Mike, 17
"Building Bridges" program, 238
Building trades, 224
Burger, Anna, 52–53, 158
Bush, George H. W., 215
Bush, George W., and administration, 19, 42, 112, 120, 154, 166
    and homeland security, 22
    Hurricane Katrina, 89–91
    labor's opposition to, 38
    and Mine Safety and Health Administration, 94, 98
    and Ohio, 107, 108
    reelection of, 146
Buy American campaign, 177

California Nurses Association (CNA), 99–100, 257
California swing shift, 46
Camarata, Pete, 222–223
Campaign issues, values vs., 113
Canton, Ohio, 107, 109–111, 114
Carey, Ron, 215, 219
Carloads for Kerry, 8, 14, 30–31, 44
Carpenters union, 245–246
Caterpillar Inc., 178
Catfish farmers, 60–63, 82
Catfish Farmers of America, 71
Catfish processing industry, xxxi, 61–64
    competition in, 62–63
    working conditions, 61–62
Catfish workers, 64, 82, 204, 250
Center for Economic and Policy Research (CEPR), 138
Center for Union Facts, 136–137
Central Conference of Teamsters, 183
Central States Pension Fund, 221
CEPR (Center for Economic and Policy Research), 138

Change to Win federation, 53, 256
    Burger, Anna, and, 52
    formation of, xxxv, 51, 158, 227, 235
    member involvement in, 236
    name of, 152
    Stern, Andy, and, 33
    and 2006 congressional elections, 118
Cheney, Dick, 108
Chicago, Illinois, 100, 138, 156–157, 165–166, 178, 183, 234, 236, 250
Chicago Federation of Labor, 188
Chicago Interfaith Committee on Worker Issues, 238
Chicago Regional Conference of Carpenters, 237–238
Chili feeds, 36, 48
China, 129, 185
City University of New York Graduate Center, 146
Civil rights, 59, 67, 69, 79–80, 85
Clark, Wesley, 32, 36
Clay, William L., 214
Cleveland, Ohio, 129–130, 183, 185, 254
Clinton, Bill, and administration, 32, 43, 124, 154, 178, 224, 225
Clinton, Hillary, 66
CNA (see California Nurses Association)
Coal miners, 250
Coal mining industry, xxxii–xxxiii, 120
    accidents, 96
    declining unionization, 95
    federal regulation of, 97
Cohen, Larry, 149, 236
Coia, Arthur, 225
Cold Storage Fire, 27–29, 37
Collective bargaining, 130, 138, 139
Columbus, Ohio, 111–112, 114
Commercial laundry workers, 237
Communication, xxx, 125–126, 151, 162, 174, 232
Communications Workers of America (CWA), 100, 149, 236, 239
Congress of Industrial Organizations, 159
Congressional elections of 2006, 50–54, 116–117, 253
    and AFL-CIO, 50–54, 118
    and AFSCME, 118
    and American labor movement, 118–119
    and Hurricane Katrina, 89
    and SEIU, 118

Consolidated Biscuit Co., 133
Construction industry, 224
Corporate power, 164, 232–233
Corruption, 220–221
Cotton, 60–62
Crancer, Barbara Hoffa, xvii–xviii, xxxv, 258
Csako, Mihaly, 207
Cultural populism, 114

Darby Mine, 96
Davis-Bacon Act, 90–92
Dean, Howard, 6, 7, 14–17, 27, 32–34,
    36, 39, 43, 44, 50, 52
Death rates, workplace, xxii, 120
Declaration on Fundamental Principles
    and Rights at Work (ILO), 140
Delta Pride, 59, 60, 249, 257
Delta Pride strike, 57–87, 230
  boycott, 73–78, 81
  and civil rights, 67, 85
  and consumer behavior, 86
  and media relations, 80–83
  return of workers to job, 72
  and St. Louis, 83–85
  and UFCW, 64–88
  union tactics, 79–87
  violence in, 67
Democratic Leadership Council (DLC), 52
Democratic Party:
  and labor movement, 128, 158
  1964 Convention, 69
  and 2006 midterm elections, 116–117,
    119, 120, 122–123, 125
  and unions, 147
  and "values," 165–168, 171, 173
  (See also Iowa Democratic caucus)
Democratization, of International
    Brotherhood of Teamsters,
    211–224
Des Moines, Iowa, 2, 12–14, 22–23, 34
Detroit, Michigan, 156, 178, 185, 221
Deutscher Gewerkschaftsbund (DGB), 220
DiMaggio, Joe, 129, 130, 183
Domjan, Laszlo, 66, 187
Dudzic, Mark, 146–147, 149, 152
Durham, R. V., 215

East Germany, 149–150, 207, 208, 212
East Missouri Laborers' District Council,
    187, 188

Eastern Conference of Teamsters, 216
Eastern Europe, trade unions in,
    xxiii–xxiv, 205–209
  and AFL-CIO, 205–206, 208
  and Communist hegemony, 206
  and transition to free market economy,
    207–208
Economic issues:
  justice, 115
  mobility, xix–xxi
  in presidential elections, 125
Economic values, 169–170
Education and Labor Committee (U.S.
    House of Representatives), 117
Education and the Workforce Committee
    (U.S. House of Representatives),
    117
Edwards, John, 13, 17, 27, 32, 39, 41, 108
Elections (see Congressional elections of
    2006; Presidential elections)
Employee Free Choice Act, 232
Employer resistance to organizing,
    130–137, 141
Endorsements:
  AFL-CIO and, 42
  IAFF and, 24–26
  SEIU and, 33
Europe, labor movements in, 220 (See also
    Eastern Europe, trade unions in)
Exclusive bargaining contracts, 220

Fairness and Accuracy in Reporting
    (FAIR), 190–191
Father Judd Act, 29
Federal Bureau of Investigation (FBI), 214
Federal Mediation & Conciliation Service
    (FMCS), 138
Federal regulation(s):
  of coal mining industry, 97
  enforcement of, xxii, 123–124
Fiedler, Jeff, 68–69
Fino, Ronald M., 226
Fire Act, 29
Fire departments, management of, 20
Firefighters, 257
  characteristics of, 23–24
  expanding role of, 18
  as first responders, 18
  homogeneity of, 46
  and Iowa Democratic caucus, 14–17

Firefighters (*continued*)
in New Hampshire campaign, 36–37
political activism of, 20–21
and September 11th terrorist attacks, 5
Firings, of pro-union workers, 134
Florida, 43, 185, 205, 254
FMCS (Federal Mediation &
Conciliation Service), 138
Food processing workers, 237
Ford Motor Company, xxviii
Forgacs, Pal, 207
Fox, Michael J., 121
France, labor movement in, 220
Frank, Thomas, 114, 168
Freeman, Michael W., 78
Free-trade pact with Mexico, 178
From, Al, 53

Gaines, Thomas A., Jr., 19
Gates, Robert, xxxii
Gay, Lori, 130–133, 143
GDP (Gross Domestic Product), 120
Gephardt, Richard (Dick), 6, 7, 12, 14–16,
26, 27, 31, 33–35, 38–40, 50, 52
German, Verdell, 70
Germany, labor movement in, 220 (*See
also* East Germany)
Giblin, Vincent, 240
Gorbachev, Mikhail, 213
Gore, Al, 7, 39, 185
Grassroots democracy, xxxii–xxxiii, 148,
209, 221–222, 227–230, 256
Greyhound Strike, 182

Hamer, Fannie Lou, 69
Harvill, Tommy, 187–188
Health and safety, xxii–xxiii, 78, 103, 120,
249
Sago mine explosion, 92–98
unions' role in, 93–97
Health care, national, 103, 255
Health insurance, 108, 113
Heinsohn, Tommy, 27
Hhorn, Charley, 70–71
Hispanics, 134, 236
Hoffa, James P. (Jim), xvi–xix, xxxv, 7, 31,
44, 117, 153–158, 163, 213,
215–216, 219, 258
Hoffa, Jimmy, xi, xiv, 156, 185, 196,
220–221, 225

Homeland Security Committee (U.S.
House of Representatives), 71
Hostile Takeover (David Sirota), 114
"Hotel workers rising" program, 236–237
Human Rights Watch, 139–140
Hungary, xxxiii, 66, 206, 207
Hurricane Katrina, xvii, 88–92, 120
Bush, George W., and, 89–91
and Davis-Bacon Act, 90–92
and media relations, 89
and 2006 congressional elections, 89

ILCA (International Labor
Communications Association), 151
ILO (International Labor Organization),
140
Immigration, as issue in 2008 presidential
election, 257–258
Indianola, Mississippi, 57–58, 60, 63, 69,
78, 83, 88, 143, 204, 230
International Association of Fire Fighters
(IAFF), xxxi, 18, 230, 231
and Carloads for Kerry program,
14–15
and chili feeds, 36
endorsement process of, 24–26
and homeland security, 3
and Iowa Democratic caucus, 14–17,
35, 44–45
local autonomy in, 24
nonconventional approach of, 53–54
and political activism, 20–21
rank and file involvement in, 24, 30
regional focus of, 29–30
and Republican party, 25
and September 11th terrorist attacks, 5
strategy of, 24–26
International Association of Machinists
(IAM), 182, 201
International Brotherhood of
Boilermakers, 139
International Brotherhood of Electrical
Workers (IBEW), 42, 48, 237–238
International Brotherhood of Teamsters
(IBT), xvii, xviii, xxxii–xxxiii, 31,
188, 201, 209, 211–224
and AFL-CIO, 159
changing image of, 128
Gephardt, Dick, and, 34, 50
and media, 183–186

and Mr. Coffee plant, 129
1986 Las Vegas convention of,
    211–212
nominating convention of, 214
opposition within, 212–214
racketeering suit against, 214
reform movement in, 222–223
and SEIU, 153, 156
International Coal Group, 95
International Federation of Professional
    and Technical Engineers, 228
International Labor Communications
    Association (ILCA), 151
International Labor Organization (ILO),
    140
International trade agreements, 124,
    127
International Union of Operating
    Engineers (IUOE), 234–235
Iowa, 49, 143, 257
Iowa 2004 Democratic caucus, 1–9
    "Carloads for Kerry," 8
    effect of, on Kerry presidential
        campaign, 6–7
    firefighters' tactics in, 14–17
    second choice candidates, 11–12
Iraq war, 89, 112, 120, 122
Italy, labor movement in, 220

Jim Crow, 58
Judiciary Committee (U.S. House of
    Representatives), 225
"Jump Start" program, 238
Junemann, Gregory, 148, 228

Kelley, Bob, 186–188
Kennedy, Bobby, 225
Kennedy, Edward, 117
Kentucky, 96, 97
Kentucky River decision, 98–105, 131,
    139
Kerry, John, 14, 19, 107, 108, 154
    and AFL-CIO, 7, 37–44
    and Cold Storage Fire, 28
    collaboration of, with firefighters, 28
    military veterans' and reservists'
        support for, 16
    obligation of, to firefighters, 42–43
    presidential campaign of, 6–19, 27,
        29–54

pro-labor voting record of, 39
    as second choice caucus candidate,
        11–12
    women's support for, 16
Kindred, Steve, 223
King, B. B., 58
King, Maurice, 238
Kleinman, Ricky, 1–2, 5, 8, 11–12, 22–23,
    31, 45, 49

La Cosa Nostra, 219, 226
La Sala, James, 181
Labor at the Crossroads (conference),
    145–150, 228
Labor Department, 94–95
Labor law reform, 55
Labor movement (see American labor
    movement)
Labor Party (U.S.), 147
Laborers' International Union of North
    America (LIUNA), 153, 156,
    224–227
Las Vegas, Nevada, 117, 153, 212
Lattimore, Neel, 66
Lauriski, David, 94
Lawhorn, Bill, 133–136, 143
Lewis, John L., 196
Lieberman, Joe, 36
Liga (Hungarian union), 206, 207
Limbaugh, Rush, 26, 121
LIUNA (see Laborers' International
    Union of North America)
Local autonomy, in IAFF, 24
Lockheed Martin Corporation, 148
Lowery, Joseph, 69

Magnolia, Mississippi, 102, 139
Management-labor-government relations,
    104
Manchin, Joe, 95
Manufacturing job loss, xxvii–xxix, 108,
    124, 127, 129, 141, 237
Massachusetts, 27–29
McCarthy, William, 215
McCarthy era, 176
McCollum, Bill, 225, 226
McComb, Ohio, 133, 135
McCree, Harry, 113
McEntee, Gerald, 32, 33, 38, 43–44, 52,
    118, 155, 165–166, 234, 239

McWilliams, Tommy, 58, 72
Meany, George, 196
Media relations, xxxiv–xxxv, 9, 33, 72,
    100, 125–126, 151, 162, 174,
    190–199
  access to media, 183–189
  avoidance of media, 179–182
  character of journalists, 196
  Delta Pride strike, 80–83, 85
  and editorial boards, 202
  Fairness and Accuracy in Reporting
    (FAIR), 190–191
  and human interest stories, 203–204
  Hurricane Katrina, 89
  intimidation of media, 175–179
  lack of context in reporting, 192
  lack of coverage, 197–198
  and local level communication,
    200
  and regional stories, 204–205
  research groups, 190–191
  sensationalism in reporting, 192
  strategy for, 199–209
  and Teamsters, 183–186
  and UAW, 175–179
  unfairness in reporting, 192
  and union hours, 195
  use of biased language, 191–192
Memphis, Tennessee, 64, 80
Mexico, 129, 178, 183, 185
Middle class, xix–xx, 251, 252, 258
Miller, Arnold, 221–222
Mine Safety and Health Administration
    (MSHA), 94, 98
MINER Act, 97–98
Miners for Democracy, 221
Mississippi, 85, 230–231, 257
Mississippi Baptist Association, 70
Mississippi Delta, 55, 57, 60, 61, 65
Mississippi Freedom Democratic
    delegation, 69
Mississippi Workers Center for Human
    Rights, 82
Missouri, 26–27, 31
Mob (*see* Organized crime)
Mondale, Walter, 7, 39, 172
Mowbray, Ken, 111–112, 143, 164, 184
Mr. Coffee plant, 129, 130, 183
MSHA (*see* Mine Safety and Health
    Administration)

NAACP (National Association for the
    Advancement of Colored People),
    69
National Association for the Advancement
    of Colored People (NAACP), 69
National Labor Relations Act, 140
National Labor Relations Board (NLRB),
    69, 98–100, 102, 131–133, 135,
    136, 138, 139, 240
New Directions Movement, 176
New England, 35–36
New Hampshire 2004 presidential cam-
    paign, 35–37, 48
  and Cold Storage Fire, 37
  role of firefighters, 36–37
  and small-town demographics, 37
New Jersey, 69, 216, 250
New Orleans, Louisiana, 88–89, 103, 139
New York City, 178, 208, 216, 219, 228
Newsroom operations, 193–196
NLRB (*see* National Labor Relations
    Board)
North Carolina, 66, 215
Nurses, 101, 249–250

OCAW (Oil, Chemical and Atomic
    Workers International Union), 146
Occupational Safety and Health
    Administration (OSHA), xxii
Oglesby, Joe, 60, 61, 63
Ohio, 108, 115, 129, 254, 257
Oil, Chemical and Atomic Workers
    International Union (OCAW), 146
Operating Engineers Local 150, 239–240
Organized crime, 213, 218–221, 223,
    225–226, 243
Organizing, 130–136, 154–155
O'Sullivan, Terence, 227
Ottumwa, Iowa, 1–2, 11, 12, 22
Ouellette, Mark, 48

Parise, Carmen, 184
Pelosi, Nancy, 117
Pennsylvania, 98, 108–109, 113, 254
Pentagon, 21–22
Peoples Bank of the Delta, 68
Peter D. Hart Research Associates,
    xxv–xxvi, 140–142
Podkrepa (Bulgarian trade union movement),
    208

Poland, 206, 207
Polish immigrants, 236
political action committees, 49–50
Political activism:
    AFL-CIO and, 154–155
    IAFF and, 20–21
Post, Bill, 5, 13, 49
Pre-apprenticeship programs, 237–238
Presidential appointments, 123–124
Presidential campaigns (*see* Iowa 2004
    Democratic caucus; New
    Hampshire 2004 presidential cam-
    paign)
Presidential elections, 165
    of 2004, 145–146
    of 2008, 117, 257–258
    and economic issues, 125
    and immigration issue, 257–258
Presser, Jackie, 184, 211
Productivity, 251–252
Professional Air Traffic Controllers
    Organization (PATCO), xxvi, 124
Profits, 251–252
Pulitzer, Joseph, 65, 66, 187
Putin, Vladimir, 213

Racketeer Influenced and Corrupt
    Organizations (RICO) Act, 222
Raffa, Frank, 28
Raynor, Bruce, 149
Reagan, Ronald, 124
"Reagan Democrats," 47, 109
Red Menace, 176
Reed, Jack, 22–23
Religious values, 110–112, 115
Republican Party, 25, 46, 53, 119, 122,
    125, 128, 165, 166, 173, 254
Reuther, Walter, 176, 196
Right to organize, 52, 55
Right-to-work states, 237
Rumsfeld, Donald, xviii, xxxiii, 122
Ryan, John, 254–255

SAFER Act, 28
Safety committees, 95–96
Safety issues (*see* Health and safety)
Sago mine explosion, xxii–xxiii, 92–98
St. Louis, Missouri, 58, 64, 66, 83–85,
    157–158, 178, 179, 181, 183, 187,
    206–207

St. Louis Labor Council, 186–188
St. Louis Post-Dispatch, 65
St. Louis/Southern Illinois Labor Tribune,
    83, 188
Salt Lake Regional Medical Center,
    130–132
San Diego, California, 175, 177, 179
Sansone, Bobby, 184, 188
Sarah Lawrence College, 147, 256
Schaitberger, Harold, 3, 4, 7, 9–10,
    19–22, 25, 26, 30–31, 38–41, 43,
    44, 49, 231
School of Industrial and Labor Relations
    (Columbia University), 137
Schumer, Chuck, 120, 125
September 11th terrorist attacks, 5,
    21–22, 29, 234
Service Employees International Union
    (SEIU), xxiii, 7, 153, 159, 256
    endorsement process of, 33
    member participation in, 150–151, 236
    organizing by, 237, 246, 255
    Stern, Andy, and, 32, 33, 156
    and 2006 congressional elections, 118
    "Unite to Win" proposal of, 147
Shaffer, Robert, 139
Shaiken, Harley, 246–247
Shanker, Al, 205–209
Shinseki, Eric, 122
Sirota, David, 114
Solidarity (Polish trade union), 206
Soviet Union, 207, 212, 213
Spellane, Jim, 47–48
Springsteen, Bruce, 10, 41
Stern, Andrew (Andy), 7, 32–33, 44, 118,
    151, 153–158, 163, 173
"Steward's Army," 236
Sunbeam Corporation, 129
Sunflower County, Mississippi, 57, 59, 60
Superdome (New Orleans), 88
Sweeney, John, 38, 40, 41, 43, 44, 50, 52,
    99, 150, 151, 154–158, 163, 173,
    222

Teamsters (*see* International Brotherhood
    of Teamsters (IBT))
The Teamsters: Perception and Reality
    (report), 221
Teamsters for a Democratic Union
    (TDU), 212, 222–223

TeKippe, John, 2, 5, 12–13, 18, 40
Thompson, Bennie, 70–71
Through Jaundiced Eyes: How the Media View Organized Labor, 191
Tort reform, 112
Transport distribution, 237
Trerotola, Joe (Joe T), 216–219
Trumka, Richard, 222
Tucker, Jerry, 176–177
TWA, 182
Twelve-Counties Laborers District Council, 182

UAN (United American Nurses), 131
Unfair labor practices, 133, 135
Unionization, 159, 237, 254
    and AFL-CIO debate, 154–155
    benefits of, 250
    in coal mining industry, 95
    of firefighters, 46
    of nurses, 249–250
    opposition to, xxvi–xxvii
    in service sector, xxvii
    of Virginia firefighters, 19–20
    worker support for, xxvi, 141
Unions:
    achievements of, xix, xxxi–xxxiv
    and American labor movement, 161
    current need for, xxiv–xxvi
    decline of, xx–xxi
    fragmentation of, xix
    health and safety role of, 93–97
    relevance of, xxi
    role of, in society, xix
UNITE (clothing workers' union), 41, 42
UNITE HERE, 149, 153, 156, 236–237, 255–256
"Unite to Win," 147, 151–152
United American Nurses (UAN), 131
United Auto Workers (UAW), 31, 42, 175–179, 201
    anticommunism of, 176
    and Buy American campaign, 177
    and intimidation of media, 175–179
    and New Directions Movement, 176
United Brotherhood of Carpenters, 158
United Farm Workers, 157–158

United Food and Commercial Workers (UFCW), xxii, 34–35, 64–88, 153, 204
United Mine Workers of America (UMWA), 95–96, 221–222
United Nurses of America, 100
United Parcel Service (UPS), 209, 212, 218
United Steel Workers of America (USWA), 31, 100, 244–245
Universal Declaration of Human Rights, 140
U.S. Chamber of Commerce, 99

Values, 165–171
Vilsack, Tom, 14, 31, 49, 53
Virginia, 19–21
Voter turnout, 14–15

Wall Street Journal, 208–209
Wal-Mart, xxviii
War on terrorism, 5
Warsaw Pact, 207
Washington, D.C., 68, 80, 185, 215, 236
Wealth, disparity of, xxiv–xxv, 120, 127, 201–202, 251, 258
Weiss, Jeff, 188–189
West Virginia, 92, 96–98
White, Sarah, 64, 82
White, Tangelia, 64
White Citizens Council, 58
Williams, Sue, 110–112, 115, 143, 164, 167
Worcester, Massachusetts, firefighters tragedy (*see* Cold Storage Fire)
Workers' rights, xxi–xxii, xxvi, 105, 120–121, 127, 135, 139–140, 164
World Trade Center, attacks on (*see* September 11th terrorist attacks)
Wright, Louie, 26, 29–30

Yablonski, Jock, 221–222
Yanda, Rachel, 147, 152–153, 256

Zack, Al, 64–66, 82–83
Zeller, Duke, 224
Zipperer, Ben, 138